SCHEMES OF SATAN

by
Michael A. Warnke

Victory House, Inc.
Tulsa, Oklahoma

DEDICATION

To all my children
and all my grandchildren

Acknowledgments

I would like to express my gratitude to:

Rose, Neale and Tracy

Doug, Tom and Tim

Georgia, Linda, Pat, Kim, Michaelle
Bev, Debbie, Tammy, Christina
Ronnie, Ed, Ruby, Kirk, Brendon
Quanita, Dewitt, Jerry, Jim

and

Hubba

My strength, my comrades and my friends.

Table of Contents

Table of Contents

Introduction

And do not participate in the unfruitful deeds of darkness, but instead even expose them.

(Eph. 5:11, NASB)

Like so many others have reported, my fascination with the dark world of the occult began in my childhood. I loved ghost stories, for example, and I wanted to learn all I could about things in the supernatural realm.

Scarred by years of physical and emotional abuse, I was looking for a way to regain control of my world and myself. I enjoyed being "spooked," because such adventures with fear and evil enabled me to escape the real horrors of my life.

Watching Samantha twitch her nose on "Bewitched" (a sign that her supernatural powers were at work), intrigued me and this simple way of revealing her powers inspired my curiosity regarding the world of the unknown. To my way of thinking, she embodied all that I wanted to be — someone who could actually control the circumstances of life and other people, if need be. Someone who was not a victim.

A friend who was a librarian put me in touch with books on occultism, satanism and eastern religions. My extraordinary interest in the "hidden knowledge" of the occult led me to devour everything I could find on the subject.

I read about Aleister Crowley, Edgar Cayce, the Druids, shamanism, witchcraft and many other topics related to the occult. On television and at movie theaters I watched every horror flick and program on mysterious subjects I could find. I was a devoted fan of "Creature Feature," and I tried to be certain that nothing would interfere with my watching this program each Saturday night.

My search for spiritual truth and power would not end, I determined within myself, until I found what I was looking for. I would make certain that others would look up to me because of the special powers I believed I could acquire and use.

I learned about talismans, amulets and charms, and I wore as many of these as I could because I believed in their ability to give me special powers. I studied and memorized spells, chants and incantations to gain control over the forces of nature and the lives of others.

One thing led to another, and I began to experiment with certain occult games such as the Ouija Board and tarot cards, in order to establish contact with spiritual forces. At first, these were just games to me, but eventually I learned to look to them for guidance.

It was all very exciting — a heady thrill for a young man who had been put down all his life. The greatest part was the sense of power I enjoyed. By yielding my life to spiritual forces, I reasoned, I would become invincible much like the comic-book super heroes I greatly revered.

Little did I realize how I was being ensnared, however. I was losing touch with my own identity and the values I once held to as Satan led me down his primrose path of power. I was too young and inexperienced to realize that power does in fact corrupt, and absolute power does corrupt absolutely.

Eventually, my search led me into the demonic Bedlam of satanism. The three-inch-long scar on my arm testifies to the extremes my involvement with this diabolical religion took. Four times a year — during our special festivals — my fellow satanists would slash my arm with a sacramental knife and drain my blood into our common chalice for ritual communion. They would mix my blood with urine, wine and blood from an animal sacrifice so we could partake together in an oblation to our god — Satan himself!

I believed I had arrived at the pinnacle of power for I was a satanist high priest. To appease my dark lord, I would offer my own blood as a sacrifice. It was a dark world indeed, and only the power of the Lord Jesus Christ — the Light of the world — was able to dispell that darkness.

From "Bewitched" to satanic high priest was a long and arduous journey into hell. Much of my story has been shared in *The Satan Seller,* my earlier book. In this present volume, however, I am writing both to warn and to inform about the dangers of occultism and satanism in our world today.

In the past few years a great number of books about satanism have appeared on the shelves. While some have been informative, many have tended simply to sensationalize the subject in line with recent media coverage.

What is often missed in all of this stir over satanism and occultism is that their activities are simply part of a much-larger social crisis. As sociologist Martin Marty points out, it is now possible to speak of an "occult establishment." In all the upheaval and change, one notices how society's attitudes toward non-traditional and deviant religions have changed.

Some wonder, "What will be next? I wouldn't be surprised to hear anything!" The attitude too often is more like a shrug-of-the-shoulders nonchalance rather than an expression of concern.

Satanism is only one of countless religions or philosophies that fall under the general umbrella of occultism. Although satanism is the primary focus of this book, it must be remembered that many occult religions present problems for our society today. We will touch on some of these in an effort to better understand satanism.

On the other hand, it must not be assumed that all satanists are criminals. The actual percentage of satanists involved in criminal activity is small but the numbers are definitely increasing. Not all satanists deviate significantly from what is generally accepted to be normal social behavior. Actually, satanism, like many forms of the occult, is the religion of choice for a very diverse group of people.

The freedom to practice one's religion is considered to be an almost-sacred privilege in our pluralistic society. It is guaranteed by the Constitution of the United States that declares in Article 3: "Congress shall make no law respecting the establishment of religion, or prohibiting the free exercise thereof. . . ."

Clearly, it is important for us to recognize this basic right upon which our society was built. However, when the activities of any religious group infringe on the rights of others, that freedom has been abused.

Much of this book is devoted to helping us discern the difference. Law-enforcement officials, educators, pastors, counselors, parents, young people and every concerned citizen can use this book as a resource concerning occult practices, satanism, ritual abuse and related matters in an effort to protect the rights of all members of our society, especially those who have been victimized by followers of occult religions.

Our ministry's counseling staff has worked with countless kids and adults whose lives have taken the same course mine followed. It's frightening to see how many young people are being innocently lured into occult involvement as a result of seemingly benign activities.

The door to satanism is being opened in a variety of creative ways. Some rock music and rock musicians, for example, openly advocate Satan-worship. Many television programs and motion pictures lead individuals into spiritualist and occult realms.

Recently, for example, Hollywood has produced more than five major films with occultic themes, as well as several lesser-known horror flicks to fill the demands of a spiritually hungry world. We see Bill Cosby cutting up in "Ghost Dad," and

Patrick Swayze learning the ropes as a disembodied spirit in "Ghost."

In "Field of Dreams," handsome Kevin Costner finds heaven in his Iowa cornfield where he encounters the specters of former baseball stars and is reconciled with his deceased father. "Flatliners" tries to find the same answers by showing how five medical students are haunted by their past misdeeds, leading them to experience death first-hand. Their experimental approaches to the after-life result in forgiveness and reconciliation with the power of love.

Following up on the success of earlier occult-inspired films, "The Exorcist — Part III" casts George C. Scott in the role of a detective who loses his faith in God because of all the evil in the world.

This genre is nothing new. In video stores everywhere one can find large sections offering films like "Rosemary's Baby," "Nightmare on Elm Street," "Halloween," and countless other videos that depict the powers of the dark side. Any of these can open windows to impressionable souls, letting in the ominous fog of occult interest that may lead the individual into personal involvement.

Time-Life Books is successfully marketing a series of hardcover books — "Mysteries of the Unknown" — to an audience of thousands. As a special incentive to buy these books, a gift is offered — a black velvet bag containing stones and crystals purported to possess supernatural powers. These polished pieces of rocks offer mental clarity, healing, improved memory, joy, happiness, creativity, prosperity, efficiency, wisdom, stress relief, a better love life, protection and other blessings to those who learn to use them. (Who wouldn't want such benefits, and many turn to the occult to find them.)

More than 2,500 New Age bookstores exist in the United States, offering a potpourri of books and items related to the occult. In bookstores in malls and shopping centers everywhere one can find large occult sections that offer everything from *You Can Heal Your Body* by Louise Hay to *The Satanic Bible* by Anton LaVey. When contrasted with sections of Christian books and Bibles in most of these same bookstores, the occult section is often at least ten times larger!

Even comic books and television cartoons are picking up on the themes of occultism. Many children and young people are learning fantasy role-playing games as well, such as "Dungeons and Dragons" and "The Quest." Some have lost their contact with reality as a result, and occult involvement and suicide related to the playing of these games have been widely reported.

Make no mistake about it, there is great interest in spiritual matters today. No matter how scientific and technological we have become, growing numbers are seeking answers to the issues of life through occult activities. A needy world cries for something to believe in.

All too often, people have tried to discount the cause-and-effect relationship that exists between occult involvement and crime today. Occultism also has dramatic effects in the realm of mental and physical health.

When it comes to satanism's influences in society, many would prefer to engage in denial rather than accurately perceiving its existence and its power over the lives of so many. The rise in reported child abuse, kidnapping, ritual abuse, suicide and murder is clear evidence of Satan's power being unleashed in the world today.

I have written this book to address these problems both as a former satanist and now as a Christian minister who deals with lives that have been affected by "the prince of darkness" every day. A massive onslaught is underway to gain control of individuals who have been marked by Satan for destruction in our society. It is time for us to recognize many of our contemporary problems for what they actually are — the schemes of Satan to destroy individual lives and society in general. It is time for us to launch a counter-offensive by becoming well-armed through prayer and the study of God's Word so we will be able to discern and expose the works of darkness wherever we can.

The greatest weapon we have at our disposal is truth, and finding the truth is the aim of this book. Jesus said it best: ''And you shall know the truth, and the truth shall make you free'' (John 8:32, NASB)

The sword of truth always gives us victory over Satan and all his works.

Mike Warnke
Burgin, Kentucky

1

Origins of Occultism

There shall not be found among you anyone who makes
his son or his daughter pass through the fire, one who uses
divination, one who practices witchcraft, or one who interprets
omens, or a sorcerer, or one who casts a spell, or a medium,
or a spiritist, or one who calls up the dead. For whoever does
these things is detestable to the Lord....

(Deut. 18:10-12a NASB)

Ritual Abuse

Let me begin this book by sharing some excerpts from a letter we received at Warnke Ministries: "The first memory I had was of my father taking me to someone's home....I was four years old. My father went down the basement stairs ahead of me. I did not want to go down the stairs. I had been there before, and I knew I was going to be hurt. A woman took my hand and pulled me down the stairs.

"The room was very dark, but it was still daytime. The basement window curtains were drawn. All the basement furniture was moved to the outside walls of the room. The room had dark paneling and an asphalt tile floor. There were some markings on the floor — I can remember a circle but nothing more specific.

"There were four other men present, plus the woman and my father. All of them were wearing black robes with hoods and had no clothing on underneath. My clothes were taken off and I was forced to lie on my back. One by one, the men removed their robes and tried [description of graphic sexual abuse deleted]...and poured something wet on top of my

17

chest — I can't tell what it was. My arms were being held down by one man and my legs by another.

"After they were through, I laid on the floor in pain while they all walked around me with their robes on, carrying candles and chanting.

"The next memory I had was of being taken to some property that my father owned. . . .I was nine years old. my sister was with me and she was four. I think it was in the summer because no one was wearing coats. It was about dusk when the ritual started.

"My first memory [of this occasion] involves standing around the body of a young boy. He was laying on a jagged slab of stone or wood. The boy did not move. He was not tied down. So I figure he was either drugged or dead already. He had a headband on. His hair was mostly straight and went down below his ear, but there were a few waves. He did not have any clothes on. There were some markings on his chest — a straight line down the center of his chest and stomach with some kind of dots or small markings to both sides of the chest.

"I was standing at the boy's left foot and my sister was standing to my right. To her right, was the leader of the ritual. He had a black robe on with a hood, long sleeves that were cuffed and a tunic went down to his calves. There was an emblem on his sleeve. I could not see his face.

"On my left was my father. On the other side of the boy's body were three men who I can describe but I cannot fix their identity. The other men were not wearing robes. They were wearing pants and a shirt, but wrapped around their waist was a sash that hung down their side. It had the same emblem on it.

"The leader moved out away from my sister and stood in front of me, but to the left. He raised a large knife like a machete. It was at least a foot long. He pounded it down on the boy's chest. He then sliced open the chest cavity and stomach. My sister and I were given some of the boy's organs to hold in our hands. Then we had to carry them in some kind of a procession to another area of the property. I haven't remembered exactly what we did yet, but I suspect we buried them there. . . ."

This ghastly description of satanic ritual abuse comes from a young woman who is now a Christian. Our staff has received hundred of letters similar to this one.

We are blessed to be able to minister to these victims of occultism, and we endeavor in every possible way to help them find freedom and healing. Thousands of young people are wandering in the maze of occult involvement, scarred by years of ritual abuse and other activities. Sometimes, as was the case with the young woman above, they have been led into the schemes of Satan by their own parents!

Our calling is to reach out to the oppressed with the love and power of God. It is because of these innocent victims that I knew the time had come for me to write this book. Let's get involved in the challenges that face us. The enemy of our souls is real. He goes to and fro across the earth, seeking victims everywhere.

The Bible says, "Be self-controlled and alert. Your enemy the devil prowls around like a roaring lion looking for someone to devour. Resist him, standing firm in the faith. . . . And the God of all grace. . . . will himself restore you" (1 Pet. 5:8-11 NIV).

The World of Hidden Knowledge

Most occultists (including satanists) hold to an esoteric (designed to be understood by the specially initiated alone) approach to their philosophies and practices. This aspect of ''specialness'' helps them to feel better about themselves and to consider themselves as being somewhat above the common lot of people. It would be accurate, therefore, to call them elitists (people who believe their group is superior to others).

Since satanism is the main subject of this book, we will focus on rites, rituals and practices that relate most closely to satanism. Satanism is a specific religion within the gigantic sphere of occultism.

Satanists are occultists, but not all occultists are satanists. Very few occultists actually surrender their souls to Satan, but many of their activities are governed by Satan who is "the father of lies."

Occultism, in general terms, can best be defined as a belief in the action or influence of supernatural, unseen forces. Sometimes these forces are given names from various early religious systems, such as Babylonian, Hindu, native American, Eskimo, Norse, Celtic, Roman, barbarian, Chinese and Egyptian mythologies, theologies and traditions. At other times, the "deities" of occultists might take a more vague form, involving the exaltation and/or worship of impersonal forces such as nature, universal oneness, the spirit of love, harmony, etc.

Magical Practices

Already, it is clear that not all occultists are the same. Beliefs and practices differ with each group and often even among individual members of each group. The same could be said of two specific types of occultism: satanism and witchcraft. In looking at the origins of occultism, therefore, it is important to realize that ancient practices often associated with occultism do not necessarily apply to all occultists.

The word "occult" derives from the idea that certain forms of knowledge can be acquired from "secret" or "hidden" sources. The occultist, therefore, believes that various magical practices can be employed to give him spiritual understanding that transcends (goes beyond) the five physical senses and the intellect.

The epigram at the beginning of this chapter is a quote from the Old Testament — Deuteronomy 18:10-12a. It shows the ancient origins of many occult customs. When the Israelites of those times (approximately 3,500 years ago) sojourned as exiles and captives in foreign lands, they learned about many already-established occult practices that had grown out of man's need to find answers to the unknown. Specifically, God was referring to the Egyptians, Babylonians, Chaldeans and others who worshiped "foreign gods."

God warned them not to get involved with these rites and rituals because He loved the Hebrew people and did not want them to become influenced by the destructive, harmful practices of the other nations' religions.

Let's take a closer look at the specific practices He warned against, realizing that these same forms are followed by many occultists today:

1. *Divination* — the interpretation of omens by the aid of supernatural powers and specific magical devices.

2. *Witchcraft* — the use of sorcery (white and black magic) to cast spells and bring about changes in the natural world.

3. *Sorcery* — the use of magical powers gained from evil spirits.

4. *Spiritualism* — communicating with the departed by way of a medium.

5. *Necromancy* — conjuring up the spirits of the dead for fortune-telling and other magical purposes.

These five occult practices, and various adaptations of them, continue to have great influence in occultism, satanism and the New Age Movement today. One can even find certain groups that advocate fire-walking in many places today, another behavior that God finds detestable, according to Deuteronomy 18.

The Most Fundamental Motive

A psychologist who has done extensive research in the field of human values, Dr. Spangler, has stated, "The love of power is the most fundamental of all human motives." It is this craving for personal (and supernatural) power that impels many to enter the world of occultism. This was the drive that led me to know more about witchcraft and satanism.

The basic tenets of occult philosophy have been with us since Eve's encounter with Satan in the Garden of Eden. Essentially, the serpent offered four things to Eve:

> 1. *Escape from death.* ("You will not surely die, the serpent said to the woman" — Gen. 3:4 NIV).
> 2. *Special knowledge.* ("Your eyes will be opened..." — Gen. 3:5 NIV).
> 3. *Realization of inner godhood.* ("You will be like God..." — Gen. 3:5 NIV).
> 4. *A knowledge of both good and evil.* ("...knowing good and evil" — Gen. 3:5 NIV).

It is interesting to consider the currently popular, trendy New Age Movement (a modern-day hodge-podge of occultic teachings and practices) in light of Satan's earliest temptations addressed to Eve. The lies are the same.

In one way or another, each of the various occult philosophies offer the promise of power and special knowledge to their adherents. Sometimes, they even offer immortality (especially through reincarnation) and esoteric knowledge available to a select few. Woven into much occultic literature is the belief that each person can become a god in his own right, and good and evil can be experienced through the practice of magic.

The sixth chapter of the Book of Genesis describes the marriage of "sons of God" to the "daughters of men." Not all Bible scholars agree on the interpretation of this passage, but many believe that the "sons of God" were fallen angelic beings. If this is so, and I believe it to be the case, we see in the early chapters of the first book of the Bible the origination of occultism in ancient times.

Ancient Occult Adaptations

We have already shown how many ancient cultures employed occultic practices in their rites and rituals. All of the forms of occult involvement mentioned in Deuteronomy 18 continue to be utilized today. Because this is true, it is important to realize that the "New Age Movement" is actually a misnomer; there is really nothing new about it at all — it is simply ancient occultism wrapped up in a shiny new package!

Some specific occult concepts that endure from ancient origins include the following:

1. *Astrology* — consulting the stars of the Zodiac for guidance. Many well-known figures, such as Nancy Reagan, have turned to this form of occult knowledge, and many newspapers and television programs promulgate this belief.

2. *Black Magic* — the use of extraordinary powers to cast spells and gain dominance over others. Many witches, warlocks (male witches who practice the black arts), followers of Wicca (a specific occult religion) and satanists practice black magic.

3. *White magic* — the use of extraordinary powers to produce beneficient results such as healing. This system includes the use of herbs, oils, candles, incense and the power of the constructive will to attract and harness the occult forces.

4. *Fortune-telling* — Gaining insights into the future through the use of occult paraphernalia such as crystal balls, tarot cards and other items of occult significance.

5. *ESP* — extra-sensory perception that seeks special knowledge about individuals and events through techniques that involve clairvoyance (the ability to see beyond the physical senses).

6. *Psychic research* — gaining special knowledge through spiritual forces.

7. *Theosophy* — a system of thought that is based upon mystical insights that come to the individual through dreams and visions.

8. *Shamanism* — a primitive religion that presupposes special powers from the occult being passed through a specially gifted

person known as a shaman (or witch doctor). Many primitive
tribes in various cultures practice shamanism.

Although the above list is not by any means comprehensive,
when understood in conjunction with our earlier list of occultic
forms (i.e. divination, witchcraft, sorcery, spiritualism,
necromancy and fire-walking, as warned against in
Deuteronomy 18), we gain from it an understanding of general
occult styles and approaches that have existed since ancient
times.

Satanism, the central subject of this book, incorporates
many of the rites and rituals from the world of the occult, in
the worship of Lucifer (the fallen rebel archangel now known
as Satan or the devil). Later chapters will deal specifically, and
in much greater depth, with satanism.

At the outset, however, it is important for us to make a
clear distinction between general occultic practices and specific
religious systems that adhere to certain of these practices. Some
of these specific occult religions are: satanism, shamanism,
animism (a primitive religion that attributes conscious life to
nature and holds to a belief in spirits that inhabit various parts
of nature), and other cults and sects.

Some eastern and native American religions incorporate
specific occult practices into their worship as well. Hinduism,
for example, teaches reincarnation and other doctrines such as
karma — the belief that a person's actions in this life predispose
him to the level of existence he will find in his next reincarnation.

As you can tell from the above briefly stated definitions,
there is much borrowing from various philosophies in many
occult orientations and a great overlapping exists among many
of these systems. Satanism, witchcraft and the New Age
Movement have borrowed thoughts, ideas and practices from
most ancient occult traditions.

"I Just Know They're Satanists!"

Although Satan has certainly utilized many of these occult
activities to his advantage, it would be inaccurate to state that

they are all aspects of satanism. Satanism's fundamental premise focuses on the worship of Satan himself, and many occult systems do not hold to satanic worship. (Even some satanists would say they don't worship Satan as a personal deity, but rather they hold to beliefs that stem from counter-Christian ideals.)

As a case in point, I was ministering in southern California several years ago at an evangelical church. After one service, a lady came up to me, and with obvious deep concern, she announced, "I've got satanists living next door. I just know they're satanists! Mike, the things they do are awful! You've got to do something!"

In an effort to calm her down, I said, "Okay, I'll go with you to your home and see what I can do."

Normally, I don't have the opportunity (or the time) to get so personally involved in such a situation, but this time I sensed that God was directing me to go with this distressed elderly lady and her quiet husband.

She went on, "They have morning and evening sessions every day. I can hear them chanting and calling upon the devil. It makes me so nervous!"

One of these "sessions" was taking place when we arrived in the palm-tree-lined residential neighborhood. As I stood on the older couple's front porch, I could hear chants emanating from the living room next door.

I excused myself and walked over to the neighbors' front lawn so I could listen more carefully. Immediately, I realized that what I was hearing was not a satanic ritual. Rather, it was a Buddhist religious service that was taking place in the home of the Japanese businessman next door.

Not bashful by nature, I walked up the steps and knocked on the door. "Hi! I'm Mike Warnke. Your next-door neighbors asked me if I would come over to invite you to special services I'm conducting at their church. I can tell that you are very religious people, and I thought you might be interested in learning about Christianity.''

The young couple smiled back at me through the screen door and thanked me for the invitation. Surprisingly, they nodded at each other and then said, ''Yes, we'd like to come.''

Back at the home of my Christian brother and sister, I explained, ''Your neighbors aren't satanists at all — they're Buddhists. How long have they lived next to you?''

''Oh, a couple of years,'' the man replied.

''Did you ever visit them?'' I inquired.

''No,'' the lady indicated with an embarrassed nod of her head, ''quite frankly, we were afraid to go over there!''

To make a long story short, the Japanese couple did come to our services and they received Jesus as their Lord and Savior. As time went on, I learned that they eventually joined that church and became devoted followers of the Lord.

Needless to say, I'm glad I obeyed the Lord that evening. In so doing, two Buddhists came to know Jesus and two Christians learned that God's ''perfect love drives out fear'' (1 John 4:18 NIV).

Followers of Eastern religions are not satanists and neither are most occultists. The fact is, most occultists (and even satanists) are sincerely engaged in a spiritual search for supernatural reality and power, and many will respond to the genuine love of a Christian who expresses heart-felt concern for them. Our response to every person, regardless of his or her religious or philosophical orientation, must be the same — to show him or her the love of Christ and the power of God by the way we live and the way we deal with him or her. In so doing, we must always remember, ''the one who is in you is greater than the one who is in the world'' (1 John 4:4 NIV).

''Mystery Schools''

Rosicrucians and others who follow hermetic traditions (occult teachings that arose during the first three centuries A.D.)

maintain that special knowledge has been passed from generation to generation via Egyptian "mystery schools." Many occultists maintain that these insights are still available to those who are counted as being "worthy."

Not long after the Flood (see Gen. 6), people planned to construct a tower that could "reach to the heavens." Some archaeologists have speculated that the Tower of Babel was, in fact, a tower to be used in making astrological calculations.

The people involved were Chaldeans and much of their religion was occultic in nature. Contemporary with them was the culture of the Egyptians who also engaged in many occult rites and rituals.

Ancient Egyptians practiced sun worship, personifying their god with the name Re. Their use of pyramids for the burial of the pharaohs was based on this religion. They believed that the angled walls of the pyramids resembled the outspread rays of the sun, and it was their desire in constructing these gigantic temples to use them as stairways to the heavens.[1]

The Great Beast

Many occultists today continue to believe in the magical powers of pyramids. Aleister Crowley, one well-known occultist of the twentieth century who was known as "The Great Beast," formed a secret society devoted to what he called "sexual magic."

On his honeymoon in 1903, he and his bride went to the Egyptian pyramids in the hope that if they spent one night in the king's tomb, they would experience extreme sexual fulfillment in their marriage.

Crowley later reported that they followed through on their plans. On that particular evening he lighted candles and began to read an unspecified incantation. He said that while he was performing this ritual, a pale lilac light filled the king's chambers, enabling him to continue the meditation without the aid of a candle!

Curiously missing from his account, however, is any report of having derived special sexual powers from the experience. He did say that it was most uncomfortable to sleep on the cold, stone floor.[2]

Some modern-day occultists place pyramids under their beds in the hope of gaining sexual powers, and many suggest that pyramids are useful for restoring energy and health. A few have even built their homes in the shape of pyramids because of their belief in pyramidic powers.

The Book of the Dead

Several occultists study the ancient Egyptian *Book of the Dead* in order to gain insights into the realm of supernatural knowledge. One Egyptologist, a contemporary occultist writer, Manly P. Hall, suggests that the pyramids are much more than symbols of the passage from this life to the next. He explains that the pyramids were used as secret temples where certain "enlightened ones" could go to be transformed into gods. They would lie on the temple floor for three days in trance-like states and their souls would leave their bodies, enabling them to become one with their immortal gods, according to this teaching.[3]

How quickly one is reminded of Lucifer — the bright and morning star — who held the highest position in the angelic hierarchy of heaven. He was the most beautiful of all the angelic host, but his pride caused him to think that he could become like God. This rebellion brought about his fall from heavenly glory as recorded in Isaiah 14:12 — "How you have fallen from heaven, O star of the morning, son of the dawn! You have been cut down to the earth. You have been weakened by the nations" (NASB).

The sin of rebellion brought about his fall as it has done in the lives of all occultists since the time of Eve. Small wonder, then, that the Bible says, "For rebellion is like the sin of divination [witchcraft], and arrogance like the evil of idolatry" (1 Sam. 15:23 NIV).

When Moses went before Pharaoh to negotiate for the release of his people, court magicians were able to duplicate many of the feats of Moses and Aaron by calling upon occult powers.

Ancient Child Sacrifices

Another culture of that ancient time — the Canaanites — practiced many occult rites and rituals too. Among these were the sacrifice of children to Molech (a Semitic god), fortune-telling, various forms of witchcraft, spiritism, calling up demons and necromancy. The Israelites' failure to completely do away with these practices in the Promised Land (overt rebellion), greatly contributed to the problems they later faced.

Although many of these early customs could be accurately described as being pre-satanic, outright worship of Satan did not evolve until the Middle Ages. By the second century A.D., church leaders were accusing the Gnostics (people who believed that matter is evil and spiritual emancipation comes through knowledge) and others of perverting Christian ceremonies by worshiping "other gods."

On the other side of the Atlantic, the Aztecs and Incas also practiced human sacrifices in their religious rituals. Some of these Indians even volunteered to give up their lives, believing that such a voluntary sacrifice would unite them to their gods.

The Black Mass

The earliest evidence of actual participation in the Black Mass comes from the thirteenth and fourteenth centuries. Peasants and serfs saw themselves as victims of oppressive social and economic institutions, including the Church. They reacted to this perceived victimization by developing a parody (or burlesque) of the Roman Catholic Mass. Their focus was primarily on social and political concerns, but their version of the Black Mass led to religious misunderstandings as well.

Many participants failed to see the satire behind the Black Mass, and they began to blame God for their plight instead of fixing the blame where it belonged — on the corrupt men who were using them for their own selfish purposes.

By observing and participating in satanic rituals, the people were saying in effect, "If the God of the Church and the aristocracy really approves of the way things are, then who else can we talk to if not Him?" Some arrived at the conclusion that they must worship the one who opposes God and all He stands for — Satan! To them, the devil had become "the god of liberty" or "the god of the serfs." Some of these Black Masses were attended by 15,000 people or more!

The challenge to Christianity grew. Consecrated communion wafers and sacramental wines were frequently stolen for use in the Black Mass. In light of the Roman Catholic teaching on transubstantiation (a belief that the communion elements actually become the literal body and blood of the Lord Jesus), this thievery is especially significant. The participants in the satanic rituals believed they were actually desecrating the body and blood of Jesus!

Eventually, other substitutions were made for the communion elements and this led to the practice of animal sacrifices being incorporated into satanic rituals. One account, for example, mentions the killing of a toad over the chalice that had originally held communion wine.

In the traditional Black Mass, a nude woman served as the altar. She symbolized the fleshly or physical nature of the satanic ritual as opposed to the spiritual emphasis in Christian services. At this time, also, these early satanists began to reintroduce a wide range of pagan rites from ancient times.

Spiritual Perversion

While the peasants were exhibiting their special form of disrespect for the Church, a few members of the established aristocracy became involved in their own forms of spiritual perversion. Because they believed that spiritual power was contained in the various liturgies of the Church, they began to see magical connotations in the actions of the priests. This led some to believe that if they changed some of the liturgies and rituals by substituting certain words or forms, they could invoke special powers in their behalf. Some priests were corrupted through bribery to engage in these surreptitious activities.

One well-known proponent of some perverted masses was Catherine de Medici. From an attempt to communicate with spirits of the dead through one of these perversions, she came to believe that her sons were destined to become kings of France.

According to a number of historical sources, Catherine performed a variety of blasphemous rituals in order to help this "prophecy" to come true. On one occasion, she brought in a priest to say the Last Rites, not over someone who was actually dying, but symbolically over an enemy so he would die. In another instance, when her son Philip was ill, she ordered a ceremony performed in which a young boy was sacrificed and his blood was drunk from a communion chalice. She also learned to use poisons in the apparent belief that Satan helps those who help themselves.

The "magical satanism" of the aristocracy eventually merged with the "political satanism" of the peasantry and a more standardized form of the Black Mass emerged.

The Black, Horned Goat

A record dating back to 1597 describes the "presiding deity" of the satanic ritual as a black, horned goat. Judging from the rest of the account, the "goat" was most likely a man wearing a headdress. Another man, dressed in priest's robes and attended by two women helpers, conducted most of the actual ceremony. Initiates into the group were presented to the "goat," and they paid him homage with the "kiss of shame" on his buttocks. Since that time, the goat has been recognized as one symbol of Satan, and he was given worship and devotion as the satanists' master, god and creator.

As time passed, the Black Mass began to lose its appeal. Gradually, people began to turn to science rather than magic for the help and meaning they sought, and for special knowledge.

The Protestant Reformation (sixteenth century) offered some disenchanted Christians the opportunity to find alternatives to Catholicism. At the same time, a more non-religious view of magic began to develop, partly as entertainment.

Hellfire Clubs

During the eighteenth and nineteenth centuries, the satanic mass began to resurface in certain parts of Europe. Groups known as "Hellfire Clubs" reintroduced some satanic practices in their meetings. Less interested in magic than their predecessors, however, the "Hellfire" members seemed primarily concerned with matters involving sexual immorality. There is no evidence to suggest that the members of these groups took any of the satanic rituals seriously, at least from a spiritual standpoint. They did employ many of the "trappings" of the Black Mass to provide them with extra stimulation for their already-jaded senses that were preoccupied with sexual excesses.

The Cabala

During the sixteenth century, a system of Jewish theosophy, mysticism and thaumaturgy (the performance of miracles) began to spread over the face of Europe. This mystical expression of Judaism is called the Cabala.

Cabalism was never accepted by mainstream Judaism, but its teachings have held attraction for many. Its basic tenets were embraced by such magical fraternities as the Hermetic Order of the Golden Dawn and the *Ordo Templi Orientis*. One of the key figures in both of these organizations (around the turn of the twentieth century) was none other than Aleister Crowley.

Aleister Crowley

Crowley referred to himself as *"Tau Mega Therion,"* or "The Great Beast," yet he apparently did not consider himself to be a satanist, or even a black magician. According to one occult researcher, Richard Cavendish, Crowley did take part in satanic rituals:

> The most notorious and most brilliantly gifted of modern magicians, Aleister Crowley, was regarded as a black sorcerer by many other occultists, and his rituals are saturated with sex and blood to an extent which, to put it mildly, scarcely fits the normal conception of white magic. But he himself professed nothing but contempt for black magicians.[4]

In spite of Crowley's claims to the contrary, his writings have inspired many who are involved in witchcraft, satanism and other manifestations of the occult.

One of Crowley's teachings, for example, concerns the division of prior history into eras that he termed as "aeons." The first aeon was that of Isis, the mother, and was characterized by the rule of the goddess and by matriarchal religions (approaches that worship female deities). In many of the ancient witchcraft and pagan religions, worship of a goddess was predominant over the worship of a god.

The second aeon, according to Crowley, was that of Osiris, the father; this period was characterized by patriarchal religions such as Judaism, Buddhism, Islam and Christianity.

The year 1904 supposedly marked the dawn of the third aeon. This final era, considered the greatest of all by many occultists, centers on the worship of Horus, the child.

Through this chronology, Crowley was able to claim that the time had come for people to reject all external authority whether it derived from men or from gods. Now the emphasis was to be on one's own will which Crowley considered to be the true self. In 1916 he proclaimed his creed: "Do what thou wilt shall be the whole of the law."

In this way, Crowley was able to get the focus of his followers off of the concept of an ethereal god and he substituted himself in the role of "god."

His writings reveal that he blended magical ceremonies from groups like the Golden Dawn with eastern occult philosophies. He was particularly interested in sex as a means of harnessing internal and external power. In fact, he believed that sexual activities in rituals set up energy forces or "vibrations" that could be harnessed for magical purposes. The sexual excesses that he advocated, along with the emphasis on self and on one's own will, have contributed to the popularity of his teachings among many occultists today.

Aleister Crowley was perhaps the most influential occultist of this century. By incorporating elements of widely diverse occult/magical beliefs, his philosophies have set the stage for twentieth-century occultism in its diverse forms.

The Search for Supernatural Power

All of the forms and styles of occultism from ancient times to the present day began with an earnest search for supernatural power. This is an innate need in the human heart.

Many seekers have failed to comprehend the declaration of Jesus Christ: "All authority [supernatural power] in heaven and on earth has been given to me" (Matt. 28:18 NIV).

Occultism is not simply anti-Christian; it is counter-Christian. Occult teachings and practices foster rebellion against the Creator. It is for this reason that we have set about to "expose the works of darkness" (Eph. 5:11).

2

Satanism in Today's Society

Even though times have changed, and always will, man remains basically the same. For two thousand years man has done penance for something he never should have had to feel guilty about in the first place. We are tired of denying ourselves the pleasures of life which we deserve. Today, as always, man needs to enjoy himself here and now, instead of waiting for his rewards in heaven. So, why not have a religion based on indulgence? Certainly it is consistent with the nature of the beast. We are no longer supplicating weaklings trembling before an unmerciful "God" who cares not whether we live or die. We are self-respecting, prideful people — we are Satanists!

(From THE SATANIC BIBLE by
Anton Szandor LaVey)[1]

Occult Commonalities

In the first chapter — "Origins of Occultism" — we address some of the general beliefs and practices associated with occultism. For example, the drive for personal and supernatural power is prevalent among occultists. Sexual immorality as a means for obtaining this power is quite common as well. Likewise, most occultists hold to a belief in magical or mystical forces, and they believe they have access to special, "hidden" knowledge.

All of the above commonalities apply to satanism in very overt and direct ways, as the above quotation from *The Satanic Bible* reveals.

The Lies of Satan

Very frequently Satan repeatedly employs similar schemes in his nefarious attempts to bring people down with him. The three primary approaches he uses are:

1. Gratification of the flesh
2. Gratification of the ego.
3. Gratification of the lust for power.

When Jesus was in the wilderness, Satan tempted Him in these three areas.

Gratification of the Flesh

> **Then Jesus was led by the Spirit into the desert to be tempted by the devil. After fasting forty days and forty nights, he was hungry. The tempter came to him and said, "If you are the Son of God, tell these stones to become bread."**
>
> **Jesus answered, "It is written: 'Man does not live on bread alone, but on every word that comes from the mouth of God.' "**
>
> **(Matt. 4:1-4 NIV)**

Jesus was hungry and, with the supernatural power He had available to Him, He could have chosen to turn the rocks into bread. After all, He had created the universe! The tempter (who is not described in this passage with personification or any other image) came to Him, and knowing the extent of Jesus' hunger, suggested (probably in our Lord's mind) that He prepare himself some food. A seemingly reasonable suggestion in light of the circumstances!

But Jesus knew that such a choice would stem from disobedience to the Spirit of God who had purposely led Him into the wilderness so that He would know what it is to experience temptation. Because of this wilderness experience, Jesus is able to empathize with us when we face temptations. (See Heb. 4:14-15.)

Often Satan will tempt us to gratify our physical appetites in ways that are contradictory to the will of God for our lives.

Certainly he has succeeded in doing this in the lives of people who make decisions based on whether something *feels* good or not.

Aleister Crowley's creed — "Do what thou wilt shall be the whole of the law" — is followed by satanists today. Its corollary may be stated as: "Do whatever feels good."

Gratification of the Ego

> Then the devil took him to the holy city and had him stand on the highest point of the temple. "If you are the Son of God," he said, "throw yourself down. For it is written: 'He will command his angels concerning you, and they will lift you up in their hands, so that you will not strike your foot against a stone.'
>
> Jesus answered him, "It is also written: "Do not put the Lord your God to the test.' "
>
> (Matt. 4:5-7 NIV)

Here we see the tempter attacking Jesus with an appeal to the gratification of the ego — the very weakness to which Satan himself had succumbed. Notice how Satan uses the Scriptures within this temptation. Many satanists are adept at twisting the Scriptures, usually taken out of context, to their own advantage.

The satanic "if" opens up Pandora's box in the lives of many unsuspecting souls. "If you...no one will know...''; "If only you would...they will like you better"; "If you will try this...you won't be hurt." If, if, if — but what *if* his enticements are lies? They always are.

Jesus immediately recognized the seductive schemes of His enemy and He sent the devil fleeing with one verse from the Word of God.

Gratification of the Lust for Power

> Again, the devil took him to a very high mountain and showed him all the kingdoms of the world and their splendor.

> "All this I will give you," he said, "if you will bow down and worship me."
>
> Jesus said to him, "Away from me, Satan! For it is written: 'Worship the Lord your God, and serve him only.' "
>
> (Matt. 4:8-10 NIV)

These verses reveal the persistence of the enemy in endeavoring to capture his intended victims. His ploy was to appeal to the lust for power that exists within many. Again, he was unsuccessful in these attempts because Jesus recognized who he was and what he was doing. Jesus also knew that He did not need satanic power.

We are warned time and time again by the Scriptures to recognize these schemes of Satan when he (or one of his underlings) attempts to victimize us. The Apostle John, for example, wrote:

> Do not love the world or anything in the world. If anyone loves the world the love of the Father is not in him. For everything in the world — the cravings of sinful man, the lust of his eyes and the boasting of what he has and does — comes not from the Father but from the world.
>
> (1 John 2:15-16 NIV)

The true satanist ignores this warning. Instead, he willfully practices the very things God counsels against. This counter-Christian approach forms the basis of his beliefs and actions. In essence, therefore, it would be accurate to say that satanists often endeavor to behave in a manner that is consistently opposite to the teachings of Christianity, and they do this deliberately.

The Church of Satan

When Anton Szandor LaVey founded the Church of Satan in 1966, his purpose was to build a religion based on self-interest and self-indulgence. On *Walpurgisnacht* — a spring festival celebrated and observed by witchcraft followers — LaVey announced, "Since worship of fleshly things produces pleasure, there would then be a temple of glorious indulgence."[2]

Now known as "the Black Pope" by many of his followers, this satanist prelate serves as Satan's representative to thousands of his followers around the world, although he alleges that his devotion is to satanic ideals, not to Satan himself. Close to one million copies of his *The Satanic Bible* have been sold in bookstores around the world. In preparing this book, I went to one bookstore to ask if they sold *The Satanic Bible*. The shop was in a small shopping center in a rural community.

The young woman behind the counter replied, "Yes, we do, but we keep it under the counter because the public might not like it to be displayed on the shelf." She seemed almost embarrassed to admit this.

"Are there other books that you keep under there too?" I asked.

"No, just this one. We do have people who come and ask for it every once in a while." She handed me the small, black paperback. On the front there is a satanic symbol — the Sigil of Baphomet.

This sign consists of two concentric circles and a pentagram (five-pointed star) within the smaller circle. The points of the pentagram touch the inside of the circle, and within the star itself there is the face of a goat.

The Sigil of Baphomet is used exclusively in the worship of Satan. The goat is known as the Goat of Mendes which represents the opposite of the sacrificial Lamb of God — Jesus. (For more about this symbol and other occultic signs, refer to the later chapter that deals exclusively with this topic.)

On the back cover of *The Satanic Bible* one sees the face of its author superimposed over the pentagram as if to suggest that Anton Szandor LaVey is the personification of Satan. It is a sinister picture indeed; the man's dark eyes stare from the cover without a hint of warmth. His countenance is severely dark and foreboding. The black mustache and goatee that surround his unsmiling lips add to the aura of mystery this photograph evokes. This is Anton LaVey, the best-known satanist in the world.

"The Black Pope"

LaVey reports that his interest in satanism evolved as a result of hypocrisies he had observed in the lives of people who claimed to be Christians. As a sixteen-year-old boy, he played the organ for carnivals and "tent-show evangelists."

Here's how he described the experiences that led him to seek answers in satanism: "On Saturday night I would see men lusting after half-naked girls dancing at the carnival, and on Sunday morning when I was playing the organ for tent-show evangelists at the other end of the carnival lot, I would see these same men sitting in the pews asking God to forgive them and purge them of carnal desires. And the next Saturday night they'd be back at the carnival or some other place of indulgence."

Finally, the youth concluded, "I knew then that the Christian Church thrives on hypocrisy, and that man's carnal nature will out!"[3] It certainly did in LaVey's case, for his books are replete with admonitions to gratify the lusts of the flesh.

Many contemporary satanists, like LaVey, report that their involvement with the occult began as a result of perceived hypocrisy they had experienced in a church setting.

One young lady I counseled with explained, "I was searching for something that was real — not plastic like the phony people I saw at church. Among satanists, I found love and acceptance that I had never seen anywhere else."

I could identify with her statement because I had been on a similar search. Like this young lady, I was looking for reality. There were a few times in those early days when I even went to church, hoping to find answers for all my questions. Each time I did so, I left feeling bitterly disappointed.

A Country Church in Texas

Once, for example, before I became directly involved in satanism, I was riding my motorcycle across the Texas plains when I heard a ringing church bell. It was a Sunday morning.

I had just concluded a successful drug deal in Louisiana and I was on my way to California with a wad of money in my knapsack and great emptiness in my soul. When I heard those church bells chiming from the steeple of the white-frame country church, something began to gnaw at my feelings. Was God trying to break through to me? I decided I would go to church to try and find out.

I turned my Harley-Davidson in the direction of the steeple I saw in the distance. When I got to the church parking lot, I pulled my bike up, then headed toward the stairs leading to the entrance.

I was dirty and disheveled, dressed in blue jeans and a sleeveless denim jacket. My long hair had not been washed in days.

Four well-dressed deacons confronted me at the top of the stairs. "Where do you think you're going?" one of them challenged.

"To church," I replied with a smile. "I'm going to meet God."

"Not with these decent folks, you're not," an overweight, balding man stated with finality in his voice as he moved in front of the door to block my way.

I couldn't believe what was happening. Those four men came toward me, grabbed me and threw me down the steps! As a result of the fall, I broke my thumb.

As I got up, I stared at them with tears in my eyes. They just looked back and laughed. As I headed toward the parking lot, I heard one of them say, "I guess we showed that hippie what he deserved!"

In my heart of hearts I made a vow that day, "If this is what Christianity is all about, then I want nothing to do with it!"

At a nearby restaurant, a kind waitress with bleached blonde hair saw my need for nurturing and T.L.C. She took two wooden ice cream spoons and made a splint for my thumb.

She asked, "What happened to you?"

I told her the story of my attempt to go to church and her response was simple and direct, "I wouldn't give you five cents for all the Christians in the world!"

Several days later I was in California, and soon thereafter I took my first steps toward becoming a satanist high priest!

Satan Wants You!

During the 1950's, the anti-witchcraft laws that had existed on the books in England were repealed. Almost immediately thereafter, paganism (in its multitudinous forms) began to resurface there.

Gerald Gardner, the founder of Gardnerian witchcraft, claimed direct descent from earlier pagan traditions. Although this assertion is not generally taken seriously by historians, those looking for legitimacy within the framework of their occult interests find his claims appealing.

Other occult researchers, such as Stewart Farrar, describe four separate branches within the Wiccan (white witchcraft) tradition.[4] These four types of witchcraft are:

1. Hereditary
2. Traditional
3. Gardnerian
4. Alexandrian

Hereditary witches, according to Farrar, were initiated by a family member who can trace an unbroken line of descent from earlier traditions. The validity of these claims is difficult to prove.

Gardnerian witches form their belief system and practices from the teachings of Gerald Gardner who claims he was initiated into witchcraft by a hereditary witch.

Alexandrian witches are those who trace their initiation to Alex Sanders and/or his wife, Maxine, who formed a rapidly growing, somewhat self-styled movement within traditional witchcraft.

Traditional witches are those who look to ancient writings for guidance.

The sixties were a time of great social unrest with all the upheaval related to the Vietnam War, political assassinations and racial problems providing a fertile ground for the sprouting of new religions on both sides of the Atlantic.

People were becoming quite disenchanted with the trends of society and they began to search for alternatives to established practices. I was one of the many who turned to drugs and Eastern religions for guidance.

A number of satanic and quasi-satanic groups grew out of the drug sub-culture, including the Process Church of the Final Judgment and Charles Manson's "family."

In the mid-sixties, as we have already discovered, the Church of Satan was organized. Arthur Lyons has pointed out in his book, *Satan Wants You,* that Susan Atkins, one of the Tate-LaBianca killers, was briefly associated with the Church of Satan before getting involved with Charles Manson.[5]

This fact, in and of itself, does not establish a direct involvement of the Church of Satan in those ritual murders, but it does serve to show how easily one can drift from a presumably legal organization into a violent, criminal expression of satanism.

The Satanic Bible

In order to understand some of the principles and practices associated with satanism there is no better place to look than in *The Satanic Bible*. Not all satanists, however, use it as their sourcebook. Although the book does not overtly advocate any illegal activity, its philosophy of total self-indulgence and self-interest has undoubtedly contributed to the rise of satanically motivated crimes in the 1980's.

In *The Satanic Bible* one finds the nine satanic statements:

"1. Satan represents indulgence, instead of abstinence!

"2. Satan represents vital existence, instead of spiritual pipe dreams!

"3. Satan represents undefiled wisdom, instead of hypocritical self-deceit!

"4. Satan represents kindness to those who deserve it, instead of love wasted on ingrates!

"5. Satan represents vengeance, instead of turning the other cheek!

"6. Satan represents responsibility to the responsible, instead of concern for psychic vampires!

"7. Satan represents man as just another animal, sometimes better, more often worse than those that walk on all-fours, who, because of his 'divine spiritual and intellectual development,' has become the most vicious animal of all!

"8. Satan represents all of the so-called sins, as they all lead to physical, mental, or emotional gratification!

"9. Satan has been the best friend the church has ever had, as he has kept it in business all these years!"[6]

These nine creeds form the basis of the satanic philosophy. Presumably, they are a parody of the Ten Commandments which Jews and Christians strive to follow. Simply stated, then, the laws of satanism are:

1. Practice indulgence.
2. Seek vengeance when someone wrongs you.
3. Look for sensual and emotional gratification.
4. Come from self-interest at all times.

Within *The Satanic Bible* one also finds the following: The Book of Satan — the Infernal Diatribe; The Book of Lucifer — the Enlightenment; The Book of Belial — the Mastery of the Earth; and The Book of Leviathan — the Raging Sea. Each of these four sections contains teachings on a wide range of subjects: love and hate, evidence of a "new satanic age," satanic sex, sacrifices, the black mass, religious holidays, theories and practices of satanic magic, satanic rituals, invocations and incantations.

Other Satanic Organizations

A colonel in the military reserve of the United States, Dr. Michael Aquino, broke away from The Church of Satan to form the Temple of Set. ("Set" is the Egyptian name for Satan, the mythological god of death.)

Like the Church of Satan, the Temple of Set has a tax-exempt status as a legal religion in the United States.

On June 21, 1975, according to Aquino, Satan appeared to him as Set. This account is similar to the one given much earlier by Aleister Crowley who claimed he was visited in Egypt by the spirit Aiwaz. Like Crowley, Aquino sees himself as the antichrist mentioned in the Bible and he has even tattooed the number 666 on his forehead![7]

Aquino's great visibility in the media allows many young people to learn about his satanist ideals. Currently, he is facing charges of child molestation.[8]

The Process Church of the Final Judgment is another contemporary organization of satanists. It is reported that this group had some degree of influence in the life of David Berkowitz (alias, "the son of Sam") whose murder spree in New York City left six dead and several others injured during the seventies.

Berkowitz left a copy of *The Anatomy of Witchcraft* in his room. On one of its pages these words were highlighted:

Thou shalt kill. They say they are dedicated to bringing about the end of the world by murder, violence and chaos — but they, the chosen, will survive to build a new world of satanic glory.[9]

It is believed that at least 450 identifiable satanic groups exist in the United States alone. Many others are hidden.

Some satanists form their own groups and covens apart from mainstream satanism. They call themselves self-styled (or solitary) satanists because they create their own rites and rituals based on their understanding of occultic concepts.

A Former Satanist on Death Row

One of these self-styled satanists was Sean Sellers, a twenty-one-year-old man who is on death row at Oklahoma State Penitentiary for the murder of his parents and a convenience store clerk.

Sean entered the frightening world of satanism by way of his involvement in a role-playing game called "Dungeons and Dragons" and other occult games. Through these influences and personal research in occult literature, Sean developed his own approach to satanism while he was a young teen-ager.

The results were tragic. Now an earnest Christian, Sean reaches out to other young people in an effort to help them avoid the horrendous mistakes he made. He writes, "...satanism leads to nowhere. Fear, pain, and loneliness are the inevitable results of the occult, and all the perverted ideals and so-called occult games are doorways into the pathway to nowhere."[10]

Generational Satanists

In recent years many have reported involvement with generational satanism. Most of those who have extricated themselves from this form of satanism report that they were sexually abused by members of their own families. Some have developed multiple personalities (alters) as a result of growing up in homes where satanism and sexual abuse were practiced.

There is evidence to suggest that some of these families have been involved in Satan worship for several generations, even centuries.

I have spoken with several people who have come from generational satanist families. Without exception, their stories are filled with reports of ritual abuse, human sacrifices, sexual immorality and diabolical schemes of Satan.

We have received countless letters at Warnke Ministries from men and women and young people whose lives have been shattered by generational satanism. The following excerpt expresses the concern of one mother whose children were raped, sodomized and tortured by their satanist father:

> Last February, my seven-year-old daughter told me about being sexually molested. Approximately a month later, her ten-year-old brother also admitted that he had been raped and sodomized. My family and I have borne up under these tragic revelations as, little by little, my children recalled how they had been taken to meetings in the wooded areas, left with strangers who sexually molested them and tortured them to ensure they would never tell anyone. They have drawn diadems that they remember seeing and have described the garbs of those attending the meetings. They were forced to do so many unthinkable things that my family and I don't know how we have kept our sanity because our hearts have been ripped out. Not only for what they have been through, but also wondering just how we help heal their wounds. Sometimes I wonder if it is even possible.
>
> My daughter is currently in a home for abused children, and my son is awaiting placement. My son worries me most of all at this point because, in his adolescent way of so strongly wanting to be normal, he refuses to let out his deep hurting.
>
> The perpetrator is their natural father. We had been divorced for three years before the children "told." My children relate that these events had gone on since they can remember and continued on through weekend visitations. They have both participated in and witnessed human infant sacrifices.

Please, Mr. Warnke, where was I? Why, didn't I know? Why didn't they tell sooner?

We have been able to work with this mother to help her see that she is not at fault. She is learning how to be more gentle with herself so that she will be able to help her abused children. The grace of God is at work in her life and the lives of her children.

All too often, people choose to deny the possibility of satanism and specific satanic acts. This is one of Satan's schemes — to get our focus off the problem by dodging the issues.

Infiltration

Some of the letters and telephone calls we receive tell us incredible stories of individuals who pretend to be Christians in order to gain respectability and other benefits, but who are actually satanists disguising themselves as born-again believers in Christ.

This phenomenon may come directly out of the corrupt schemes of Satan or it may be a manifestation of multiple personality disorder which exists quite often in satanism. Someone with a multiple personality disorder has created different personalities within himself or herself in order to protect himself or herself from hurt, prosecution, guilt and insanity.

Many people with multiple-personality disorders were sexually abused in childhood. In such cases, the psyche literally shatters into several pieces. Unless integration occurs through the grace and power of Jesus Christ, the individual is consigned to a life of drifting in and out of several identities and personalities. There have been certain cases reported where people with this disorder have had as many as ninety different personalities, but it is far more common for them to have less than ten.

In satanic circles, the phenomenon of multiple-personality disorder is known as ''alters.'' At one moment, the person may be meek and loving (Christ-like) but within seconds he can be transformed into a sinister, angry personality (Satan-like). Everything changes in the life and appearance of someone who undergoes such an ''altering.''' Even the vocal sounds change. So do the values, beliefs, feelings and thoughts. The facial countenance is altered according to the personality change as well.

We have even received reports of pastors who have preached to a Christian flock on Sunday morning and to a satanic coven on Friday evening! In most cases, because of the secrecy of satanism, such an imposter is not discovered.

Some children who grew up in secretly satanic homes have reported to us that their parents pretended to be born-again Christians during the daytime hours but were actually practicing satanists at night! Can you imagine how confusing it would be to grow up in such a home?

Other practicing satanists will infiltrate church congregations from time to time in order to manipulate believers into doing something for them. Actually, most infiltration comes in this form. These satanists enjoy ''putting one over'' on Christians and they do so with a fiendish sense of delight.

In the Sermon on the Mount, Jesus foretold of this kind of infiltration:

> **Watch out for false prophets. They come to you in sheep's clothing, but inwardly they are ferocious wolves. By their fruit you will recognize them.**
>
> **(Matt. 7:15-16a NIV)**

God has given us the Spirit of His Son Jesus Christ to help us discern between the true and the false. This is one of the gifts of the Spirit (see 1 Cor. 12).

The Apostle John shows us how to use this gift:

> **Dear children, this is the last hour; and as you have heard that the anti-christ is coming, even now many anti-christs have come. This is how we know it is the last hour. . . . But you have an anointing from the Holy One, and all of you know the truth. . . . no lie comes from the truth. Who is the liar? It is the man who denies that Jesus is the Christ. . . .**
>
> **(1 John 2:18-23 NIV)**

Because such things are taking place today, we know we are in the last days. We have already entered that long-ago-prophesied era when Satan will unleash every possible weapon at his disposal. Our response should not be fear, however, but we should become equipped for the spiritual warfare that such an age demands. Let us always remember these words: "The reason the Son of God appeared was to destroy the devil's work" (1 John 3:8b NIV). The wonderful truth is that this has already been accomplished through the finished work of Jesus on the cross.

How Satan Works

I became one of the self-styled satanists we mentioned earlier. I started my journey into darkness when I was just a little boy.

When I was six years old my alcoholic father who had been drinking heavily called me to climb up on his lap. I was eager to respond because I very much wanted closeness with my father. Happy and trustingly, I did as he asked, but as I turned to smile at him, he smashed one of his empty beer bottles in my face!

The glass shattered in a thousand pieces after tearing my nose and check in such a way that my face looked as if it had been mauled by a lion. At first I whimpered out of fear, but when I touched my face and saw the blood on my fingers, I began to sob and scream. My drunken father grabbed me and shook me. "Don't you ever trust anyone!" he admonished as he pushed me to the floor and stormed out of the room.

I'll never forget that experience and the import of those harsh words from my own father. I did love him and, even then, I realized that it was his concern for me, mixed with his own pain and confusion, that had caused him to use such an "object lesson" in my training that day.

One thing I knew for certain was that I couldn't trust him again! That experience and several subsequent blows to my ego left me feeling empty and lost. I grew up feeling both unloved and unlovable.

By the time I was eleven years old, both of my parents had died, and I was raised by foster parents. Even though my foster-home situation was basically a good one, growing up in that environment can still, to this day, cause feelings of not being wanted and fear of being an outsider within me.

As a child, I had a great deal of interest in spiritual things, but, even though I often went to church, there was no clear spiritual direction in my upbringing. My parents were Catholics, and I was brought up with strict Catholic teachings. After my father died, I lived with two aunts for about six months. They exposed me to biblical teaching, but it did not have time to sink in. Soon after, when I went to live with my foster family in California, I experienced a very different situation. Although they were moral people, there was not very much spiritual training in the household.

During high school I began to adopt the role of a seeker. I developed an active interest in occult/witchcraft literature and attained a relatively high degree of understanding in occult philosophy. Also, as I reported earlier, I watched "Bewitched" and other TV shows with occult themes regularly. When watching such programs, I had a note pad with me and I wrote down any new word or concept that was incorporated into the programs. One could say that my interest in spiritual things at the time was very intense, but also quite generic.

As time went on, however, I left the "dabbling phase" of occult involvement and went wholeheartedly in the direction of satanism.

Many teen-agers get started in satanism the same way I did — innocently. Eventually they learn that Satan offers them power and control over difficult circumstances in their lives.

Many of these kids have been abused psychologically, physically and/or sexually, and they have become anti-social in their orientation to other people. They frequently do poorly in school.

Their fantasy lives, on the other hand, are filled with excitement — even thoughts of revenge. In satanism they find a way to justify all of these feelings and rebellious behaviors. It offers them a social context in which to express their pent-up frustrations and animosities. In effect, then, they become "rebels *with* a cause," instead of being simply rebels.

We would throw parties in an effort to find others who felt like us — such individuals, we realized, were "ripe for the picking." We would watch them to see if they were rebels too. If they were, we knew we had likely candidates for satanism.

Step by step, and little by little, we would lead them into deeper involvement with the occult. If they continued to show interest along the way, we would show them even deeper satanic secrets. This is known as *progressive entrapment,* because the individuals didn't realize that we were setting them up, whetting their appetites, getting them used to their craving and hunger for "devil's food."

When you think about it realistically, there are only two kinds of spiritual food from which to choose, either "devil's food" or "angel's food." I have partaken of both, and, believe me, the taste of "angel's food" (the Bread of Life — Jesus Christ) is incomparably better than the alternative. It is spiritually nutritious, leading the eater to eternal and abundant life; whereas, "devil's food" is poisonous — it always leads to death!

"Taste and see that the Lord is good; blessed is the man who takes refuge in him" (Ps. 34:8 NIV).

3

The Satanic Revolution

Every Friday evening just before midnight, a group of
men and women gathers at a home in San Francisco, and
there, under the guidance of their high priest, a sorcerer or
magus sometimes called the "Black Pope of Satanism," they
study and practice the ancient art of black magic. Precisely
at midnight they perform satanic rituals that apparently differ
little from those allegedly performed by European satanists
and witches at least as early as the seventh century. By the
dim and flickering light of black candles, hooded figures
perform their rites upon the traditional satanic altar — the
naked body of a beautiful young witch calling forth the
mysterious powers of darkness to do their bidding. Beneath
the emblem of Baphomet, the horned god, they engage in
indulgences of flesh and sense for whose performance their
forebears suffered death and torture at the hand of earlier
Christian zealots.[1]

(Edward A. Moody)

The End Justifies the Means

Why do satanists do what they do? What motivates them
to cross over the boundary that separates the Kingdom of Light
from the kingdom of darkness? Just what are their goals?

In order to answer these questions, we must examine the
goals of Satan himself. It is clear that Satan is fomenting a
spiritual revolution in the world today, and all his goals center
on this primary aim. These goals are clearly defined in the Bible.
The means used to reach those goals are rooted in deception
and confusion.

55

To Be Greater Than God

Isaiah reveals the primary motive of Satan:

> **You said in your heart, "I will ascend to heaven; I will raise my throne above the stars of God; I will sit enthroned on the mount of the assembly, on the utmost heights of the sacred mountain. I will ascend above the tops of the clouds; I will make myself like the most High."**
>
> **(Isa. 14:13,14 NIV)**

Satan is building a kingdom — the kingdom of darkness — on this earth. As my good friend, Hal Lindsey, has pointed out, "Satan is alive and well on planet earth."

Satan's primary purpose is to take people to hell. He will do whatever needs to be done to accomplish this purpose. He wants to keep people from finding Jesus. By doing this he knows that he is doing the one thing that hurts the Lord the most.

Satan knows that he cannot win a head-on confrontation with God. He tried that and lost. Now all he can do is try and get even.

Human beings are only tools to be used and discarded in Satan's quest for vengeance. The devil knows that each time one of us steps into eternity without a saving knowledge of Jesus, it breaks the Lord's heart and puts Jesus on the cross all over again.

Satanism and satanists are just two of his many ploys.

> **And no wonder, for Satan himself masquerades as an angel of light. It is not surprising, then, if his servants [oftentimes satanists and occultists] masquerade as servants of righteousness. Their end will be what their actions deserve.**
>
> **(2 Cor. 11:14,15 NIV)**

Many occultists, such as white witches and Wicca followers, will say that they employ supernatural powers to accomplish good goals, such as healing. They are simply masquerading as servants of righteousness, oftentimes unwittingly.

To Destroy the Church

Many means are employed by satanists in order to attack the Church of Jesus Christ. As we have already pointed out, the Black Mass is a mockery of Holy Communion. In *Occult Shock and Psychic Forces,* Clifford Wilson and John Weldon describe the anti-Christian symbolism of the Black Mass:

> **A high priest stands by the table dressed in bishop's robes. On his person he wears an inverted cross. He throws a larger cross to the floor . . . . He then spits upon the cross, with an obscene gesture, and cries, "Hail Satan!" Thus begins the sickening and blasphemous ritual, as the devil worshippers repeat the Lord's Prayer backward and make mockery of the ordinances of the church.[2]**

The Black Mass deceives people by leading them in rebellion against the teachings and practices of the Church. Often, satanists will try to do the exact opposite of what the Church advocates. They emphasize hate instead of love, lies instead of truth, and the fulfillment of the sensuous lusts instead of self-control.

Man is basically a spiritual creature. He will look for spiritual comfort somewhere. If we Christians are not doing our jobs, Satan will do everything he can to take up the slack.

The Satanic Method

Satan is pragmatic. He will do whatever he can to accomplish his goals. Deception, one of his schemes that we've already alluded to, is his primary tactic.

Jesus said this about His enemy — and ours:

> **He was a murderer from the beginning, not holding to the truth, for there is no truth in him. When he lies, he speaks his native language, for he is a liar and the father of lies.**
>
> **(John 8:44-45 NIV)**

Satan's greatest lie that he perpetuates is that somehow he's going to get out of what he's got coming. He uses all kinds of deceptions and lies to enlist soldiers who will fight for him. The truth is, he has even deceived himself!

Jesus said:

> **On this rock I will build my church, and the gates of Hades [hell] will not overcome it.**
>
> **(Matt. 16:18 NIV)**

Though he apparently doesn't realize it, Satan is already a defeated foe. His host of human followers does not realize that they have been lied to. The demons, however, know that there is only one God, and this knowledge causes them to tremble. (See James 2:19). So many of the people we work with at Warnke Ministries have been victims of the lying schemes of Satan.

I Don't Have Anything to Live For

One of those victims was a teenager named Marcie. She chose satanism as a way to make friends. Little by little, the satanists led her down a darkened pathway that was paved with deception.

As a child, Marcie had been sexually abused. There was a history of alcoholism in her family. Her parents frequently beat her. Her self-esteem was totally shattered.

To make matters worse, she had been attacked by a German shepherd when she was quite little. The dog had ripped into her face and neck with a fury, tearing open her scalp and leaving ugly scars all over her face.

She began taking drugs to ease her psychic pain. At this stage in her life, satanists moved in to complete the destruction of her life.

Twice she had overdosed on heroin. As she began to advance in the satanic power structure, she found herself enmeshed in a power play with other leaders in the group.

All of this had left her confused and without hope. She began to contemplate suicide.

In the midst of all this turmoil, a person who had attended one of my concerts gave her a tape that I had made.

She listened intently to my words: "God loves you and accepts you just as you are. No matter what you have done, He wants to receive you unto himself. When Jesus died on the cross, it was for *you*. The blood of Jesus Christ will cleanse you of your sins and make you into a lovely new creature. If you will accept Jesus as your Savior, you will be washed in His blood. When the blood of Jesus takes away your sins, it will be just as if you had never sinned...."

Marcie learned that I was coming to her city to hold a concert. A week before my arrival, she sent me this note:

> **I don't have anything to live for. I'm going to cash it in. When you're here [in my city], I will be in the audience. You'd better be good, because if you don't convince me, right after the show, I'm going to kill myself.**

When I received this letter I felt overwhelmed by the responsibility she challenged me with. Her plan of suicide weighed heavily on my heart. Immediately, I began to pray. I prayed all that week, and when I got to my hotel room on the day of the concert, I continually asked the Lord for guidance. "Show me what to say, Lord. Help me to say the right thing."

His gentle voice responded with a reminder in my spirit, "Marcie's not really *your* problem. She's *my* responsibility. You just get up there on stage and do your regular thing, because that's what I've called you to do."

I needed that word from the Lord. It lifted the tremendous weight I'd been carrying off my shoulders. When I got to the auditorium I felt free and refreshed.

As the Lord had directed, I simply did my thing. The response to my message was overwhelming. More than one hundred people came forward to receive Jesus as their Savior.

One of those who did so was Marcie! I talked to her after the service. "You really spoke to me," she said.

"No, Marcie, I didn't speak to you. The Lord did."

"Thank you so much, Mike, for letting Him use you. I feel like a brand-new baby!"

"You are, Marcie, you are," I affirmed as I put my arms around her. "Jesus will always be with you."

I put Marcie in touch with good Christian people who I knew would have great patience with her. They helped her get away from her old associates and begin her new life in Christ. It was the love of God that reached her, giving great light to her darkened soul.

Satan's lies had nearly killed her, but Jesus had given her a whole new purpose for living. Every once in a while I still hear from Marcie. She's living for the Lord, in complete victory over the schemes of Satan.

Criminally-Oriented Satanic Covens

Many satanists will say that they are not responsible for most of the crimes that appear to have satanic overtones. Often, they will claim that child abuse, rape, murder and other crimes are committed by "crazy kids" or by individual psychopaths who are working on their own.

While the majority of the cases that have reached the courts have involved individuals rather than groups, group involvement in satanic criminal activities cannot be altogether discounted. Researchers like Maury Terry, the author of *The Ultimate Evil*, have been able to document the operations of criminally-oriented satanic covens.[3]

In a paper entitled "Contemporary Satanism: Establishment or Underground?", Lawrence Nelson and Diane Taub have used the terms "satanic establishment" and "satanic underground" to differentiate between legal and illegal satanic groups.[4]

Not all satanists give great credibility to *The Satanic Bible* as their source for inspiration. Whereas members of the organized Church of Satan describe their religion as being based purely on self-interest and self-indulgence rather than overt Satan-worship, other groups do get involved in specific criminal acts that stem from their worship of Satan.

In *The Black Arts,* a book by Richard Cavendish, there is a description of how animal and/or human sacrifices might play an important role in the occultist's quest for power:

> The sacrifice tends to be...closely associated with the ceremony itself and in modern rituals, the victim is sometimes slaughtered at the height of the ceremony....The most important reason for the sacrifice, however, is the psychological charge which the magician obtains from it. The frenzy which he induces in himself by ceremonious preparations, by incantations, by burning fumes, Is heightened by the savage act of slaughter and the pumping gush of red blood....It would obviously be more effective to sacrifice a human being because of the far greater psychological "kick" involved.[5]

It is inaccurate to say that all satanists perform human sacrifices. At the same time, however, it is equally inaccurate to dismiss all forms of satanism as being harmless, as certain satanists would claim.

The Satanic Bible itself contains a section entitled, "On the Choice of a Human Sacrifice." LaVey writes:

> The question arises, "Who, then, would be considered a fit and proper human sacrifice, and how is one qualified to pass judgment on such a person?" The answer is brutally simple. Anyone who has unjustly wronged you — one who has "gone out of his way" to hurt you — to deliberately cause trouble and hardship for you or those dear to you. In short, a person asking to be cursed by their very actions.[6]

Although LaVey qualifies this subject by suggesting that the sacrifice should be symbolic only, by way of a curse, he concludes with this remark, "...if your curse provokes their actual annihilation, rejoice that you have been instrumental in ridding the world of a pest!"[7]

Animal Sacrifices

There is a definite increase in newspaper reports around the world that link mysterious deaths of animals to satanism. One such report appeared recently in a newspaper published in Scranton, Pennsylvania:

Dog's Death Linked to Satanism

A skinned and dismembered dog found Thursday in Taylor is being linked with satanist activity in the area, according to police.... It was skinned and its feet, genitals, tail and ears had been cut off....Police theorize that the animal parts will be used in a satanic ritual, as this weekend marks the beginning of the rites leading to Halloween, satanism's "high holy days"....[8]

Similar accounts appear in newspapers around the world just prior to and following satanic holidays. (We will discuss those holidays in more detail in a later chapter.)

United Press International reported the following case of sacrificial activities from Sacramento, California:

Animal, Human Sacrifices Claimed in Devil Cult Case

Bizarre details of a child molestation ring that involved "devil movies," witchcraft, mock wedding ceremonies and drinking rat's blood were made public Monday in court documents.

Deputy District Attorney Rick Lewkowitz said investigators were still looking into the possibility that some of the five men arrested may have produced a so-called snuff movie in which a child was killed while being photographed.[9]

Although there is a giant leap from making animal sacrifices to human sacrifices, there is plenty of evidence to suggest that some satanists see it as only a small step.

Police records abound with gruesome tales of children and adults who have been used to satisfy the aberrant lusts for power, sexual gratification and evil manifested by many satanists. (A later chapter will deal with occult crimes in more detail.)

Human Sacrifices

A few years ago I was called by a police department in a western state to help them with an investigation of alleged ritual abuse. They showed me some gruesome photographs of a four-year-old girl who had been brutally murdered. The individuals who had committed this abominable act actually went so far as to skin the baby. It was believed that the little child had been flayed while she was alive!

Such experiences have caused me to realize how serious the present-day spiritual battle has become. Fortunately, public officials and law-enforcement agents are becoming aware of the problem too. Warnke Ministries is often called upon to assist criminal investigators in unraveling crimes of ritual abuse. Indeed, we feel called to assist in whatever way we can.

Many of the mass murderers and child abductors who have been apprehended have had occult experiences in their backgrounds. Even Adolph Hitler, it has been reported, was heavily involved in the occult long before he rose to the position of Germany's leader. It has been suggested that he planned his suicide to coincide with *Walpurgisnacht,* a significant date in the witches' calendar. According to these reports, Hitler believed he was making the supreme sacrifice to Satan by committing suicide.[10]

Breeders

In 1988 a special broadcast of the "Geraldo!" program was devoted to satanism in America. Three women on this show testified to their experience of having been used at very young ages to be "breeders" of babies to be used as child sacrifices in satanic rituals.

One of these women, named Cheryl, described her baby being impaled through the heart by a cross!

It is believed that such "baby breeding" is employed by some satanists because it minimizes the possibilities of their being caught. After the sacrifice is completed, the child's body is burned and buried to avoid detection.

Who Satan Is

Although satanism shares many characteristics that are common to other occult orientations, it has its own set of unique features. The most obvious of these is that true satanists literally worship Satan, the enemy of God. Without Christianity (which defines the nature and character of Satan), it is unlikely that satanism, as we now know it, would exist. In other words, satanists derive their understanding of Satan and his purposes from the Bible, at least in part.

In both Hebrew and Greek, the word "Satan" means "opponent" or "adversary." His depiction as the embodiment of evil stems from this concept.

It is important to realize that Satan does not have powers and abilities that are equal to God's. Whereas God is omnipotent (all-powerful), omniscient (all-knowing), and omnipresent (present everywhere), Satan does not have all power, he does not know everything and *he can be in only one place at a time.* His representatives, both satanists and demonic entities, help him to accomplish his purposes, but he himself can be only in one place at a time.

Satan will never be able to produce evil in the same degree that God produces good. A satanist is usually deceived into thinking that Satan's capabilities are at least equal to God's. Most believe that he is even more powerful than God.

Attractions to Satanism

Given that many different expressions of satanism exist, it is difficult to make universal statements about what attracts people to satanism. Usually, however, a person who is fascinated by the mysterious, unexplainable aspects of life is susceptible to occult lures.

Most of the attempts to study satanism have focused on visible, organized groups like the Church of Satan headquartered in San Francisco. This is because such groups are more accessible than hidden covens that are more likely to be involved in criminal activities.

Randall H. Alfred did such a study in which he identifies six specific attractions to satanism that are applicable in a variety of settings:

1. *Hedonism* (living for pleasure). Since satanism advocates self-indulgence and self-gratification, some people find the lack of self-restraint desirable.

2. *Magical Power.* Satanists believe in the effectiveness of supernatural powers for reaching their goals. They incorporate spells, ceremonies, incantations, symbols and rituals to tap into this power.

3. *Participation in Forbidden Acts.* This possibility grabs the attention of those who are in a state of anti-social rebellion. This aspect of diabolism (devil-worship) serves two functions: it supposedly "frees" a person from the "bondage" of his or her past training, particularly traditional religious training; it also enhances the bond between group members while isolating the group from the outside influences.

4. *Iconoclasm.* This refers to the symbolic destruction of established attitudes or institutions. The desecration of crosses and other Christian symbols is appealing to those who wish to rebel.

5. *Leadership Charm.* The high priests of many satanic cults often are charming individuals who possess the ability to influence others. Those who have weak self-concepts frequently find such strong and charming authority figures very appealing.

6. *Safety From End-Times Catastrophes.* Some leaders tell their followers that their group will be victorious

at the final battle (Armageddon). Such teachings fall into a general occult category known as millenarianism. Charles Manson taught his followers that in a future war known as "Helter Skelter," the black peoples of the world will unite to overthrow the whites. In the "new world" that will follow this conflict, Manson and his followers will be in charge, he taught.

The Church of Satan, also, is somewhat millenarian in that its followers believe that a new satanic order will emerge in which satanists will have a governing role. This is the satanic revolution.[11]

When these philosophical orientations are combined with a variety of promises and practices, such as the provision of drugs, free sex, power and other inducements, the making of the modern-day satanist is facilitated (made easier). Satanism becomes an effective way to express rebellion against society and its established values and traditions.

Satanic Strategies

Terry Ann Modica has written an informative book on this subject entitled, *The Power of the Occult*. In the book, she lists twelve favorite strategies employed by Satan (and satanists) in order to lure people in:

"1. He gets people to attribute all spiritual experiences to God.

"2. He twists and perverts Scripture.

"3. He makes life so comfortable, we see no need for Jesus.

"4. He gives us reasons to doubt God's promises, so he can separate us from God's power.

"5. He bombards our minds with thoughts, desires, and motives that lead us away from God.

"6. He feeds us fear and other negative emotions that keep us from knowing the joy of Christ.

"7. He gives us illnesses and diseases, to discourage us and blind us or deafen us to God's Word.

"8. He desensitizes us to immorality through such repeated exposure as violent or morally lacking television shows.

"9. He tempts us, although he cannot do anything against the will of God, and God does not permit him to test us beyond our powers to resist.

"10. He falsely accuses us, making us feel guilty or unforgiveable or unworthy of God's love.

"11. He puts us in bondage, i.e. controls parts of our lives to prevent us from receiving the abundance Christ came to give us.

"12. He possesses us, if possible, occupying our whole lives to keep Christ out."[12]

Although the above list reveals Satan's strategies against Christians, in particular, it is important to realize that these same schemes are used to keep people who do not know Christ in a confused and blinded condition.

One glance at television programing in the nineties shows us how the desensitization process works. Little by little, the foundational values of our civilization are being eroded.

Recently, while watching the late-night news on television, I was taken aback by a video clip that was inserted into the middle of the program. They showed an actual murder that appeared to have ritual-abuse overtones, in its entirety! The video recorded the murder of a nineteen-year-old boy who was tied in a kneeling position. His assassin, a young woman of his approximate age, took a revolver and fired at his chest from a range of fifteen feet or so. Still alive, the young man cried for mercy. His murderess walked up to him, grabbed him by the hair, and shot him in the head! Then, she turned to the camera and grinned!

This same video (known as a "snuff film") had been used as evidence against the young woman in her trial for murder. Why it was shown on television I will never understand.

A couple of days later, I called the news producer of the station. "What was your rationale in showing that tape?" I asked point-blankly.

He fumbled and faltered with his words and tried to come up with some kind of defense for showing it. He was totally unsuccessful in giving any reason for it.

Then I asked him, "Did anyone else call to protest it?"

"No, you are the only one."

Has our society become so desensitized by Satan that we can watch such a scene without any reaction? Such certainly appears to be the case. Because this desensensitization is taking place all around us, we need to be especially alert. We need to see what is happening and to take a stand against it!

Other Motivations for Involvement in the Occult

Despite recent extensive media coverage of witchcraft and satanism, many people choose to ignore the possibility that there are large numbers of witches, satanists and occultists in our society today. For over 500 years, western cultures have emphasized science over magic and rationalism over religion. Nevertheless, as anthropologist Arthur Lyons has pointed out, the proclamation of the death of magical religions has been premature. In his book, *The Second Coming: Satanism in America,* he states:

> **Western man, trained from birth to discard and smother any belief he might have in a supernatural realm, extends this field of vision to any of those people he might encounter who do believe. One must not necessarily postulate the existence of a supernatural realm, however, to acknowledge the existence of a hard-care, fanatical group that does.[13]**

In other words, whether we believe in the power of magic or not does not prohibit others from having these beliefs.

In order, therefore, to really grasp the attraction of witchcraft, satanism and occultism, it is not sufficient just to accept their existence. One must also understand the means in which persons are motivated to pursue occult philosophies and the meanings their adherents find in occult beliefs. Already we have discussed various social conditions which permit an increase in occult activity and we have identified certain steps in the process of getting involved. (In the next chapter we will go into even more detail to explain further steps in the conversion process.)

We do not have a complete picture of these factors until we consider the expectations and motivations of individuals who choose the occult. In most instances, the individual must come to a point of personal choice. Usually this is a gradual process. In fact, it is not a single choice, but the accumulation of a series of choices made over an extended period of time.

Even in these "enlightened times," the distance between rationality and superstition is not as great as we usually suppose. British author G.K. Chesterton maintains that "Superstition occurs in all ages, and especially in rationalistic ones."[14] He goes on to describe a luncheon meeting in which he participated in a defense of Christianity against a large group of agnostics (people who insist that no knowledge of God is possible). Despite their rationalistic convictions, every person there admitted to carrying some charm or talisman (perhaps a rabbit's foot or "lucky coin," for example)!

Chesterton further suggests a connection between superstition and both skepticism and agnosticism:

> If [superstition] rests on something that is really a very human and intelligible sentiment. . . . It rests on two feelings: first, that we do not really know the laws of the universe; and second, that they may be very different to all that we call reason.[15]

Despite the rationalism of our culture and the disregard of what cannot be scientifically measured, a "sense of the mystic" is often regarded as a fundamental attribute of humanity, even by many social scientists. They are quick to point to "magical thinking" when it is observed in people who use wishing and hoping as devices for coping.

Magical Thinking

In *The Black Arts,* Richard Cavendish describes the magical perspective as a complex belief system that has its own laws and its own logic. The basis for the magical system lies not in observable or measurable phenomena, but in the thoughts, perceptions and emotions of the individual magician. Cavendish points out, ". . . [magical thinking] leaps to conclusions which are usually scientifically unwarranted but which often seem poetically right."[16]

Social research indicates that the followers of magical religions receive certain mental or emotional benefits from their beliefs. For example, nothing is left to chance in the magical mind-set. Every person, place, or thing has a purpose. Thus, magic provides an orderly model of the universe for its believers. This is especially attractive to an individual who has felt a lack of purpose in his or her life. Further, magical thinking puts the individual magician at the center of his her own universe. Not only does this make the magician feel powerful, but it provides relief (in the short term, at least) from the problems that result in one's everyday existence.

We are living in times of rapid cultural change, moral upheaval and reevaluation. In such times people experience great stress and pressure. Often, individuals find their personal moral and ethical values shaking, and even collapsing, in the face of such pressure to change and conform. Sociologists call this "anomie," (the state of normlessness in which the individual is unable to determine what is normal).

When political and religious leaders fall prey to this anomie themselves, the mainstream of society begins to question what is acceptable and unacceptable behavior as well. Recent scandals involving well-known figures have contributed to this societal response. Individuals so affected are likely to be attracted to a group-oriented occultic expression which gives them a new standard for determining what is acceptable and unacceptable.

Then there are those "magical thinkers" who choose to pursue a solitary expression of their craft. According to Emile Durkheim, a sociologist who wrote *The Elementary Forms of the Religious Life,* "There is no Church of magic."[17] He was implying that the practice of magic remains solitary rather than communal even if the individual is a member of a larger group.

In spite of this finding, many occult groups meet on a regular basis and perform communal rituals. this permits the group members to find validation for their beliefs and it gives them a sense of social solidarity.

Intense affiliation with an occult group usually involves submission to a leader who makes decisions not only about the group, but also about many private aspects of members' lives. In this way the individual member is relieved of the stresses associated with decision-making. Many leaders of occult groups possess sociopathic or psychopathic personalities which enable them to manipulate others to serve their personal whims.

Sex in Satan's Service

Carl A. Raschke, Professor of Religious Studies at the University of Denver, compares the worship of Satan to the uninhibited expression of man's most base nature:

> **The satanist mind-set is not 'religion' in the regular sense of the word, but a mystification of the most corrupt secular passions and values. LaVey in his public pronouncements about 'satanism' was merely presenting an artificial religious handle for good, old-fashioned lust and libertinism.[18]**

Although satanists are most outspoken about their rejection of traditional morals and values, the actions of many occultists go so far as to violate social norms. Sexuality is one area where this violation is especially common. For example, a number of rituals in "white" witchcraft are performed "sky-clad," another way of saying that they are performed in the nude. Commonly, witches will deny an association between ritual nudity and sexuality; it is nonetheless one of the attractions employed to get people involved.

Open sexual activity is quite common in the practice of satanism. *The Satanic Bible,* for example, describes an "Invocation for the Conjuration of Lust." In this section, LaVey offers "invocations" for both men and women. As we have already mentioned, Aleister Crowley was an occultist who became well-known for his use of sexual rituals. It is believed that he was a bisexual. There is even a report of an occasion when Crowley influenced a female follower to have sexual intercourse with a goat and, while she was doing so, the master occultist castrated the animal as an act of sacrifice![19]

One book that can be found on occult bookshelves, *Helping Yourself With White Witchcraft* by Al G. Manning, has a chapter entitled, "How to Use Rituals and Spells to Attract and Hold a Lover." He tells his readers how to pray to Venus and other "deities" in order to capture a lover and gives case studies of individuals who reportedly were successful in doing so.[20]

Sean Sellers, a former satanist who is now on death row, describes one of his first encounters with black magic as follows:

> This one, knowing I was interested in witchcraft, introduced me to a witch. Her name was Glasheeon. Some of her first words to me were, "You can go white magic or black magic. White magic is sorta hypocritical. If you want real power, go black magic."
>
> "Let's go black magic," I replied.
>
> She told me that the first step involved praying to Satan. She then gave me a special incantation to use to call forth the powers of evil. Now I was mad at God, but it still took me a day to get up the nerve to pray to the devil. That night was a turning point in my life.
>
> By Glasheeon's instructions, I stripped naked and laid down. "Satan, I call you forth to serve you," I prayed aloud

as I recited Glasheeon's incantation. I felt the room grow cold
and experienced the unmistakable presence of utter evil. My
pulse rate went up. The veins on my arm bulged. I experienced
an erection and began to feel a lifting sensation. Then
something touched me.

My eyes flew open but I saw only spots, as they had been
closed so tightly. Again I felt something touch me, and I shut
my eyes, feeling both terrified and thrilled. It felt like ice-
cold claws began to rake my body caressingly, and I literally
shook in erotic pleasure as they explored every inch of my
body. I heard an audible voice speak three words in a whisper,
"I love you."

I continued to pray, telling Satan I accepted and would
serve him. One by one, the invisible clawed hands touching
me disappeared, and my pulse rate fell. I was alone.

I sat up exhausted, hooked, unbelieving. I hadn't been
on drugs. I hadn't smoked a joint. It had been incredible,
and I knew it was real. I had found what I was looking for
— or so I thought....[21]

I understand what Sean experienced because through
witchcraft and satanism I had often known Satan's sexual lust
in rituals I had engaged in. As satanists, we would frequently
participate in full-blown sexual orgies laced with witchcraft.
Sometimes, members of the coven would entice others into the
group with sexual allurements.

On more than one occasion, I regret to admit, we
participated in ritual sexual abuse that even involved rape. Most
of the time I was too doped up to perform sexually, but I would
watch these lust rituals with great desire.

All over the world these kinds of activities are practiced
by occultists and satanists on a regular basis. People of all ages,
including children, are abducted to serve Satan's lusts. Many
times such rituals will end in murder for fear that the victim
will report the group.

Social and Political Motivations

Some writers look to the moral decay of our culture as a factor that contributes to the deliberate pursuit of evil. G.K. Chesterton wrote:

> There comes an hour in the afternoon when the child is tired of "pretending"; when he is weary of being a robber or red Indian. It is then that he torments the cat. There comes a time in the routine of an ordered civilization when the man is tired at playing at mythology and pretending that each tree is a maiden or that the moon made love to a man....Men seek stranger sins or more startling obscenities as stimulants to their jaded senses....they try to stab their nerves to life, if it were with the knives of Baal. They are walking in their sleep and try to wake themselves up with nightmares.[22]

This well-described transformation is what causes a "white witch," for example, to drift into "black magic" and satanism.

A sociologist, Gini Graham Scott, studied one satanic group that she called "The Church of Hu." The following represents part of her findings:

> Its members are alienated from society; the group's beliefs and structure encourage this alienation; members seek group and individual power through a tightly knit, almost military hierarchy and the group is increasingly turning inward to protect itself from the threat of impending doom.[23]

The War Rages On

Whatever the motivations, it is clear that satanists and occultists are engaged in a contemporary revolution to change society. Without realizing it, perhaps, they are intent on destroying the very foundations of our culture and the Church of Jesus Christ.

In studying the satanic revolution, we must always remember the words of the Apostle Paul:

> For our struggle is not against flesh and blood, but against the rulers, against the authorities, against the powers of this dark world and against the spiritual forces of evil in the heavenly realms. Therefore put on the full armor of God, so

**that when that day of evil comes, you may be able to stand
your ground, and after you have done everything, to stand.
(Eph. 6:12-13, NIV)**

We do not need to fear the enemy. We simply need to stand
against him. Paul wrote, "Finally, be strong in the Lord and
in his mighty power. Put on the full armor of God so that you
can taken your stand against the devil's schemes" (Eph. 6:10-11
NIV).

Dressing daily in the armor of God, we are prepared to
do battle. James wrote, "Submit yourselves, then, to God. *Resist
the devil,* and he will flee from you. Come near to God and
he will come near to you" (James 4:7-8 NIV).

4

Surrendering the Soul

What good will it be for a man if he gains the whole world, yet forfeits his soul? Or what can a man give in exchange for his soul?

(Jesus, as recorded in Matt. 16:26 NIV)

The Decision to Become a Satanist

The Satanic Bible teaches, "To become a Satanist, it is unnecessary to sell your soul to the Devil or make a pact with Satan. This threat was devised by Christianity to terrorize people so they would not stray from the fold."[1] Whether a satanist or an occultist actually goes through a formal ritual in which he makes a pact with Satan is not the issue. Knowingly or not, an individual who gets involved with the occult goes through a gradual process of surrendering his soul to "the prince of evil."

Many people, however, do sell their souls to Satan. Psychiatrist M. Scott Peck wrote about a man who did so in his best-selling book, *People of the Lie.* The man was named George and he had an obsessive-compulsive disorder. In order to deal with his compulsion that stemmed from a fear of death, George made a pact with the devil. Here is how he explained it:

> I made a pact with the devil. I mean, I really don't believe in the devil, but I had to do something, didn't I? So I made this agreement that if I did give in to my compulsion and go back, then the devil would see to it that my thought came true. Do you understand?...Then it occurred to me that the one thing I love most in the world is my son Christopher. So I made it part of the agreement that if I did give into the

77

compulsion and go back, the devil would see to it that
Christopher died an early death. Not only would I die but
Christopher would too. Now you know why I can't go back
anymore. Even if the devil's not real, I'm not willing to risk
Christopher's life on the issue — I love him so much.[2]

Dr. Peck worked with George over a period of time,
helping him to see that his pact with the devil involved the literal
surrender of his soul to evil whether George actually believed
in the devil or not. He confronted his client as follows:

You plead that you shouldn't be held accountable for
your pact with the devil because it was made under duress.
Why else would one contract with the devil, except to rid
oneself of some kind of suffering? If the devil is lurking
around, as some suggest, looking for souls who'll sell out to
him, I'm damn sure he's focusing all his attention on those
people who are suffering some kind of duress. The question
is not duress. The question is how people deal with duress.
Some withstand it, and overcome it, ennobled. Some break
and sell out. You sell out, and, I must say, you do it rather
easily. . . .

I think you really did make a pact with the devil, and
because you did, I think, for you, the devil became real. In
your desire to avoid pain, I think you called the devil into
existence. . . .[3]

This was the first time the psychotherapist had encountered
a client who had made a pact with the devil. He helped George
to see that the pact was reversible. He led him to assume personal
responsibility for his problems, and George began to grow
stronger.

Satan had deceived George to such an extent that he
wandered for several months in a dark maze of confusion, guilt
and fear. So many people are caught in that same web today
and, try as they might, they can't get out? It is our responsibility
to help them.

Newspapers are filled with stories of Satan's victims —
"The people of the lie." One case involving a fourteen-year-
old boy was reported in *The Chicago Tribune* on April 27, 1986:

Chicago, Illinois — The arrest last week of a 14-year-old DuPage County youth who allegedly threatened to kill two young boys as a sacrifice to the devil is the latest evidence of what some authorities believe is a growing incidence of Satan worship by young people in the Chicago area.[4]

At Warnke Ministries, we have met and worked with hundreds of youths and adults who have made a decision to follow Satan. It is a growing problem resulting from the great stresses people face in our day. Two sociologists, John Lofland and Rodney Stark, have studied the phenomenon of conversion to occultism and satanism. Their findings were reported in the *American Sociological Review.*

In their study, Lofland and Stark present a model that shows how one might be converted to satanism. They developed this model by studying a specific occult group known as "Divine Precepts." They identified seven conditions that often exist in the lives of those who turn to the occult. We will list those conditions here and then elaborate on them throughout this chapter:

1. **The perception of stress.**
2. **Religious Perspective**
3. **Seekership.**
4. **A Specific Turning Point**
5. **Cult-Affective Bonds.**
6. **Absence of Outside Ties.**
7. **Intensive Interaction.**[5]

These seven conditions form a useful model that shows the phases an individual may go through in making the ultimate decision to join a specific group or, ultimately, to make a pact with Satan. One by one, we will examine these seven steps to help us better understand the problem. This model is a useful tool for counseling, police detective work and other forms of intervention. Most importantly, by understanding how an individual may get started on the satanic path, we are better prepared to help them change their course. In so doing, however, it is essential to realize that the process of selling one's soul is usually gradual — a series of choices rather than a single decision.

The Perception of Stress

When a person realizes the stress he is experiencing in life, his perception of that stress causes him to seek ways to overcome it. In George's case, as in so many others, he made a conscious decision to make a pact with the devil, thinking that this act would enable him to cope. The perception of stress is a "predisposing condition" — a fertile garden in which seeds of occult philosophies can germinate and grow.

Feelings of tension, frustration or being "at odds" with one's circumstances or surroundings commonly appear in those who become vulnerable to occult or satanist recruitment. Those who are aware of this kind of stress in their lives are most vulnerable to occult approaches, because they are consciously looking for ways to resolve their tensions and difficulties.

Young people, in particular, experience a literal onslaught of "stress bombs" from various sources: peer pressure, parental expectations, fear of failure, academic achievement, etc. One letter I received from a teen-aged girl clearly shows how her perception of stress in her life led her to consider satanism:

> **Dear Mike, I can't stand it any longer! I want help! It's so hard to put a smile on my face and pretend that everything's okay. I hate myself so much! I'm such a pushover and I hate myself for that!**
>
> **Why is my whole life falling apart? I hate everyone and I hate the world. My ex-best-friend got a whole bunch of people against me today at school, even one of my best friends. I hate her!**
>
> **I'm sick of doing the right thing. I didn't do a thing to her. Please understand how horrible it is to go around school without your best friend. I shared everything with her. I gave her a part of my life. Now, it's gone. This has been going on for two weeks now. When I was trying to live for God, I knew He wanted me to be best friends with her, because she really needed a friend then. I gave of myself to her so much. I**

ignored all my problems so that I could help her. I was always there for her and I hardly ever talked about myself. And she just threw it all back in my face. Why?

I have nothing to live for, I really don't. I take voice lessons, but I must not have a good voice or I would've gotten a part in the musical. I used to be good at acting, but I got a small part in this play. I quit piano... 'cause I kept on getting sick or hurt....I hate life and I hate myself for feeling this way. I'm a normal person, what's wrong with me? I feel so awful....I can't even cry any more!

I'm starting to get interested in the things of Satan....I keep on hearing this voice [telling me] to surrender over to Satan. Each time it becomes more tempting. He has power and I could hurt all those people who hurt me in the past.

This talented young lady was a ripe candidate for satanic recruitment because of her weakened self-concept and all the negative experiences of her life. Feelings of stress, isolation, self-hatred, inadequacy and anger threatened to overwhelm her. She was looking for a way to deal with these problems. As these things were happening to her she saw a video about Satan in which certain rock singers testified that they were sold out to Satan. They told of his power and this was what led her to consider satanism as a viable alternative for her life.

In working with her, we were able to show her how the "voice" she heard was lying to her. Through prayer and counseling we were able to lead her back to the Son of God. But I can't help but wonder how many other teens and adults begin to deal with their perceived stresses by turning to Satan. How many never seek help and feel that they have no one to turn to except Satan himself? The statistics of increased occult involvement give us the answer — an answer which too many choose to deny.

Religious Perspective

This second condition, cited by Lofland and Stark, refers to the perspective that many have about God. Religious people are folks who find a religious significance in everything that happens to them. Sometimes this is a desirable attribute, but far too often people grow up with a view of God and religion that is anything but healthy.

Oftentimes, religious people are loaded with guilt, and when bad things happen to them, they frequently blame God for their problems. One teen-ager I know attended an evangelical church with his family before turning to satanism. How could such a thing happen in a Christian home, many wondered. The precipitating event in this young man's life was the death of his father. The youth began to blame himself because he felt that God was somehow punishing him by taking his father's life through a massive coronary. He concluded, "If that's the way God is, then I will turn to Satan."

Fortunately, the boy's mother and pastor saw what was happening and they were able to help him see that his view of God and himself was not in line with the Scriptures. But so many others continue to view God as a "critical parent" who seeks only to punish them every time they step out of line. Under such pressure it is easy to understand why such an individual would turn away from God.

This condition is particularly acute in the lives of people who have been abused by their parents, especially fathers, during childhood. Such people often find it difficult to relate to God as their Father. Their view of God is colored by earlier experiences to such an extent that God is seen as a vengeful, arbitrary disciplinarian.

Unless such an individual is able to experience the love of God, through Jesus Christ, he is likely to turn to occult philosophies that try to mask the truth by offering only good things to their followers. Being religious by nature, the individual looks for a "religious" way to deal with his or her erroneous views.

Seekership

Most people who turn to witchcraft, satanism and the occult identify themselves as religious seekers. I was one such seeker. I read every book I could find that dealt with philosophy, religion and supernatural power. I sincerely believed that I was seeking truth and I also believed I could find it in my study of the ancient "masters."

I studied Eastern religions — Zen Buddhism, Taoism, Hinduism and Confucianism. I read the *Tao te Ching,* the ancient Egyptian *Book of the Dead,* the writings of the Dalai Lama, the Rosicrucians, and many others.

When I turned to witchcraft, I examined every book and magazine I could find. I learned about transcendental meditation, yoga, reincarnation and satanism.

I watched every film that dealt with occult themes, especially the horror flicks that starred Boris Karloff and Bela Lugosi.

My search was a quest for ultimate truth and when I turned to satanism, I felt I had found it!

In their study of an occult group known as "Divine Precepts," Lofland and Stark noted how many of the group's members had tried traditional churches, prayer groups and/or Bible studies prior to turning to the cult. As I did, many members of this group had formed their own religious philosophy, drawing on a wide variety of sources. Often, however, there may be no clear connection between the beliefs of the converts prior to contact with the occult and the beliefs they subsequently adopted.

One young man wrote to us about how his search, like mine also had done, nearly ended in death:

> **I came across an ad in the paper that said, "Witchcraft, and All the Things You Could Get." Sounded good to me, so I ordered an interesting book. The author was Anton LaVey, so I tried some of these things. . . . The one thing that fascinated me was astral projection. I tried this a few times,**

but that scared me pretty bad, so I didn't do it anymore....I hit the drug scene hard enough where I would have died....

Like so many others who turn to satanism and the occult for answers, this young man became a drug addict. It was easy for me to identify with him because my own search had led me into hard-care drug use. If you could drink it, smoke it, drop it or shoot it — I did it!

Surrendering one's soul to the powers of the dark leads one into a foggy maze that all-too-frequently ends in death!

Despite the wide variety of beliefs held by those who may be caught in this tangled web, two ideas remain consistent:

1. That spirits, deities, or beings of some kind come from somewhere other than the physical realm to affect our lives here.

2. That some sort of spiritual purpose exists for every person, place and thing.

The purpose of their search, then, comes to be a search for personal meaning which they (for whatever reason) did not find in traditional religion.

The Turning Point

The fourth condition in the conversion model we are examining is the presence of a circumstance or event that can be identified as "the turning point." For some it may be a move to a new location; for others it may be the death of a friend or relative or even the loss of a job. Whatever the precipitating circumstance, it serves to create an environment in which "the rules" or the available responses to life situations are changed. In most cases, this turning point provides a freedom from old obligations or inhibitions, and it usually occurs just prior to or at the same time as the initial contact with an occult group.

The turning point for me occurred when I went to college. Being away from home removed some of my former inhibitions against activities that my foster family would not have approved of. It also contributed to feelings of unrest and loneliness, and it was in college that I also began to use drugs.

Generally speaking, exposure to occult philosophies may have its greatest effect at this time in a person's life. Most teen-agers would like to see significant changes in their lives. In looking for help, they continue with their search. Many have reported that they could not find the answers they sought in church, so they looked for alternatives. They may feel somewhat "out of touch" with traditional values and they open themselves to new approaches.

Recently, we received a letter from a Christian mother who was concerned about her daughter who is a co-ed at an undergraduate school. The mother wrote:

> **My 20-year-old daughter has become involved in satanic activities. She has, within the past few weeks, become quite open about it. She states that she is practicing Wicca, and she asked her father for a sacrificial knife and a large amethyst wrapped in a specific way (to be worn around the neck) as Christmas gifts!**

Wicca, to which this mother refers, is a currently popular form of witchcraft that is attractive to many college students and adults. Its name is derived from the Saxon word *wica,* which means "wise one." It is also the feminine form of an old English word that means "witch," and it has worship as its main object. Wicca bases many of its tenets on ancient fertility rites. It is especially attractive to young women although some men become members of wicca as well. The cult is highly matriarchal, however, and most of its leaders are high priestesses. Wiccans worship the deity of witchlore — the Queen of Heaven, and her symbols are the stars and the moon.

Cult-Affective Bonds

The next step is the development of cult-affective bonds. This refers to the building of a relationship with at least one member of the group. "Affective" is a term that refers to the emotional aspect that influences one's attraction to a specific group. "Cult-affective bonds," therefore, are the emotional ties that pull a prospective recruit toward the group.

If a positive relationship between one or more members of a cult/occult group does not already exist, it will probably develop at this point. The existence of cult-affective bonds does not necessarily mean that the individual who is considering the group shares the religious beliefs of the group; actual acceptance of those beliefs can come much later.

The cult-affective bonds began to develop in my search when Dean, the dealer who was supplying me with drugs, began inviting me to parties. At the time, I had no idea that the group of people I was partying with were satanists. All I knew at that stage was that I was attracted to Dean and his friends because of the drugs, sex and ego-reinforcement they provided for me. My exposure to the deeper activities and beliefs of the group was very gradual.

Absence of Outside Ties

The sixth factor in the conversion model we are studying is the absence of or neutralizing of affective bonds outside the group. This can occur in a number of ways, but it seems clear that some sort of isolation from the "outside world" is necessary. The odds of a potential recruit actually being converted are greatly reduced if he or she retains strong ties to someone who is outside of the group.

Lofland and Stark observed that a move to a new location or a serious "falling out" with family or friends was often sufficient to isolate the future convert. Geographical distances may separate the recruit from his family and this enables him or her to avoid discussing anything that would help others see the changes that are taking place within him or her.

In my own case, being away from home at college and not having any close friends there meant that almost no one could have known what was happening to me except, of course, the members of the Satanic Brotherhood, and they were not telling!

Lofland and Stark noted that in instances in which "extra-cult" (outside of the group) relationships withstood the strain of this crucial time, conversion did not happen. They specifically note the case of a spouse who had begun to show interest in Divine Precepts, but because his relationship with his wife remained strong and she resisted his urging to join, he did not continue to pursue involvement with the group.

This factor helps us to understand the importance of maintaining open and positive communication with our children as one means of knowing what individuals and philosophies may be influencing them. Such a strong and caring relationship goes a long way in preventing someone from getting involved with occult and satanist orientations.

Intensive Interaction

The final condition is that of intensive interaction with the group. Prior to this step, a convert may verbally claim allegiance to the cult. If he or she experiences regular and frequent contact with group members, however, it becomes likely that the recruit will place increasing amounts of control over his or her life into the hands of the group leaders. Repeated exposure to the group and its philosophies creates in the individual a growing feeling of acceptance.

Closely allied with intensive interaction, particularly in the case of satanic and black-magic cults, is the concept of the "cult of confession." This refers to activities that bind the group together while at the same time isolating it from the outside.

The activities may be specifically criminal, or they may be immoral, offensive and anti-social without breaking any laws.

However, the common denominator among cult of confession activities is the producing of extreme attitudes and emotions. When I was a satanic high priest, for example, my coven regularly performed a ritual of the Black Mass. My blood was bled into a chalice, mixed with communion wine and urine, and consumed by coven members. Strictly speaking, this is not illegal if all parties are consenting adults.

Such a ritual produces two effects in its participants. First, the sharing of the experience brings a sense of unity (precarious and fragile though it may be) to the structure of the group. At the same time, it separates the participant from the outside.

It is unlikely that someone who takes this final, secretive step will communicate the experience to those outside of the group. To do so would cause others to label the individual as "weird" or even "sick" — someone to be avoided at all costs! This isolation becomes even more pronounced when the group's rituals and activities involve illegal acts. How, for example, does a person tell others about a ritual involving human sacrifice?

The seven steps of this conversion model represent the means Satan employs to lead an individual to surrender his soul to him. There are a broad range of circumstances that fit into each condition. There are also exceptions to the rule and circumstances which cannot be explained by these steps.

Understanding how a person gets involved with the occult provides important clues for helping a person get out. By relying on the Lord's wisdom and wielding "the sword of the Spirit, which is the word of God" (Eph. 6:17 NIV), we can find ways to break the pattern of circumstances that eventually trap the potential convert. In fact, this is a specific application of Paul's admonition to "See to it that no one takes you captive through hollow and deceptive philosophy, which depends on human tradition and the basic principles of this world rather than on Christ'' (Col. 2:8 NIV).

Selling Out to Satan — the Results

Sanford, Maine — The bizarre story of a Devil worshipper who killed a 12-year-old girl began last year when Scott Waterhouse walked into a bookstore and bought a copy of *The Satanic Bible*.

It ended last week when a jury convicted Waterhouse, 18, of luring Gycelle Cote into the woods and strangling her ''for the heck of it.''

Between the time Waterhouse bought the book and his conviction, he experimented with LSD, got heavily involved in Devil worship, became obsessed with a 15-year-old girl and allegedly threatened to kill her, and, finally, murdered Cote.

''The Satanism bit...just changed him,'' Doug Waterhouse, the killer's brother, said when the trial ended.

It was sometime last year that Waterhouse, then a junior at Sanford High School, bought *The Satanic Bible*, by Anton S. LaVey of The Church of Satan in San Francisco. He studied it and started calling Satanism his ''religion.''[6]

This article from *Rocky Mountain News*, dated November 18, 1984, shows how one young man was seduced by Satan, step by step, into an all-out surrender of his soul. His brother observed, ''Satanism...just changed him.''

In the case of Sean Sellers, a former satanist who murdered three people to please the devil, his pact with Satan changed him from being an honor-roll student and football star into a murderer! Prisons and mental hospitals are full of people who started out well only to be sidetracked by Satan into crime and mental illness.

It must never be forgotten that Satan's work is to destroy whatever is good. The Bible says:

Woe to those who call evil good and good evil, who put darkness for light and light for darkness.

(Isa. 5:20 NIV)

This verse is prophetic with regard to satanism in our present day because one of the greatest lies the satanist perpetuates is to say that good is evil and evil is good. The resulting confusion causes the newly indoctrinated satanist to reject former values and replace them with satanic ideals. These ideals are the direct opposite of Christian values.

> **The god of this age has blinded the minds of unbelievers,
> so that they cannot see the light of the gospel of the glory of
> Christ, who is the image of God.**
>
> **(2 Cor. 4:4 NIV)**

The god of this age is none other than Satan himself. He leads people into deception by blinding them spiritually so that they will not be able to see God's light. This blindness imprisons the victim in a world of darkness. All the while, however, the person so entrapped feels that he has arrived at the pinnacle of spiritual enlightenment!

> **For although they knew God, they neither glorified him
> as God nor gave thanks to him, but their thinking became
> futile and their foolish hearts were darkened. Although they
> claimed to be wise, they became fools and exchanged the glory
> of the immortal God for images made to look like mortal man
> and birds and animals and reptiles.**
>
> **(Rom. 1:21-23 NIV)**

Spiritual blindness, Paul points out, results in the darkening of the human heart, emotional blindness, if you will. Someone with a darkened heart is a person who has lost touch with his emotions; they no longer guide him to do what is right. This condition is further addressed by Paul, the Apostle:

> **Because of this, God gave them over to shameful lusts.
> Even their women exchanged natural relations for unnatural
> ones. In the same way the men also abandoned natural
> relations with women and were inflamed with lust for one
> another....They have become filled with every kind of
> wickedness, evil, greed and depravity. They are full of envy,
> murder, strife, deceit and malice.**
>
> **(Rom. 1:26,27,29 NIV)**

The darkened heart leads to darkened behaviors that are self-defeating as well as being damaging to others. The modern-day satanist fits the description given by St. Paul of what men will be like in the last days:

> **But mark this: There will be terrible times in the last days. People will be lovers of themselves, lovers of money, boastful, proud, abusive, disobedient to their parents, ungrateful, unholy, without love, unforgiving, slanderous, without self-control, brutal, not lovers of the good, treacherous, rash, conceited, lovers of pleasure rather than lovers of God....Have nothing to do with them.**
>
> **(2 Tim. 3:1-5 NIV)**

Those "terrible times in the last days" are upon us. Paul's description of people in the last days is an apt description of today's satanist. His list of characteristics of our age shows what happens when a person surrenders his soul to the devil, and those attributes always lead to tragedy, confusion and destruction both in this life and the life that is to come.

5

Satan's New Age

The eye never has enough of seeing, or the ear its fill of hearing. What has been will be again, what has been done will be done again; there is nothing new under the sun.

(Eccles. 1:8-9 NIV)

Crisis of Confidence

A stately church with gray stone walls and splendid stained-glass windows stands like a silent sentinel on the corner of Main Street. Its towering steeple points to the One in the heavens who gave His life for the Church. The heavy oak doors at the entrance are painted red to remind us of His blood.

It is Sunday morning and those doors are open. But only a handful of people, mostly older women with gray hair, climb the steps to go to church. The cavernous sanctuary, so well-cared-for, seems more like a tomb than a temple. It is so empty, so devoid of life.

Salaried employees — the pastor, the organist, the members of the choir and the sexton — perform the services of the church. But the ceremony of worship is more like a memorial elegy to the life that used to be there. The church itself, a monument to what once was.

Where is this church? It can be found in almost every town and city in the Western World. I've been to this church in the United States, Canada, Sweden, Denmark, New Zealand, South Africa, and Australia. Whenever I attend its services, I ask myself, "What happened? Where is the life of Christ? Where are the people?"

93

Once in a church in southern California I was introduced to a congregation by a very liberal pastor. He told his people how glad he was that I was with them. He went on to say, "Mike is a wonderfully funny man, but he is a very conservative Bible believer. I hope you have a good time with the humor, but be ready to take what he says about Jesus in the light of what I have taught you."

I learned that he had taught his congregation that Jesus was not the Son of God, but just a bastard son of a Palestinian prostitute! You could have knocked me over with a feather when I heard that! Needless to say, I dropped a sermon that night that registered on the Richter scale!

There is a crisis of confidence toward the Church in many quarters today. A growing disenchantment with traditional religious values has reached crisis proportions in many churches and communities. In the face of this, I've heard so many young people say, "The church doesn't mean anything to me!"

In one city where I ministered I spoke with the pastor of a denominational church about this problem. He reported, "Our young people attend Sunday school through their childhood years. Then, in ninth grade, they begin their preparations for Confirmation. By the springtime they are ready for Confirmation Sunday. They learn the Apostles' Creed, the Ten Commandments, various Scriptures and the doctrines of the Church. Ironically, however, after the Confirmation service in May, you never see them again!"

This phenomenon is one characteristic of our age. At the same time, however, I would be remiss if I did not point out the tremendous revival of Christianity that is taking place in many parts of the world. This polarization was prophesied by Jude when he contrasted the two extremes to be found among people in the last days:

> **But you, dear friends, remember what the apostles of our Lord Jesus Christ foretold. They said to you, "In the last times there will be scoffers who will follow their own ungodly**

desires." These are the men who divide you, who follow mere natural instincts and do not have the Spirit.

> **But you, dear friends, build yourselves up in your most holy faith and pray in the Holy Spirit. Keep yourselves in God's love as you wait for the mercy of our Lord Jesus Christ to bring you to eternal life. Be merciful to those who doubt; snatch others from the fire and save them. . . .**
>
> **(Jude 20-23 NIV)**

We have entered those last times. A clear line of demarcation separates the sheep from the goats, and the ones who have been made righteous through the grace of Christ from those who practice unrighteousness.

Many recent surveys reveal that orthodox Christian values have been replaced by humanistic ideals in the lives of many people, including some who call themselves Christian. In many church programs, spiritual concepts have fallen by the wayside.

It is interesting to note what one study shows regarding Christians' beliefs about the devil. The following list reports the results of this survey by showing what percentage of the members of the denominations surveyed actually believe in a personal devil:

Roman Catholics	**66%**
Congregationalists	**6%**
Methodists	**13%**
Presbyterians	**31%**
Southern Baptists	**92%**
Pentecostals	**100%**

In these last days, Satan has succeeded in convincing millions of Christians that he doesn't even exist! The end result of all this watering down of Christian truths is the weakening of the Church. Is it any wonder, then, that many people see the Church as being irrelevant to the problems of our modern day? When this attitude is entertained in the human heart, it opens one up to a wide range of satanically inspired ideas, no matter how anti-Christian those concepts may be.

One lady I met said to me, "Mike, I'm a Christian humanist." She was attempting to justify her position by mixing ideas from two diametrically opposing systems together.

I responded, "That's impossible. You cannot be both a Christian and a humanist. The value systems of Christians are irreconcilable with the beliefs of humanists."

"But don't both hold to the value of love?" she countered.

"Yes, but a Christian's view of love is that it is a *divine* imperative and the ability to love stems from his faith in Christ. The humanist, on the other hand, believes that love arises from the *human* heart."

As our discussion continued, I could see that this lady had become a humanist who used to be a Christian rather than a Christian humanist. Very subtly, she had been seduced into thinking that love was the only thing that matters, and I realized it would be futile to continue the discussion.

So many of the people who are attracted to humanism and other "new religions," feel the same way. This is why we must always remember Jude's admonition: ". . . Build yourselves up in the most holy faith and pray in the Holy Spirit. Keep yourselves *in God's love* as you wait for the mercy of our Lord Jesus Christ to bring you to eternal life" (Jude 20-21, italics mine).

The Attractions of the New Age

One of the things about the New Age Movement that makes it so dangerous (more dangerous in some ways even than satanism) is that it's so nice. The people are nice, the doctrines are nice and, for the most part, the practices are nice.

This makes it appealing to people who would *never* dream of putting on a black robe and slaughtering a cat.

We must always remember, however, that anything that takes people away from God, that causes them to lose their salvation, plays right into Satan's hand!

When an individual perceives the church to be weak and without power, he begins to look for alternatives that will minister to his spiritual needs. For many, the attractions of "new religions," such as the New Age Movement, have become very appealing. In fact, the New Age Movement has become the religion of choice for many disillusioned Christians.

Trying to mix ideas from the occult with orthodox Christianity is nothing new. Many groups who came to the New World to escape religious persecution in Europe borrowed ideas from the occult in their religious practices. Such mixtures exist in certain countries where missionaries have endeavored to preach the Gospel. In some countries of South America, for example, you can find people who claim the name of Christ but still continue pagan, occultic practices. Some forms of Santeria and voodoo do this.

During the 1950's well-known Bishop James Pike of the Episcopal Church fell victim to one of Satan's schemes to bring mixture to the church. Bishop Pike tried to contact his dead son through a spiritualist medium named Arthur Ford. Similarly Edgar Cayce was an occultist who claimed to be a Christian and Jeane Dixon, well-known astrologer, also claims to be a Christian.

The search for personal meaning is certainly a valid quest. If the Church fails to provide the answers for that search, people will turn elsewhere.

The great actress Shirley MacLaine has become a leading advocate of the New Age approach to finding personal meaning. She has written several autobiographical books that describe her search and her findings. In one of her books, Ms. MacLaine reports that in a former existence she was Asana, "a princess of the elephants."[1] She is a firm believer in reincarnation and *karma*.

Characteristics of the New Age

Shirley MacLaine's approach to spirituality, like that of most New Agers, draws heavily from occult sources. Typical beliefs of the New Age Movement include:

1. *Reincarnation.* This teaching has its origins in Hinduism. One who believes in reincarnation holds to the idea that the soul reappears throughout various lifetimes in different bodies. Some also believe that it is possible to get in touch with one's former embodiments through hypnosis and other means known as past-life recall. In *Dancing in the Light,* Ms. MacLaine describes some of her previous incarnations: a dancer in a harem, a monk who practiced meditation in a cave, a voodoo practitioner in South America, etc.[2]

2. *Astral Projection.* This refers to out-of-the-body experiences such as "soul travel." Presumably, the individual who practices astral projection is able to project his soul to leave the body and visit other places and/or times. Many have reported that this experience may take place involuntarily when the individual is near death.

3. *Mental Telepathy.* This involves supernatural communication between the minds of people, sending messages via thought waves and the reading of minds. This practice is followed by people who believe in ESP. It often leads to the psychic practice of mind control that is popular with many occult groups.

4. *Past-Life Memories.* Many who believe in reincarnation seek to discover who they may have been in previous lifetimes. Through trances, hypnosis and other techniques they endeavor to gain insights into their former embodiments. The case of Bridey Murphy who was reported to be able to recall a previous existence through hypnosis, brought great public attention to this possibility during the 1950's.

5. *Spirit Channeling.* This is a current fad in many circles today. It is simply a new word for old-fashioned spiritism through which a living person is able to contact a departed loved one or spiritual entity by way of a medium. The medium is known as a channeler.

6. *Higher Consciousness.* In his book, *Handbook to Higher Consciousness,* Ken Keyes defines the "law of higher consciousness" as being "Love everyone unconditionally —

including yourself.'' He lists twelve pathways to ''The Living Love System.''[3]

  7. *Inner Human Potential.* The belief in the inner abundance of the human soul leads some New Agers to conclude that they can become like God or even a part of God by getting in touch with the inner self. In so doing, some New Agers believe they have become ''little Gods.''

  8. *Karma.* This belief goes hand in hand with reincarnation. Its origins are Hinduistic and Buddhistic. It is the process by which the transmigration of the soul is perpetuated and its ethical consequences determine the individual's destiny in his next existence. This process is believed to be ongoing until the individual reaches *nirvana* — the state of being at one with God.

Main emphases of the New Age Movement include supernatural abilities and the supremacy of love. As Ken Keyes stated in the dedication to *Handbook to Higher Consciousness,* ''This book is dedicated to us — all of us four billion human beings on earth who, by Living Love, can make our planet a here-and-now paradise.''[4]

Visualization

Many New Agers use visualization as a technique to deal with problems that occur in human existence. By visualizing peace, they tell us, mankind will be able to put an end to war. Often, holistic approaches to healing also utilize visualization as a means of therapy. To the cancer patient, for example, the practitioner will tell his client to visualize the healing process by using the imagination to ''see'' healthy cells defeating the disease, and to visualize himself as being completely well. The use of visualization techniques is very much akin to the practice of meditation, such as Transcendental Meditation (the ability to transcend one's problems and the material world through meditation).

The Extent of the "New Religions"

Polls taken during the 1980's show that the majority of Americans believe in psychic phenomena. One study reveals that two-thirds of American adults believe they have experienced psychic events at some time in their lives.[5] This group of millions forms what is known as "the New Age subculture."

New Agers search for personal meaning in life. They look for ways to transcend (go beyond) the mundane experiences of human existence. They may also look for ways to escape the reality of death.

There are some specific New Age groups but there is no central organization from which all New Agers receive direction. Many self-help groups fit within the general classification of New Age thinking. For example, the Spiritual Frontiers Fellowship in New York bases many of its teachings on the work of Edgar Cayce. Another group called Free Soul, headquartered in Arizona, uses meditation, biofeedback and mind and body control.[6]

Trance Channeling

One of the latest fads in the New Age Movement is known as "spirit channeling" or "trance channeling." Shirley MacLaine, along with thousands of others, believes in this practice that involves a living person who enters a trance-like state in order to serve as a "channel" through which a "spirit" or "spirit being" may speak.

J.Z. Knight is one of the best-known of these modern-day spiritist mediums (channelers). She serves as a "conduit" through which her spirit-guide named Ramtha dispenses his philosophy to thousands of people who attend expensive seminars to receive Ramtha's insights about life and death. Incidentally, Ramtha is purported to be a 35,000-year-old warrior from a lost continent called Lemuria![7]

New-Age channeling has become a multi-million dollar industry in the United States. Many adherents of the movement believe that the nineties are the continuation of the Age of Aquarius that dawned during the sixties.

The Satanic New Age

Anton LaVey has suggested that the world has entered "the satanic new age."[8] The phenomenal growth of New Age approaches lends credence to his statement.

As one professor has pointed out, the New Age Movement is ". . . really good old-fashioned occultism and superstition gussied up with pseudo-scientific jargon to give it an air of legitimacy."[9]

The "new religions" of humanism, the New Age Movement, witchcraft and satanism are certainly not new. Hundreds of years ago, the Bible identified these practices as follows:

> **The acts of the sinful nature are obvious: sexual immorality, impurity and debauchery; idolatry and witchcraft; hatred, discord, jealousy, fits of rage, selfish ambition, dissensions, factions, and envy; drunkenness, orgies, and the like. I warn you, as I did before, that those who live like this will not inherit the kingdom of God.**
>
> **(Gal. 5:19-21 NIV)**

The emphasis on love that is espoused by most New Agers understandably, is very appealing to people. "Love bombing" (the free and frequent expression of love) is, in fact, a technique that is employed by many cults and occult groups to lure in prospective recruits. Dr. Walter Martin was recognized as a leading expert on cults and the occult prior to his recent death. He suggested that the attraction to such groups as the New Age Movement stems from "the church's unpaid debt to society."

It is true that many turn to occult philosophies because they have not seen the reality of the love of Christ at work in the Church. It behooves us, as members of the Church of Jesus Christ, to remember the words of our Master:

> **A new command I give you: Love one another. As I have loved you, so you must love one another. All men will know that you are my disciples if you love one another.**
>
> **(John 13:34-35 NIV)**

Others are attracted to the new religions because they wish to avoid the commitment and responsibilities required by Christianity. In effect, the new religions tell such people that you don't have to be restricted in your search. You can become your own god.

This is the same message that proponents of satanism offer, but it is given in a much more positive vein and it is wrapped in a blanket of love. Shirley MacLaine, for example, has reported that her "Higher Self" directs her, "There is no judgment involved with life. There is only experience from incarnation to incarnation until the soul realizes its perfection and that it is total love."[10]

Such suspended judgment leads many New Agers to believe that ultimately there is no difference between good and evil, a decidedly anti-Christian concept.

Supernatural Manifestations

While traditional religions are being rejected, many studies show that interest in magic and other supernatural manifestations is quite high. When one college psychology class observed a sleight-of-hand magician (entertainer) at work, over one-half of the students attributed his act to psychic, paranormal and spiritual powers. Their belief in the performer's magical powers persisted even after their professor informed them that the magician was simply involved in trickery and "stage magic."

For the most part, society has discarded its former attitudes about witchcraft and magic. In other words, there is greater acceptance of witches now than there used to be. As sociologist Marcello Truzzi observes, "Witches today are much more likely to be invited to parties than they are to be burned at the stake!"[11] A recent broadcast of the "Geraldo!" program lends evidence to this growing acceptance of witchcraft today. His guests on the show were four witches who received considerable approval from the studio audience.

While much of society is interested in supernatural phenomena, there is a large segment of the population who regard occultism with a lack of concern. Many people find it difficult to take occultism, witchcraft and satanism seriously. An anthropologist named Arthur Lyons has observed that those who disbelieve in the supernatural often find it difficult to take seriously other people who do believe.[12] Such "unbelievers" take notice of these groups only when criminal activities of occult groups surface.

One of the consequences of these contemporary social attitudes is that information about satanism and other forms of the occult is very accessible. Hundreds of books on satanism and occultism are available in bookstores everywhere. Over 2,500 New Age bookstores exist in the United States alone. These shops carry books and magazines plus all sorts of paraphernalia, such as special candles, ingredients for magic potions, tarot cards for divination, robes for rituals and other tools of witchcraft.

As we have already pointed out, occult themes are also very prominent in the media. Rock music has often been linked to interest in satanism, especially among young people, and we will cover this subject in more depth in a later chapter. Many believe that some rock music, such as Ozzy Osbourne's "Suicide Solution" has contributed to the rise in teen-age suicides.

Movies are another source of propaganda for witchcraft and satanism. One of the best-known of these films is "Rosemary's Baby" which portrays the character Rosemary as being raped by Satan to produce an anti-Christ. In an overt way, this film that is now available on video cassette, reveals the typical satanic reversal of Christian values. Interestingly, the role of the devil was played by none other than Anton LaVey! The producer of the film, Roman Polanski, has ties to the occult as well.

Satan in the Movies

Another film that proved to be diabolic propaganda was "The Exorcist." Although its graphic portrayal of demon possession turned many people away, others found the apparent superiority of Satan over God to be quite appealing! One of its sequels — "The Exorcist III" — has just been released, pointing to the great interest in satanism that continues in our society.

Many of the films of occultism that have been released in the past two decades have served as training films for young people who decided to experiment with the occult. We have worked with several teen-agers who began their occult involvement as a result of seeing movies such as "The Believers," a film that incorporates a number of elements of Santeria (a mixture of African native rituals with the veneration of Roman Catholic saints) in its plot; "Angel Heart" deals with voodoo practices and, in this film, Robert DeNiro appears in the role of Satan; "Omen" and its sequels are based on a corruption of the account of the anti-Christ given in the Book of the Revelation; and "The Seventh Sign" contains a blend of quasi-Jewish mysticism and misinterpreted Bible prophecy.

While it is impossible to mention all the motion pictures that exist on this subject, it is important to realize that occultism remains a popular Hollywood theme. Many of these films have been box-office hits. Ideas of occultism are even presented in various comedies such as "Beetlejuice," "The Witches of Eastwick," and the two "Ghostbuster" movies.

This is not to suggest that everyone who has viewed any of these films is now possessed by Satan. Rather, these films are just very clever ways of inspiring occult-related thinking into the lives of everyday people.

One popular video that never made it to the theater deserves special mention as well. "The Faces of Death" (with sequels, of course) claims to be a documentary that studies people's attitudes about death. In one scene, a satanic ritual is shown. In this scene, participants cut open the body of a victim, take out the heart, and eat pieces of it as they smear blood over themselves. It is an extremely gruesome scenario, and I mention it only because it has played a role in the lives of many young people who have become ensnared by Satan as a result of viewing this video. I have seen this film on display in a number of video rental shops around the United States. Many times, teen-agers rent this video because they have heard about it from their friends and they may consider it to be "cool" to watch such a film.

(For more information on the influence of occultism in contemporary motion pictures; refer to the introduction of this book.)

Levels of Involvement

At any level of involvement with satanism and occultism the individual exposes himself to hidden dangers. Even those who participate at the "fun and games" level are in danger without knowing it. By "fun and games" I refer specifically to those who think that "playing" with a Ouija board, tarot cards, a crystal ball, occult role-playing games like "Dungeons and Dragons" and other tools is innocent fun. It is clear that such "fun" has resulted in many serious tragedies in the lives of some participants, leading some to go so far as to engage in ritual abuse, murder and suicide.

In order to ascertain the levels of involvement that one may engage in with regard to satanism and witchcraft, we will look specifically at the aspect of *commitment* to the ideologies represented. Commitment is reflected by the amount of time, energy and even money that one may invest in his pursuit of hidden knowledge. Levels of involvement can also be studied with regard to the amount of knowledge that one has acquired in these areas.

For our purposes, we have identified four specific levels of involvement:

1. **Superficial commitment.**
2. **Dabbling.**
3. **Serious Commitment.**
4. **Criminal Involvement.**

Superficial Commitment

One sociological study of satanism has disclosed that the majority of satanists are only superficially involved with their religion. This study describes their interests as "playful contempt" for traditional religions.[13]

Those who are superficially involved in satanism or witchcraft are often the most vocal about it. The more serious follower of these religions endeavors to maintaining an air of secrecy about his or her practices.

Secrecy is one of the foundational principles of a system known as the "Witch's Pyramid." According to this philosophy, "power shared is power lost."

Occultists at the superficial level, for the most part, have not really experienced supernatural power in this sense; their interest is centered on the gratification of physical desires or other ego-oriented needs. Thus, their wants and needs are met more by displaying their interests than by hiding them.

Initially, an individual's exposure to an occult group or philosophy usually occurs in one of two ways. In many cases, the person is introduced to a group of people who offer inducements for belonging. These allurements may take the form of parties, use of drugs and/or alcohol, sexual activities, or just an opportunity to participate in activities which seem "mysterious," "taboo," or otherwise fascinating.

In the case of "white light" occult groups, the initial interaction may be cause-oriented. Such "white light" causes might be focused on environmentalism, feminism or gay rights, for example.

The second way in which an individual might be exposed to occultism is through literature, media representation and/or advertisements. Even though this kind of initial contact is indirect, it may arouse enough interest to motivate a person to identify himself as being a Wiccan, a Cabalist, a satanist or some other kind of occultist.

The role-playing, fantasy game "Dungeons and Dragons" has frequently been reported to be the initial contact for some young people who have been lured into occultic and satanic activities. The following excerpts from two newspaper accounts show how this game served as the initial contact for particular young people who fell victim to Satan's schemes:

Deaths of Two Brothers May Be Linked to Game.

LaFayette, Colo. (UPI) — Two young brothers whose bodies were found with a pistol beneath a railroad trestle may have been carrying out a suicide fantasy associated with the game Dungeons and Dragons, the police chief said Saturday.

"The older boy was involved to some degree — I should say, quite heavily — with the Dungeons and Dragons game," said Police Chief Larry Stallcup. "We're investigating that that might have had something to do with it." ..."My understanding is that once you reach a certain point where you are the master, your only way out is death," Stallcup said. "That way no one can beat you."...[14]

The two boys, aged sixteen and twelve, also possessed materials related to the occult, including satanic ritual manuals and an occult curio catalog.

Another article on this topic appeared in the January 20, 1985, issue of *The Tampa Tribune-Times:*

Classmates Stunned By Youth's Suicide in Front of His Drama Class

Arlington, Texas (UPI) — A teen-ager who killed himself with a sawed-off shotgun in front of his drama class was a devotee of the fantasy game Dungeons and Dragons and had a lead role in this weekend's school play, friends said....[15]

The young man, James A. Stalley, was a seventeen-year-old senior at Arlington High School. The youth was a good student who practiced Tai Chi Chuan, a form of graceful martial arts exercise.

Regrettably, there are countless articles from recent newspapers that testify to similar circumstances. They show how "game-like" initial contacts with occultism and satanism have led participants into criminal activities and death.

At the superficial level of commitment, however, most participants would never consider such recourses. They may wear special clothing or carry occult symbols. They may read various occult books, such as *The Satanic Bible,* but they remain naive about the true nature of occultism and its all-too-frequent results.

Sometimes they will even express certain occultic beliefs in order to get attention while remaining oblivious to the deeper meaning of those ideas.

Recently, in a central Kentucky high school, for example, a few students began dressing in black, carrying copies of *The Satanic Bible,* and drawing pentagrams on their hands. This was apparently done for shock effect rather than for magical purposes. (In fact, few true satanists would behave this way.) Many of their fellow-students found these practices to be intimidating nonetheless.

The use of symbols and other paraphernalia related to the occult, as well as the performance of rituals, is quite often an inaccurate application of occultism, at least at this initial level of commitment. Many times, the participants themselves totally misunderstand what they are doing, and this, of course, can be a very dangerous business. Their use of occult symbols is often not clear to them because they have not studied their subject in depth, and as the old adage accurately states, "A little knowledge is a dangerous thing."

One of the most common illustrations of this misuse of occult symbols involves pentagrams. The distinction between the upright "witches' pentagram" and the upside-down satanic pentagram is often lost to those at this level, and they may use these symbols inappropriately, sometimes thinking that the two symbols may be used interchangeably. This would be unthinkable to someone who is knowledgeable in the field of occultism since the two symbols have opposite meanings.

The person who is involved at the superficial level may have read some occult literature and may even be able to quote from it, but he has not invested enough time and energy to his study to enable him to understand the significance of what he is saying and doing. In such cases, the goal is often simply ego-reinforcement, and by appearing sinister and mysterious, he feels he will get the attention of others. The respect that comes from fear that others may feel toward him is often enough of a "reward" for him to continue his superficial involvement.

Dabblers

Some who experience the superficial level of commitment eventually reject occultism altogether, deciding to go no further with their involvement after their early experimentation with it. Others, however, go on to the second phase of involvement which we are calling the level of "dabbling."

Most often, those at this level also lack a complete understanding of their involvement with the occult, but their fascination with the magical powers of the supernatural realm continues to grow. It is at this stage that the individual begins to cultivate spiritual powers for his own use. The study of available occult literature becomes more intense at this level in an effort to acquire the "hidden knowledge" that the occult offers. At this level, also, the individual begins to invest time, money and energy toward the acquisition of knowledge, power and paraphernalia.

The serious occult literature is frequently so esoteric that it is indeed difficult to understand. It requires much study, reflection and experimentation. The description of introductory rituals is usually confusing and complex. Therefore, those who pass beyond the dabbling level have had to spend considerable time with the material.

Serious Commitment

Certain individuals pass through the first two levels with continued interest in occultism and satanism. They reach the point where they are no longer just students of occultism but they have actually become practitioners. No longer is such a person interested in "playful" approaches; he or she has become very serious about his or her involvement with the occult.

At this level a strong commitment to the philosophy, ideals and practices of a particular orientation develops. The individual is committed to pursuit of occult knowledge. We can now call him or her an occultist, and as such he or she has accepted the premise that knowledge is a vital source of supernatural power.

Many times a person at this level of commitment goes beyond the available published occult material and develops his or her own personalized rituals. Also, the possession of and understanding of magical implements is more or less complete at this level.

A seeker may have become part of a group as early as the superficial level. In most cases, if a person has not already joined a group, he or she will have developed a desire to do so by this time. Membership in a group brings a degree of ''legitimacy' to the occultist and this feeling of legitimacy is achieved in a number of ways.

Within traditional witchcraft, for example, a person becomes ''legitimate'' by blood relationship to a legitimate witch, being trained by a legitimate witch or by being initiated into a legitimate coven. The claims of most covens of witches with regard to ''blood-line legitimacy'' are somewhat suspect; prior to 1950, the evidence for an unbroken line of descent is usually scarce. In spite of this, many group members and prospective members take these claims quite seriously.

Within satanism, legitimacy is usually considered to stem from a wide acceptance of the group or from national recognition; thus, the Church of Satan and the Temple of Set are usually considered legitimate.

Criminal Involvement

Not all occultists reach a criminal level of involvement, and some individuals or groups who consider themselves to be occultists may become criminal without having passed through all these stages. Similarly, the commitment of some witches and satanists to their religion may be superficial while their involvement in other activities such as drugs, pornography or child abuse is quite pronounced.

It is interesting to note that almost all publicly recognized organizations claim non-involvement in any criminal activity. Anton LaVey, high priest of the Church of Satan, has made the claim that a ''true satanist'' would never harm an animal or a baby, nor would he or she harm anyone else except for people who wish or deserve to be hurt.

In a letter to the staff of the ''File 18'' Law enforcement newsletter, Laurie Cabot claims that ''. . . a 'witch' who does harm to any living thing is no longer considered a witch.''[16]

Despite occultists' and satanists' claims of non-involvement in criminal activities, a rash of occult-motivated crimes continues to spread. In some areas these crimes have reached almost-epidemic proportions. Sometimes this is due to the "copy-cat" syndrome that often follows crimes of a mysterious nature. At other times, however, direct connections between occult involvement and criminal activities can be established.

In *The Black Arts*, Richard Cavendish maintains that even ritual murder can play a part in the activities of some occultists, and he gives three reasons for such practices. First, he points out that a common occultic belief that the shedding of blood releases the life force of a victim leads some to believe that the release of the life force through ritual sacrifice can be utilized as a source of power by the occultists. Second, it is possible that the emotional state of the victim can provide a type of "psychic fuel" for a magical spell. Third (and perhaps most important), the act of sacrifice produces an intense psychological "kick" for the occultist. All three of these beliefs may tie into the satanist's tenet that the devil requires such sacrifices in order to respond to the requests of his followers.[17]

There are at least two reasons why a person may arrive at the criminal level of involvement in his search. For some, satanism provides a handy excuse (a justification) for violent crime for someone who may already be predisposed toward criminal activity. Certain psychopathic or sociopathic individuals may need relatively little excuse for committing such crimes because something has been lacking in the development of a conscience in them.

On the other hand, the belief systems of certain occultists lead them to think that certain amounts or kinds of supernatural power are available to them only through actions that are labeled criminal. Many philosophies of occult magic teach that the magician must transcend both good and evil through experience in order to gain true power. In other words, the occultist or satanist may feel that he or she needs to experience both good and evil in order to set himself or herself above these influences.

As previously mentioned, satanic activity does not always occur in isolation. In many cases, a correlation can be established between satanic involvement and drug and alcohol abuse, bikers and the gang mentality, survivalist groups and a variety of other abusive/destructive situations. In these cases, however, it is important to realize that satanic beliefs of participants may not be the only motivating factors involved.

Drugs and the Devil

The July 23, 1984, issue of *Newsweek* reported an incident of how drugs and satanism form a combustible mixture:

> Northport, Long Island — Police arrested Ricky Kasso, 17, and James Troiano, 18, on charges of second-degree murder. Teenage members of a group which called itself the "Knights of the Black Circle" had been spray-painting satanic symbols in a local park for several years.
>
> Sometime during the night of June 16, 1984, members of the group led Gary Lauwers, 17, into a woods and conducted a four-hour ritual in which they burned Lauwers' clothing and hair, and then stabbed him to death. "I love you, Mom," Lauwers shouted during the attack. But one of his assailants, Ricky Kasso, commanded, "No! Say you love Satan."
>
> Two days after his arrest, Ricky Kasso was found hanged in his cell. Jimmy Troiano was later acquitted on murder charges. Concerned teens from the area spent time during the investigation and trial cleaning up the park the gang had frequented and decorated.[18]

The use of drugs among satanists is widely reported. The resulting disorientation may lead a satanist or occultist to do things he otherwise might never consider.

This happened to Sean Sellers, former satanist who is now on death row in Oklahoma's State Penitentiary. As a result of his involvement with satanism and drug abuse, Sean murdered a convenience store clerk and his own parents. He described his journey into darkness as follows:

> **I became obsessively involved with Dungeons & Dragons.
> I went frequently to the "Rocky Horror Picture Show" (a
> rock movie musical based on transvestism, sadomasochism,
> and other perversions). I met a lot of satanists there. I
> identified myself by wearing my left shirtsleeve rolled up and
> keeping my left pinkie fingernail unclipped and painted black.
> Through Ninjitsu, I delved into the violent aspects of the
> martial arts, learning how to conceal weapons and commit
> assassination. I once ate the leg off a live frog in biology class.**

> **Drugs played a role, too. I started out with marijuana.
> I had such a rigorous routine doing rituals at night that I took
> speed to keep me going....[19]**

A drug-induced black-out preceded Sean's murder of his
parents. He was sixteen-years-old at the time. It took him a year
after committing the murder to recall the events surrounding it:

> **I drove home, did some homework, performed a ritual
> and slept. My next clear memory is a jail cell two days later.
> I had taken my father's .44 revolver and shot both my parents
> in the head as they slept. In a year, the memories of that night
> would haunt me....But for now, all I knew was that my life
> was destroyed. I had given Satan everything, and now I sat
> in a jail cell without a family....[20]**

Don't PANIC

What is the Christian to do in response to the rising tide
of occultism in our world today? While is it true that more than
800 "new religions" have developed since the mid-1960's, we
need to continue to realize that God's power is greater than any
satanic scheme.

I once asked a bank teller, "How can you spot counterfeit
currency?"

She replied, "It's relatively simple. We become so familiar
with the real thing that we can spot a phony bill in a second."

There is no fear possible when we become totally familiar
with the Lord Jesus Christ, His love and His power. St. Paul
wrote,

> **For God did not give us a spirit of timidity [apistio (Greek) — fear and cowardice], but a spirit of power, of love and of self-discipline.**
>
> **(2 Tim. 1:7 NIV)**

God is infinitely more powerful than any scheme Satan could ever devise. In a later chapter we will discuss specific ways through which we can help individuals who have been ensnared by the occult.

By learning about the ways in which our enemy operates, we equip ourselves for the important responsibility we have to stand against them. The most effective defense we have is education and information-sharing coupled with prayer and the Word of God. No single center or organization has all the answers; we must work together on this problem.

Cooperation must also exist among agencies that deal with adolescents. Getting adults to be aware of what is going on "out there" and teaching basic moral values at home would put a big dent in this problem. There is far too much sensationalism on both sides of the warfare; we need good, positive data to provide patterns and information on how to counter occultism and satanism in a positive manner. There is a workable solution to this problem if we will all learn to pull together.

Above all, DON'T PANIC!

As John Charles Cooper wrote, "More and more people today are looking for an element of the supernatural in their everyday affairs. In their routine lives they struggle to create openings to experience mystery, adventure, and romance. In their search for meaning many seem willing to sacrifice their intellect and even to engage in illegal practices. As Christians, we believe that the various occult and Eastern religious groups cannot finally satisfy the needs of men. Only in and through Christ can man find wholeness. But if the church does not communicate this saving wholeness to people, we may well expect many to continue turning to the immoral and the absurd for healing."[21]

We have a great privilege and responsibility as Christians to fulfill what Jesus called us to do. Through Him, we can do all things. Without Him, we can do nothing. As He was called to minister to the needs of people everywhere, through His Spirit we can go forth to:

> **...preach good news to the poor.... proclaim freedom for the prisoners and recovery of sight for the blind, to release the oppressed, to proclaim the year of the Lord's favor.**
>
> **(Luke 4:18-19 NIV)**

Occultists and satanists are imprisoned in a dungeon of darkness. They are spiritually blind and oppressed. Our responsibility is to proclaim freedom to them, to release them from their oppression, to proclaim the Lord's love for them. This we can do if we look upon the problem in the light of God's eternal plan and we look upon the individual through God's eyes of love.

And remember, DON'T PANIC.

The True Church

At the beginning of this chapter I described an unnamed church that was devoid of life and power. Paul warned his young disciple Timothy to have nothing to do with those "...having a form of godliness but denying its power" (2 Tim. 3:5 NIV).

It should be no surprise to us that there will be great godlessness in these last days. But we must always remember that simultaneously Jesus, the Lord of the Church, is building a mighty army of people who have been redeemed from the schemes of Satan. I would like to conclude this chapter by describing the true Church of Jesus Christ.

A group of joyous people gather to worship their risen Lord. They tell what Jesus has done for them. They sing because they're happy. As you hear them praying, you know that they are taking to One who loves them. They are in love with Jesus because they know who He is and what He can do.

This vibrant, loving group of Christians care about other people. They share their faith and love with everyone they meet.

This was the Church that eventually reached me after all my involvement with occultism, drug addiction and satanism. It was this Church that revealed the power of God to me. Two members of this Church showed me the love of God.

The Love of Jesus Killed the Witch in Me

While I was involved in satanism, several Christians tried to witness to me. They could see the mess I was in, but they didn't know how to help me.

I was shooting $120. worth of heroin a day. My teeth were rotting and I had gone through bouts with hepatitis four times due to my use of dirty needles. My hair was coming out in clumps and my weight was down to 110 pounds.

One Christian said, "Mike, you're messed up. You're going to hell."

I knew I was messed up and I felt like I was in hell already, but I didn't know how to get free.

Thinking it might help me, I joined the U.S. Navy. During boot camp I was assigned to room with two Christians — Bob Washburn and Bill Wardel — for three months. They were like Peter and Paul. They didn't judge me. Unlike the others I had met, they didn't preach at me and tell me I was going to hell.

Bob and Bill did witness to me. They didn't speak many words about Jesus, except to say, "Mike, Jesus loves you."

I could feel their love, their genuine concern for me. Due to my background, especially my previous experiences with Christians, I was in an attack mode all the time.

Many times I sneered and cursed at my fellow sailors. "Leave me alone!" I shouted. "I don't need Jesus!"

Bill and Bob just kept on showing me the love of Jesus. Once I got so angry that I got into a fist fight with Bill. It resulted in him having a broken nose! Blood was all over Bill's face, but he just looked up at me and smiled, "Jesus loves you, Mike."

"What's love?" I shot back with hatred in my voice as I watched him wipe the blood from his face and hold out his bloody hand to me. He said, "Mike, Jesus shed His blood for you and if you're good enough for Him, you're good enough for me."

This guy was really getting to me. All my beliefs were so opposed to what he was saying. I had been taught that Jesus was Satan's younger brother. And because God had favored Jesus, I thought that He had done a great injustice to Satan (who I felt was the rightful inheritor of heaven).

It was my understanding that Satan was justified in preparing an army on earth that would overcome God and Jesus. I felt that I was a part of the satanic army, along with my fellow-satanists and one-third of the angelic host who had sided with Satan.

I believed the satanic lie that it is "better to reign in hell than rule in heaven." Up to this time, I believed that the life of Jesus had been greatly exaggerated by His disciples. To me, He was not God's Son; He was simply a man who believed He was God's Son.

By way of the Crucifixion, Satan had done away with Jesus. To my way of thinking, Jesus had been defeated. Satan had won and he would ultimately win.

In this young naval recruit, however, I came face to face with a power that was greater than anything I had ever seen in satanism. Bill had supernatural power in Jesus. The power of love.

When I saw his blood I witnessed for the first time the reality of the love of Jesus Christ. Blood had held special meaning for me as a satanist. Blood had always been a part of my religious rituals. But here was a young man who had willingly shed his blood for me. When this realization dawned on me, I saw the Crucifixion of Jesus Christ in an entirely new way.

I began to see that Jesus had died for *me*. His love was even greater than my friend's. He had shed His blood for *me*.

It was the love of Jesus Christ, so beautifully demonstrated in the lives of two of His followers, that killed the witch in me.

> **Therefore, if anyone is in Christ, he is a new creation; the old has gone the new has come!**
>
> **(2 Cor. 5:17 NIV)**

> **For God so loved the world, that he gave his only begotten Son, that whosoever believeth in him should not perish, but have everlasting life.**
>
> **(John 3:16 KJV)**

6

The Witch's Calendar

What harmony is there between Christ and Belial? What does a believer have in common with an unbeliever? What agreement is there between the temple of God and idols? For we are the temple of the living God. As God has said: "I will live with them and walk among them, and I will be their God, and they will be my people." Therefore come out from them and be separate....

(2 Cor. 6:15-17 NIV)

The Mysteries of Stonehenge

Thirty-eight megaliths (prehistoric monuments) stand in a circle on the Salisbury Plain in southwest England. Some say the stones are men who were petrified by the gods. Whatever one's belief about these monuments of Stonehenge may be, the truth surrounding their origin is clouded by mystery.

Astronomers point out that this circular formation of stones may have served as a precise observatory of the heavens. Archeologists believe this formation of gigantic rocks was erected between 3500 and 1000 BC.[1] Many occultists and satanists see strong supernatural significance in the Stonehenge megaliths.

Ancient Celtic priests known as Druids used Stonehenge as their special site for the observance of their pagan religion. They celebrated a major holiday — the Vigil of Samhain — there on October 31. Samhain was their god of the dead, and his special holiday forms the basis of our modern-day celebration of Halloween.

This 2,000-year-old "feast of the dead," like most of the Celtic religion, was based on fear and superstition. To them, October 31 was the eve of winter and the beginning the Celtic new year. With the passing of springtime, summer and harvest, the Celtic people, guided by their priest-class (the Druids), prepared for the dark, cold and foreboding days of winter. First, they celebrated a productive autumn harvest with a great feast. Then, they engaged in religious rites and rituals that included human and animal sacrifices.

Winter was a dreaded season — the time of year when storms, cold, death, disease and darkness descended on the land. The Celts believed that the night of October 31 represented "a crack in time" when the dead could revisit the living.[2] They also believed that evil spirits and ghosts roamed the land on this evening (New year's Eve, to them) and their malevolent purposes were to visit hardships and catastrophes on the living. No longer was the sun god of summer in charge; the approach of winter meant that the god of the dead — Samhain (Satan) — would now take over.

They devised as many practices and rituals as possible in an effort to appease the lord of death. They gathered the weak, prisoners and all who were considered to be evil and placed them in special baskets. Huge bonfires (believed to have the power to ward off evil spirits) blazed in the meadows surrounding the Salisbury Plain. In the center of the circle of Stonehenge one of these fires was prepared to receive the people who had been selected for the ritual sacrifices that would take place at midnight.

The Celts, like many witches today, based their calendar on the cycles of the moon. This lunar calendar guided them in the establishment of their customs and holidays.

By sacrificing those who the Druids considered to be worthy of death, the pagan priests believed they would gain favor with Samhain for themselves and their people. One by one, they would throw their victims into the raging inferno.

The screams and cries of the dying could be heard echoing throughout the valley. Samhain, their lord of darkness and of death, they believed, must have been pleased by their service to him. Surely now he would prevent them from having to face hardship during the winter months.

While engaging in their frightening rituals, the Druids dressed in dark robes and wore hideous masks. By so doing, they thought, they could fool the evil spirits and ghosts that sought to do them harm. They felt that the spirits would see their grotesque masks and think that the priests were like them. This, the Druids believed, would cause the spirits to leave them alone.

In these ancient traditions we see the beginnings of so many of the practices our children of today associate with Halloween.

Jack O'Lanterns and Black Cats

Several myths and traditions grew out of the ancient Druidic customs. Many of these persist to our present day. For example, many people still consider it to be unlucky for a black cat to cross in front of them. This superstition stems from the Celtic belief that the disembodied spirits of evil people who died take up their residence in cats, especially those that are black in color.

Jack o' lanterns carved from harvest pumpkins adorn the front porches and windows of many homes on Halloween. This custom started with the Celts as well. One myth involving jack o' lanterns originated in ancient Ireland. A fellow named Jack was a very miserly individual who played tricks on the devil and hoarded all his earthly possessions, never sharing anything with those in need. As a result, this Irish legend suggests, Jack was barred from entrance into both heaven and hell. His punishment was to walk the earth throughout all time until the Judgment Day.[3]

It was believed that his spirit took out angry vengeance on the living at every opportunity he could find to do evil. For this reason, the pumpkins with faces carved into them and candles shining through the faces, were placed in front of cottage doorways to scare Jack (and all other roaming spirits) away.

Another legend suggests that the custom of using jack o'lanterns around the time of Halloween stems from ancient England. The menfolk would go to the harvest fairs around this time of year and get drunk from the ale they consumed; their wives had to go and find them, according to this legend, and they would design special lanterns called "punkies" in order to find their husbands who might be lying alongside the roads. They felt that carving a scary face on their punkies would help to keep them safe from evil spirits while searching for their husbands.

Tricks and Treats

The Roman Catholic Church "christianized" the Vigil of Samhain during the ninth century. They named November 1 as the Feast of All Saints (or all hallows) and November 2 became the Feast of All Souls. The name "Halloween" is literally "the hallowed evening," the night before the Feast of All Hallows (Saints).

To celebrate this special time of year, Christian children would go "a-souling." This meant that they would go around their village neighborhoods begging for "soul cakes" — sweet pastries that were greatly loved. They would stand in the doorways of the cottages and chant:

> **Soul, soul, for a souling cake I pray, good missus, for a souling cake Apple or pear, plum or cherry Any good thing to make us merry[4]**

If the "missus" failed to comply with their request, the children would frequently play tricks upon her since they felt that she had failed to make them "merry." Instead, she had made them "mad."

The blending of Christian traditions with pagan customs has resulted in a contemporary holiday known as Halloween

— a time of ghosts and goblins, witches and bats, tricks and treats, haunted houses and masks. It has also led demented souls to poison candy and place razor blades and other dangerous items in apples and candy bars. In the weeks prior to and following Halloween, the numbers of child abductions and ritual sacrifices of animals and humans show marked increases.

Though Halloween has traditionally been a time of parades and parties, in recent years the holiday has taken on increasingly sinister overtones. Some schools and communities are taking steps to curb the celebration of Halloween. In one community in Pennsylvania, for example, the parent-teachers organization has canceled the school's annual Halloween parade and party, "because the rise of satanism in our area seems to be supported by Halloween and Halloween costumes."[5] The officials cited three additional reasons for the cancellation of New Cumberland's Halloween celebration:

1. Not enough parental support
2. Costumes promote violent behavior
3. Some children have elaborate costumes while others have none.

Harvest Parties

Though many parents and children were angered by the decision made by the New Cumberland Parent-Teacher Organization, I believe they have made a wise decision. When I was involved in satanism, I learned how many witches and satanists see Halloween as their highest holiday. They seize upon the celebration as an opportunity to practice their black arts, including ritual sacrifices.

There is absolutely nothing that is Christian about Halloween, no matter how much the Church may try to legitimize it. Today, even some churches sponsor "haunted houses" in an effort to keep their youths involved.

One pastor described this phenomenon of "Christian haunted houses" in churches as follows:

A few years ago, late in the month of October, I was ministering in a small Texas town. One afternoon I decided to do some sightseeing. As I drove down one road I looked to one side and saw something that astonished me. It was an old turn-of-the-century church building, but it was neither its wonderful architecture nor its beautiful stained glass windows that caught my eye and nearly took my breath away. Instead of the beauty, what astounded me was that in front of the building were giant wooden doors with beautiful glass windows above them, and in those windows were pictures of ghosts, witches, and even the devil himself. A sign outside the church read something like, "Come, celebrate Halloween with us." I was astounded! How could anyone use the house of God in such an abominable fashion?[6]

And yet, all over the world at Halloween, we see churches opening their doors to the kingdom of darkness, even welcoming its representatives with fascination and joy. this is one of Satan's schemes to "Deceive even the elect" (Matt. 24:24).

Through seemingly "innocent" activities such as "dressing up," trick-or-treating, creating "haunted houses," etc. adults and children are being deceived into thinking that the realities of satanism and witchcraft are ridiculous — something to have fun with, to laugh at, to treat with humor. My own experience causes me to know that there is nothing funny about the powers of darkness — nothing funny at all.

As a creative alternative to Halloween parties and parades, I would like to recommend that churches, communities and schools consider the idea of harvest parties on October 31. These occasions could be great fun and they could include hayrides, contests, good food, games and even costumes. Such costumes would not need to represent the dark forces, but they could symbolize different careers, sports heroes, comic book figures, etc.

I have watched my own children struggle to discern the difference between the two kinds of Halloween celebrations. One of my daughters wanted to attend a community "haunted house" one year because her friends had encouraged her to go.

It seemed that nothing Rose and I could say or do would dissuade my daughter from going. We decided to let God take over, and so we agreed to walk with our daughter down to the center of town where the haunted house was located. As we got within twenty feet of the place, my daughter turned to me and said, "No way am I going in there! It looks and sounds so evil!"

Later that week, I decided to walk through the "haunted house" myself. A youth group from a large church was sponsoring the "haunted house" as a fund-raising endeavor in the basement of their church. It was very dark, and candles provided the only light. A ghost-like figure with a green face was my guide. He took me through the various chambers where "corpses" lay in caskets that had been provided by a local undertaker, a skeleton danced in one corner, screams and shrieks filled the air, and a Dracula-like figure "decapitated" his victim!

The experience brought back so many of the old feelings of fear and evil that I had experienced as a satanist. How glad I was that my daughter had decided not to attend. The young people were extremely creative in their depiction of evil and the satanic realm. If their purpose was to evoke fear in the hearts of those who came, I know that they succeeded. But how is God glorified by that?

> **There is no fear in love. But perfect love drives out fear,
> because fear has to do with punishment. The man who fears
> is not made perfect in love.**
>
> **(1 John 4:18 NIV)**

Our church offered an alternative to the youths of our community that was based on love, not fear. I'm happy to report that my daughter decided to attend the harvest party our church provided on Halloween night that year. The young people were just as creative in their planning and decorating for the harvest party as the other youths had been with regard to their "haunted house." None of the children left this party crying and screaming as I had observed happening in the other church. They weren't obsessed with fascination regarding the powers of darkness and fear. They were happy in their celebration because they were focused on the One who made the bountiful harvest for us to enjoy.

Mystical Powers

Halloween is the highest of "holy days" in the witch's calendar. Many modern occultists (including some followers of witchcraft and satanism) continue to believe in the mystical powers of Stonehenge (and in the traditions of the Druids).

Every June 21 (the date of the summer solstice), many people gather at Stonehenge in an effort to gain contact with the spiritual forces of the universe. Likewise, many go there on October 31 to observe the Vigil of Samhain.

Several psychics have reported that amazing supernatural experiences, such as healings and precognition (the ability to see into the future) have occurred there. It is believed by many that the stones hold the power to speak to them of eternal wisdom, to impregnate barren women and to produce spells of vengeance against one's enemies.[7] Some occultists believe that the stones possess spirits that are able to give special powers to those who accept them.

Supernatural Dreams and Visions

Tribal shamans, Druidic priests and followers of ancient Egyptian religions (among others) have believed in the powers of the occult to produce supernatural dreams and visions. Many other ancient cultures held to such occultic notions as well. From ancient Greece, Rome, Babylonia, India and China, as well as some native American cultures, reports have circulated about special occult powers that enable one to receive visions of mystical import.

The Eskimo shaman Anarqaq told of a melancholy spirit that appeared to him soon after the death of his parents. He reported, "The spirit (Giant Eye) said, 'You must not be afraid of me, for I, too, struggle with sad thoughts. Therefore, I will go with you and be your helping spirit.' ''8

Many modern-day psychics and clairvoyants (those who claim to have the power to see into a world beyond the five physical senses), including Edgar Cayce, report that similar spiritual experiences have imparted to them the ability to gain psychic powers. These spirits are known as "familiars," and the Bible reveals the source of "familiar spirits" as being the kingdom of darkness. For example, Samuel identified the witch of Endor as being one who was possessed by a "familiar spirit" from the devil. (See 1 Sam. 28:7.)

The ghosts and spirits that are depicted in Halloween costumes and parties represent the spiritual realities of the underworld — evil spirits serving the prince of darkness, none other than Satan himself.

Edgar Cayce was thirteen years old (in 1890) when he encountered one of these "familiar spirits." He was reading his Bible in the woods near his family home in rural Kentucky when this meeting occurred. He looked up and saw a woman standing before him whom he assumed was his mother. He later reported that he soon realized that he was in the presence of a spiritual apparition, a mystical entity rather than a living person. Cayce went on to describe her appearance and to relate what the "familiar spirit" said: "Your prayers have been heard. Tell me what you would like most of all, so that I may give it to you."

After getting over his initial shock, the youth responded, "Most of all,I would like to be helpful to others, especially to children when they are sick."9

The entity told him that his wish would be granted. From this experience, Edgar Cayce went on to become one of the leading practitioners of the occult arts that the world has ever known. He gave thousands of "medical readings" during his lifetime while in trance-like states, and many people reported that they received psychic healings of physical problems.

Many other psychics and occultists have reported that their special abilities came to them through similar supernatural dreams, visions and "visitations."

The Moon Goddess

Historically, the worship of the moon as goddess predates the worship of the sun god; therefore, the four most significant holidays of witchcraft are taken from the lunar calendar. These dates also correspond to the major times in the agricultural year.

The first of these is the Vigil of Samhain (or Halloween) which we have already discussed. This is "New Year's Eve" to the occultists, and much revelry is associated with its observance.

Candlemas

The next significant holiday in the witch's calendar is known as Candlemas or the Feast of St. Bride (St. Brigid). This date — February 2 — marks the soon coming of springtime, the lengthening of daytime hours, and the end of the rule of death and destruction (as typified by Samhain).

Certain "moon cults" continue to believe that the moon goddess gives birth to a new sun god on December 21 of each year (the winter solstice — the shortest day of the year). Candlemas, therefore, is to them a time to celebrate the moon goddess's recovery from giving birth six weeks previously.

To Wiccans, Candlemas is known as Oimelc, the festival of winter purification and the celebration of springtime's new life. Oimelc is also recognized by satanists as a significant holiday in their calendar.

Beltane

The holiday known as Beltane is celebrated on April 30. It is also known as Walpurgis Night and Roodmas. Beltane originated as a holiday to honor St. Walburga (The term ''Walburg'' is also an old Teutonic name for the festival given in honor of the god of the underworld — Satan.) Its date coincides with the time of the year when spring planting begins, and the Celts (represented by the Druids) often used this celebration as another opportunity to offer human sacrifices.

As you will recall, it was on Beltane (or Walpurgisnacht) that Anton Szandor LaVey founded the Church of Satan in San Francisco. This shows that satanists have adapted this holiday as a part of their calendar. Wiccans regard the feast of Beltane as a fertility festival. Symbolizing the advent of spring, Beltane is the time for them to get in touch with special powers that they believe can produce healing and other benificent results.

Lammas

Also known as Lugnassad, Lammas is observed around the date of July 31, a time in witch's calendar that represents the onset of the harvest season. During this period fruits and vegetables are ripening and farmers begin to gather their crops.

In some of the older occult religions, the priest-kings would be sacrificed in the fields as a part of the rituals surrounding Lammas. Lammas is also known as the festival of first fruits, and it was believed that the blood of the martyred priest-kings would provide fertility for the produce of the following year.

Worship of the Sun God

Generally speaking, worship of a sun god as a primary deity developed later than the worship of a moon goddess. The worship of the sun became most prevalent in cultures that had some understanding of astrology and astronomy. Ancient Egypt and Babylonia, for example, gave honor to the sun.

The Druids considered themselves to be astrologers and astronomers as well. They believed their religion was based on principles from those sciences. From their study of the heavens, they made many deductions about the divine powers of the sun and the moon.

Many of the holidays they observed were celebrated on the same dates we use to mark the changes of the seasons of the year. The holidays were as follows:

1. **Yule (December 21-22)**
2. **Vernal Equinox (March 21-22)**
3. **St. John's Eve (June 21-22)**
4. **Michaelmas (September 21-22)**

Sabbats and Esbats

Not all witches, Wiccans and satanists adhere to all of the eight holidays we have listed thus far. In general, however, it would be fair to say that these eight holidays reveal the most significant dates in the witch's calendar. The eight holidays are known as sabbats — midnight assemblies of witches, sorcerers and satanists used to renew their allegiance to Satan and/or other gods through mystic rites and orgies.

Witches of today are generally less concerned with making crops grow than they are with getting in tune with nature and "recharging their spiritual batteries." Their sabbats are regarded as times for working their spells most effectively. Many witches observe only the four lunar festivals as their sabbats, but some do celebrate all eight.

Esbats are gatherings of covens that often take place under the full moon. Some covens, however, have weekly, bi-weekly and/or monthly esbats as well. Many times these esbats coincide with the eight major holidays of the witch's calendar. The four lunar sabbats enable them to perform their rituals in the silver light of the full moon.

Yule (December 21-22)

This holiday marks the winter solstice. It comes close in the year to the Christian celebration of Christmas, the birth of the Lord Jesus. Yule to many occultists, however, represents the birth of the sun god. According to ancient traditions, the sun god is actually reborn on this date, marking the longed-for end of winter's grasp.

Vernal Equinox (March 21-22)

The advent of spring is a time of great celebration in most cultures, religions and traditions. For many occultists, the vernal equinox is especially significant because it is the date when day and night are of equal length. From this point on, the days begin to grow longer and spring planting often begins.

St. John's Eve (June 21-22)

Also called midsummer, this holiday falls on the longest day of the year. It is known as the summer solstice, the day when the sun god has the most power.

Michaelmas (September 21-22)

The autumnal equinox occurs on Michaelmas. Again, the day and night are of equal length on this date, and the days following begin to grow shorter. It is a time of celebration of the harvest.

Other Gods and Goddesses

Throughout history, many cultures have given cats the status of divinity. To kill a cat in ancient Egypt, for example, was a capital offense. The Romans believed that their goddess Diana sometimes took the form of a cat.[10]

Likewise, bats are often regarded by occultists as beings with supernatural powers. Often primitive cultures have seen sexual significance in the behavior of vampire bats. A great mythology has evolved with regard to vampirism that has its origins in bat-worship.

According to superstition, a vampire is a ghost that comes from the grave at night to suck the blood of a living person, especially young people. Supposedly, such a vampire enters the bedroom of a sleeping victim, bites his or her neck, consumes the blood and leaves the person to waste away and die. Upon death, the victim becomes a vampire himself.

The blood of the living enables the vampire to keep going. In 1897, Bram Stoker wrote a well-known book — *Dracula* — that has perpetuated this myth along with the ways to deal with vampire attacks. In order to resist a vampire, it is said, one must drive a stake through his heart. This act alone will keep the vampire confined to his grave. The use of a crucifix, it is believed by many, will help to ward off a vampire's attack.

The mythologies surrounding the worship of cats and bats as well as stories surrounding vampirism, have found their way into many occult teachings and practices. They are also a large part of Halloween customs.

Many occultists look to the religions of ancient cultures to identify their gods and goddesses. Some occultists relate to Roman or Greek gods and goddesses; others identify with Egyptian deities. Still others, look to the theologies of Norsemen and American Indians for their gods and goddesses.

Whatever their orientation, it is clear that the occultist is not worshiping Yahweh, the God of the Bible who said, "I am the Lord your God, who brought you out of Egypt, out of the land of slavery. You shall have no other gods before me" (Exod. 20:2-3 NIV).

When occultists turn away from the one true God to follow after other gods, Satan eagerly enters the picture to receive their worship and adulation.

Witches often refer to the principles of the Lady and the Lord in their teachings. "The Lord," to them, is the masculine power over animals, death and the realm of the unknown. "The Lady," on the other hand, is their primary deity — the triple goddess. This female trinity consists of the maiden, the mother and the crone. The changing phases of the moon reveal the different characteristics of the Lady.

To satanists, the goat image represents their worship of Lucifer. This goat is called "the goat of Mendes" and it is symbolized by the Sigil of Baphomet. Witches also revere the goat as their "horned god of the hunt and death." He is also known as Pan or "the lord of the forests."

Holidays of Horror

In modern times, many of the holidays we've discussed in this chapter have become "holidays of horror" because of the rise of criminal acts that have been associated with their observation. The weeks immediately preceding and following these holidays (especially Halloween and Beltane — Walpurgisnacht) are times of increased kidnapping, ritual abuse, criminal mischief, murder and suicide. In many American cities, the night before Halloween (known as "Mischief Night" or "Devil's Night") has become an evening of crime, looting, arson and other violence. It almost seems that the ancient Druids were "right on" in their belief that Halloween was the night when all the evil spirits were unleashed.

Unlike the Druids, however, Christians have no reason to fear. While the religion of Druids, satanists, witches and Wiccans is often based on fear and superstition, our faith is based on love.

> **For God so loved the world that he gave his one and only Son, that whoever believes in him shall not perish but have eternal life.**
>
> **(John 3:16 NIV)**

Faith, Not Fear

I'm sure some people must see me in the same way one might look upon Ebenezer Scrooge or "the Grinch who stole

Christmas,'' because of my views regarding Halloween. It is certainly not my desire to be "a party-pooper" or a "joy-quencher." The fact is I love to make merry and to have a good time.

It is my own experience with fear and its self-destructive manifestations that causes me to take such a serious stance regarding the topics of this book. At the same time, I want to be certain that I do not evoke fear in anyone's heart by so doing. God wants us to be happy. He is pleased when we have a good time in an atmosphere of His presence and love.

When I was a satanist I thought I was having a good time on Halloween by participating in so many evil and self-gratifying experiences. It was only when I became a Christian that I was able to discern between true happiness and false happiness, between light and darkness, love and hate, faith and fear. With real joy, I can now sing with David of old:

> **The Lord is my light and my salvation — whom shall I fear? The Lord is the stronghold of my life — of whom shall I be afraid?**
>
> **(Ps. 27:1 NIV)**

Do we need to fear "Devil's night" or any other holiday or satanic custom? The Bible gives us a clear answer:

> **When evil men advance against me to devour my flesh, when my enemies and my foes attack me, they will stumble and fall. Though an army besiege me my heart will not fear; though war break out against me, even then will I be confident. One thing I ask of the Lord, this is what I seek: that I may dwell in the house of the Lord all the days of my life, to gaze upon the beauty of the Lord and to seek him in his temple. For in the day of trouble he will keep me safe in his dwelling; he will hide me in the shelter of his tabernacle and set me high upon a rock.**
>
> **(Ps. 27:2-5 NIV)**

We have nothing to fear from satanists, witches and others. The power and love of God are our protection. We need to remember the words of our Lord Jesus:

Do not be afraid, little flock, for your Father has been pleased to give you the kingdom.

(Luke 12:32 NIV)

His kingdom is not a kingdom of fear; it is a kingdom of faith and love. Let us return Halloween to the Church's original intention: a holy evening in which we celebrate the love of our Lord Jesus Christ!

7

Inside Satan's Toolbox

Recently I have been hearing more and more about ministries coming under demonic attack, as they (and their churches) are targeted for destruction by local covens. Just yesterday I read...how ministers...are suffering from various mysterious oppressions, including nagging physical problems that physicians are not able to cure. Last week I was listening to a cassette where Benny Hinn tells how a witch who has come out of Satanic bondage shared with him that local covens gather and in their version of prayer, curse pastors by name, one by one. Then a member of our staff here has discovered that there are some 62 covens right here in Jacksonville....[1]

(Francis MacNutt in "Christian Healing Ministries Newsletter")

Magical Technology

For the most part, the "magical technology" of witchcraft, satanism and a wide variety of other magical traditions comes from similar roots and resources. Certain implements and paraphernalia tend to be used in similar ways by representatives of each magical orientation.

There are some differences, however, regarding how these "tools of the trade" are used. For example, groups that follow a "white magic" path will describe and employ these items differently from those of the "left-hand path." (i.e. satanists, witches and others). In the following pages we will endeavor to describe and explain many of the various tools, books and techniques that are employed by followers of the "magical arts."

The Athamé

Also known as a Bolline, the Athamé is the ceremonial knife of a witch or satanist. As with all the other basic tools, it needs to be "consecrated" by the user in order to become "official."

The designs of Athamés do vary, but certain guidelines always apply. First, the hilt of the knife must be black. This helps to distinguish it from the white-hilted knife that is employed for digging, engraving, cutting or piercing.

Strictly speaking, the Athamé's use in a ritual is purely symbolic. It is possible, however, for some occult practitioners to use the Athamé in ways other than symbolic. This appears to be the case, most often, among those who are at superficial or dabbling levels of occult involvement.

Most Athamés have a double-edged steel blade about five or six inches long. Ideally, both sides of the blade should be sharp, and it should be pointed at the tip. Athamés with varying degrees of ornamentation are usually available from occult bookstores or mail-order outlets. They may have curved or wave-shaped blades, and their hilts may contain symbolic carvings.

The hilt of the Athamé may be made from the horn of a goat or from some other animal, and any metal on the handle is likely to be silver. In some cases, the Athamé may simply be a kitchen knife with black tape over the handle.

According to *Mastering Witchcraft* by Paul Huson, the Athamé is used to draw magical circles or other diagrams for use in the casting of spells.[2] A practitioner, for example, may draw the outline of a pentagram in the air with the Athamé during a ritual. It is believed that the use of the Athamé during a ritual raises "the cone of power" for the magician's use in casting a spell.

The Witches' Cord

Also known as the girdle, the witches' cord is a length of rope, usually measuring from four or five feet in length to nine or ten feet. Sometimes it is known as the cingulum or cable tow.

Many witchcraft manuals suggest that the magician should make his or her own cord from flax or river rushes. The witches' cord will most often be made from some kind of natural fiber such as cotton; however, as is so often the case with matters related to the occult, this is not necessarily universal.

The witches' cord has two basic functions. For one, it is often used to measure a circle or a triangle. When used in this manner, there may be markings or knots at regular intervals in the rope (at three-foot intervals in a nine-foot rope, for example). The witches' cord is also used in various initiation rituals or in rituals involving some sort of binding (hence the name "cable tow"). In the latter scenario, one of the ritual's participants may actually be tied with the ceremonial rope.

The Chalice

The chalice, or ceremonial cup, is a goblet that is used in a magical ceremony. According to *The Satanic Bible,* the chalice should be made of silver. If a silver chalice is not available, however, one made from glass, pottery, or another metal may be used, as long as the metal is not gold. Gold is believed to represent the sun or "white-light" religions. Other sources suggest that an animal horn may be used as a chalice.

There are two purposes for the ceremonial chalice. First, it is used to contain a liquid, often either salt water for exorcism rituals or sacramental wine for drinking. A bowl may sometimes take the place of a cup, and this is most often the case when a potion is being prepared. Second, according to many magic traditions, the bowl or cup symbolizes femininity (as opposed to the ceremonial knife which represents masculinity). Often, the Athamé may be found placed in the chalice on the altar.

In *Halloween and Satanism,* a book by Phil Phillips and Joan Hake Robie, there is a vivid description of a medieval black mass ritual that is often copied by satanists today. Note how the chalice and the Athamé were used following a human sacrifice:

> ...While it is not known for sure, some early accounts place the time of the sacrifice of the victim before the actual celebration of the Black Mass as the culmination point of the hideous ritual.
>
> A mock confession followed The Lord's Prayer, then the celebrant made an inverse sign of the Cross with his left hand. The Chalice would then be passed around, to be filled with the urine of the participants or dipped in the blood of the sacrifice. Next came the elevation of the Host, which was received with wild screams and hideous yells from the congregation. The priest then stabbed the Host with the same knife which he had used for killing the victim, and the wafers composing it were dipped into the blood. After that, the Host was thrown upon the ground, where the priest spat upon it and all the participants rushed forward with growls and screams to trample it underfoot. The final desecration was the out-pouring of the contents of the Chalice upon the crushed remains.[3]

The Thurible

Also known as the witches' censer, the thurible is most often used for burning incense, giving an increased sense of a mysterious atmosphere to the ritual site. In some cases, it might be filled with burning charcoal, particularly when heat and fire are needed for a particular ritual. The thurible may be ornate, or it may be a simple metal bowl.

The Grimoire

Often called a book of shadows, the Grimoire is a record of the spells employed by particular individuals or groups. Unlike the books on witchcraft that are available on the open market, the Grimoire is generally a handwritten manual and its contents are supposed to be kept secret. It may take a variety of forms, but the cover is usually black. On the cover there may be symbols representing a particular group, or the "magical name" of the practitioner may be inscribed there.

The Grimoire describes various spells and rituals in detail. The instructions may be written in calligraphic script. Some groups may also keep a list of their members in the Grimoire as well as the dates of the groups' activities. For groups involved in sacrifices, a list of their victims and/or intended victims may possibly be found there as well. For satanists and witches, the Grimoire is a spellbook. One specific Grimoire that is often used by witches is called *The Greater Key of Solomon.*

Other Tools

The preceding five tools are the ones that are used most universally by witches and satanists. A number of other items are often employed as well. *The Satanic Bible,* for example, lists the following items:

1. *Ritual clothing.* Black robes are used by the male members in a ritual; female participants may wear black, or they may wear sexually suggestive attire. Other groups and individuals may wear robes of different colors and types. For example, red robes may be used in sexual ceremonies.

2. *Jewelry.* Amulets, charms, talismans and other objects believed to possess magical powers are likely to be worn during rituals. The specific nature and design of these pieces of jewelry differ with various groups and specific rituals.

3. *The altar.* Since satanism is a religion that is based on emphasizing the flesh instead of the spirit, the altar in a satanic mass is traditionally provided by the body of a nude woman. For other groups, any kind of table may be used and the table is generally covered with a cloth. Various magical implements are arranged on the altar, depending on the specific group's practices.

4. *The Sigil of Baphomet.* This satanic symbol is generally represented as a half-man, half-goat creature. *The Satanic Bible* recommends that the Baphomet symbol be made large enough

to be seen by all in attendance when it is placed on the wall above the altar.

5. *Candles.* In some satanic ceremonies, only black and white candles are used. Depending on the specific magical tradition involved, a wide variety of colored candles and shapes may be used. For example, a green candle is used for spells involving peace and/or prosperity. A red candle is used for sexual magic. Black candles often represent the destruction of enemies. (Somewhat surprisingly, *The Satanic Bible* recommends that a white candle be used for the destruction of enemies as well as for representation of the "hypocrisy" of those who are on the "right-hand" path.)

6. *Bells and gongs.* These instruments are used to signify the beginning and end of rituals as well as to mark specific times within particular rituals.

7. *The phallus.* A phallic symbol represents the human penis. According to *The Satanic Bible,* a phallic symbol capable of sprinkling water is used as a perversion of the Roman Catholic vessel that is used to sprinkle holy water.

8. *Parchment.* A request for a magical operation is often written on parchment, or on a plain sheet of paper, and then it is burned.

9. *The sword.* In some cases, a sword is substituted for the Athame in group rituals.

The Compass

In most rituals, at least those performed by serious magicians, most of the implements as well as the activities of a group are oriented according to compass directions.

For example, if a pentagram is drawn within a circle on the floor of a ritual site, the direction of north generally will determine how a symbol will face.

In a satanic ceremony, a pentagram drawn in this fashion may have one point facing south and two points facing north. Also, movement around the circle is dependent on the type of ritual.

Many witchcraft sources specify a counter-clockwise direction for invoking rituals (those rituals that are used to increase something or to call up a demon), and clockwise for banishing rituals (those rituals that are used to decrease or lessen something or to banish demons).

Using the Witches' Working Tools

Al G. Manning, in a book entitled *Helping Yourself With White Witchcraft*, explains how the various tools of witchcraft may be used:

> *Spellbook (or Grimoire):* When you have a highly successful demonstration of your witch power, you will certainly want to remember exactly how you did it so you can do it again should the occasion demand. A good quality loose-leaf notebook is best, so you can occasionally clean out the accumulation of not so effective spells. This should be planned as a combination of diary and recipe book. It is very personal, and the necessity for secrecy is obvious, you'll find that a degree of reverence in handling it will pay dividends. Establish this rewarding practice from the very beginning of your work: record date, time and the details of each ritual performed or spell cast. In a few months you'll find you have a priceless record of your growth and proficiency. And would you encounter the term, Grimoire, in your research, you'll know that the writer was speaking about a witch's secret recipe book.

> *Altar:* The householder's altar of Buddhism could be an interesting parallel to the altar of Witchcraft. A small table makes an ideal altar, but just as in Buddhism it could be a tray that you put away after each ceremony. The minimum requirements for your altar would be two candle holders (the style should suit your individual taste), an incense burner, 2 small cups (one each of

water and earth) and of course a candle snuffer — no self-respecting witch would ever blow out a candle! A mirror will prove very useful in advanced ritual work also.

Chalice, Mortar and Pestle, Chafing Dish: When we begin mixing your potions and witch's brews you'll need a large cup or chalice and a chafing dish (or some suitable container that can hold burning charcoal without setting fire to the place). And unless you are careful to acquire only finely powdered herbs, a simple mortar and pestle such as you will find in any hobby shop is virtually indispensable.

Cord and Knife (or Athame): Your witch's cord can be worn as a sash or belt — it is also used as a drawing compass to lay out the nine and seven foot ritual circles. Your cord should be made with your own hands by braiding together six strips of bright red ribbon. It should be knotted at the 3½ foot mark and at the 4½ foot mark to indicate the radius of the traditional circles. (Its length: 4½ to 6 feet.) The knife or athame should have a blade six to eight inches long and a plain handle on which you will inscribe your witch's name and other symbology later. This is used for drawing the symbolic circle and many other interesting parts of your rituals.

The Hat, Robes and Other Apparel (or Lack Thereof): Let me begin by commenting that the best of all Witch costumes is the lovely suit of skin in which you entered this world. For some coven (means place) work (or on an extremely cold night) one might resort to simple robes, but the physical and psychological freedom expressed by the absence of clothing fits beautifully into the ancient traditions of fertility and oneness with nature that are the great power of true Witchcraft. My favorite exception would be the pointed hat — note the similarity to the "dunce cap" and the pyramid. There is a powerful energy in the properly constructed pyramid and we can understand the cone as simply a pyramid with an infinite number of sides. A stiff paper is easiest for this purpose and if you're impelled in this direction try a diameter of seven inches for the bottom and let the altitude of the hat be just under five inches. . . . [4]

The Powers of the Gods

Whereas in Christianity we are concerned with the power of love, the satanist is preoccupied with the love of power.

Satanists and witches may call upon a pantheon of gods and goddesses in order to gain that power.

Most of these deities come from the traditions of ancient Germany, Rome, Greece, Egypt and Babylonia. Each of these cultures had a supreme god that ruled over all of creation. For the Germanic tribes, the deity's name was Woden or Frigg. The Romans called this deity Jupiter or Juno. To the Greeks the supreme deity was Zeus or Hera. The highest deity for the ancient Egyptians was the sun-god Ra, and the Babylonians worshiped Marduk.

In two of the ancient theologies, the creator-god differed from the supreme god. In Egypt, for example, the creator was called Ptah; in Babylonia he was called Anu.

Each of the ancient religious systems had gods who supervised the following realms: the sky, the sun, the moon, earth, air, fire, the sea, water, rain, light, thunder, wind, storms, dawn, fertility, harvests, vegetation, death, music, poetry, wisdom, learning, war, love messengers, healing, hunting, wine and crafts.

Modern-day witches and satanists may evoke these deities and several others in their spells and incantations in an effort to gain power in the areas of expertise represented by the gods and goddesses. For example, the gods of death — Hel (Germanic); Pluto (Roman): Hades (Greek); Osiris (Egyptian); and Nergal (Babylonian) — might be called upon in a ritual in order to bring a curse upon an enemy.

Likewise, the gods and goddesses of love would be summoned if an individual witch or satanist had designs on someone they wanted to love. The mother goddesses might be summoned as well. The following chants exemplify how this concept might be followed in witchcraft:

Chant to Attract a Lover
> Venus, Cupid, Eros, Friends,
>> Your help will serve my rightful ends.
> My loving trust appeals to thee,
>> Please send my true love straight to me.[5]

Chant to Enhance an Existing Love Affair
Aphrodite, Venus, Ishtar, Isis,
  Keep our love and bring no crisis.[6]

Chant for Business Improvement
Nature spirits of the air,
  Bring us business and to spare.
We serve them well as you do see,
  So this request is right for thee.[7]

Chant for Good Luck
Oh wondrous spirits of Pan and Puck,
  I turn to you for much good luck.
This herb maintains our contact pure
  And brings good luck that's swift and sure.[8]

The Witch's Marketplace

Publications, periodicals, books, audio and video cassettes
that deal with all aspects of occultism can be found in bookstores,
libraries, schools and magazine shops everywhere. In many of
these one can find advertisements for all kinds of occult products.

For example, in the Autumn, 1990, issue of *The Quest*
— "A Quarterly Journal of Philosophy, Science, Religion and
the Arts," one can find the following classified ads:

For Sale: Chakra-Tuned Quartz Crystal Singing Bowls.
Guaranteed lowest prices. Frosted and clear.[9]

Mind Expansion Videos. Improve memory, meditation,
confidence, sexuality, stress, healing, energy, psychic abilities,
100's more![10]

Tibetan Prayer Wheel. For over 2000 years the monks of
Tibet have known the secrets of moving the universe by churning
the ethers. The Sacred Prayer Wheels which we offer contain
the prayer "Om Mani Padme Hum," which is an invocation for
Peace and Prosperity."[11]

Back issues of *Gnosis* magazine are offered here as well.
The topics of those issues include: Oracles and Channeling;
Secret Societies; Esoteric Spirituality; Alchemy; the Northern
Mysteries; Magic and Tradition; Ritual and The Dark Side.

Another readily available magazine, *New Age Journal,* offers readers a wide array of occult ideas and products. In the classified section of July-August, 1990, issue of this magazine we find the following advertisements:

> *Firewalking* — an Ancient Ritual of Spiritual Empowerment. Instructors training — A professional training in Firewalking and spiritual leadership.[12]

> *Horoscope and interpretation.* Very accurate. $24. Send birthdate, time and place.[13]

> *Learn Tai Chi* — Strengthen your mind, body and spirit with China's most healthful and intriguing exercise.[14]

> *Personal Guidance Through Numerology.* In-depth life readings on cassette tape. Clarifies your past, present and future directions.[15]

> *Group Marriage.* New book tells how to succeed.[16]

> *Goddess Worshippers.* Isis, Ishtar, Greco-Roman, Hindu, more! $15/statue.[17]

> *Reverend George.* I am a specialist in matters that concern love spells. Uniting and reuniting lovers.[18]

Countless examples of these kinds of ads are found in new age and occult literature that is available everywhere. Also advertised are communes, herbs, jewelry, approaches to healing, etc.

Witchcraft, occultism and the New Age Movement are providing thousands of entrepreneurs with a means of luxurious livelihood, and Satan is alive and well in the marketplace.

Ouija Boards

The *Dictionary of Mysticism* defines the Ouija Board as follows:

> **An instrument for communication with the spirits of the dead. Made in various shapes and designs, some of them were used in the sixth century before Christ. The common feature of all its varieties is that an object moves under the hand of the medium, and one of its corners, or a pointer attached to it, spells out messages by successively pointing to letters of**

the alphabet marked on the board which is a part of the instrument.[19]

Parker Brothers produces Ouija Boards as parlor games. During the nineteen-seventies they sold more than seven million around the world. The "game" consists of a small, rectangular board that is made from pressed cardboard with a laminated top. On the board there are various symbols: the letters of the alphabet, numerals from 0 to 9, and the words "yes," "no," and "good-bye."

There is a plastic pointer, often shaped like a heart, that is used to spell out "messages" from "the other side." Frequently two or more people will "play" with the Ouija Board at a time. The individual who is using the pointer will place his or her fingertips on the top of this heart-shaped object at which point "unknown forces" guide the pointer to symbols on the board in an effort to spell out a message.

There have been cases reported wherein individuals have acted upon the messages they have received from the Ouija Board, leading them to murder, suicide and other acts of violence. As a case in point, one teen-aged girl endeavored to use the Ouija Board in a seance with her deceased mother. Reportedly, the spirit of her mother directed the daughter to kill her father. The fifteen-year-old girl obeyed "the spirit's message."[20]

Some people have researched the use of the Ouija Board and they almost universally report unusual phenomena arising from its use. In *On the Threshold of the Unseen,* Sir William Barrett told of circumstances in which the board "worked" even when participants were blindfolded, the symbols on the board were rearranged and the board was covered up. He concluded, "Whatever may have been the source of the intelligence displayed, it was absolutely beyond the range of normal human faculty."[21]

Spiritualism

Many occult tools from Satan's toolbox are used by spiritualists and others who practice necromancy and divination. The Ouija Board is one of these.

A primary belief of spiritualism is that the living can communicate with the dead. In order to make contact with the deceased, the services of a particularly gifted and sensitive individual (known as a medium) are employed. Frequently, the spiritualist medium will enter a trance-like state in order to establish contact with the spirit world.

Meetings of spiritualists in which they endeavor to communicate with the departed are known as seances. Most often, the seance is held around a table. Sometimes the "spirits of the dead" will communicate by rapping on the table, tilting it or moving it across the room. These occurrences are known as "manifestations."

In other seances, spirits are presumed to literally take over or "possess" the body of the medium. In these cases, the "spirit" may speak through the medium or use the hands of the medium to write out a message.

There are three main bodies of spiritualist churches in the United States:

1. **International General Assembly of Spiritualists**
2. **National Spiritual Alliance of the USA**
3. **National Spiritualist Association of Churches**

The above three branches of spiritualism involve thousands of members each.[22]

The spiritualist movement in the United States began in the mid-nineteenth century in New York State. It is reported that two young sisters — Margaret and Katherine Fox — heard rapping on the walls of their home in Hydesville, New York. They learned that a man had been murdered in their home, and they believed that the rapping they heard was the murdered man's attempt to establish contact with them.[23]

After a while, the girls learned how to communicate with the dead man's spirit. They would ask him questions that could be answered by yes or no. He would respond with a certain number of knocks for yes and a different number for no. Interest in the story of these girls and the rappings they reported spread around the world. Before long, others reported similar phenomena and the concept of mediums evolved.

Many well-known individuals have followed certain spiritualist practices and teachings, including: Sir Arthur Conan Doyle, the author of the Sherlock Holmes mysteries; two British scientists — Sir James H. Jeans and Sir Oliver Lodge; and William James, a psychologist from the United States.[24]

Spiritualist teachings have involved experiences with ectoplasm (a ghost-like misty mass that often leaves a gummy residue) that may appear during a seance. If the participants believe the ectoplasm is the ghost of a dead friend, the phenomenon is called "materialization."

Many spiritualist teachings and practices have found their way into the New Age Movement, and some satanists and witches also participate in necromancy (contacting the spirits of the dead for magical and/or fortune-telling purposes). In necromancy — objects such as bones, skulls — parts of the dead — are used.

Tarot Cards

The traditional deck of tarot cards consists of twenty-two pictorial cards that are used for divination and fortune-telling. Not all tarot cards are the same, however. The cards represent the major "Arcana" or suits which give the primary reading. There are other cards in the deck that make the reading more specific.

Certain ancient cultures, including Egypt and India, had symbolic cards that were used for fortune-telling. The cards have pictures on them that represent major forces in nature and events in life. The card numbered 13, for example, is the card for death and it is usually represented by a skeleton.

Gypsies have taught that their culture holds the original set of tarot cards, and that they are the only ones who know the true meanings of the cards.

There is also a set of witches' tarot cards. How these cards are used varies with the individual witch or fortune-teller.

Seeing the Future in Crystal

One popular tool used by gypsies and others for scrying (seeing into the future) is the crystal ball. Modern-day witches, New Agers and others use crystals of all shapes and sizes for a wide range of supernatural purposes.

Tina Turner, for example, has reported that her use of crystals takes away the loneliness she feels when she enters a hotel room.

A fortune-teller who uses a crystal ball enters an auto-hypnotic state while gazing into the shiny, clear orb. Eventually, the clearness gives way to cloudiness in the center of the globe, followed by a vision of supernatural portent.

Other rocks and minerals are used in supernatural ways as well. The following list describes the supposed benefits derived from using these rocks and minerals, according to many New Agers. Many witches, New Agers and other occultists believe in the power of these talismans (objects that are reported to produce magical and miraculous effects):

> *Amethysts* — help to clarify the thinking processes and may bring physical healing as well.
> *Aventurine* — Removes anxiety, stress and tension. Enables the user to find peace and joy.
> *Carnellian* — Makes one prosperous and successful.
> *Fluorite* — Creates greater physical and mental energy.
> *Jade* — Leads to longevity; enables one to find unity with universal powers.
> *Jasper* — Brings emotional balance.

Obsidian — Helps the individual develop his inner potential.

Petrified wood — Heals back problems.

Rhodocrosite — Emotional healing.

Rose Quartz — Improves love life and skin tone.

Snow Quartz — Cleanses the body and soul.

Tiger Eye — Provides protection. Helps one overcome bad habits.

Sodalite — Resolves inner conflicts.

Rhodonite — Protects lungs and respiration.

Unakite — Good for the heart.

Rock crystal — Used to enhance meditation. Able to store and transmit supernatural energy.

Amulets and Talismans

An amulet is a charm that usually has inscriptions of magical significance engraved on its surface. The person who wears such an amulet believes that it will protect him from evil or benefit him in some way. The list of rocks and minerals cited above is one source for amulets. The following chapter, dealing with satanic symbols, reveals additional sources.

Often talismans are associated with astrology. Like amulets, they are worn as jewelry in order to gain supernatural protection, good luck and other benefits.

Many times talismans bear symbols associated with astrology, witchcraft or satanism. Crystals are frequently the talisman of choice for modern-day occultists.

Role-Playing Fantasy Games

There are many role-playing fantasy games on today's market. The best-known of these is Dungeons & Dragons (also known simply as D&D).

In the January — February, 1985, issue of "NCTV NEWS," the newsletter of the National Coalition on Television Violence, there is a report that more than twenty-seven deaths associated with the playing of Dungeons and Dragons have occurred. They go on to describe a typical scenario:

The D&D game is played in groups, mainly by boys ages 10 to 21. Each player creates his own character to fight in a medieval fantasy world of monsters, devils, sorcery, and combat. The goal of the game is to amass power by finding treasure and killing opponents. Violence is a constant element of the game with assassination, poisoning, curses of insanity, demonology, and combat with all sorts of medieval weaponry. Satanic and horror violence is common to the game even including human sacrifice, the drinking of blood, commanding the undead and creating zombies, and desecrating religious fonts by urination. The games require many hours of fantasy development from the players and usually last for weeks and months.

The deaths are listed in two categories, (1) where D&D was the decisive factor. There are usually suicides where full information is available, often with detailed suicide notes, and (2) where D&D was a major factor in the lives of the young men at the time of their violent acts. These are usually murders and fuller details are less available because of at least four on-going murder trials. NCTV is calling for required warnings on all D&D game materials and for an enforcement of the Toy Safety Act of 1984....[25]

In many cases, it appears that the line between reality and fantasy has been crossed over by the D&D participant so many times that his perspective is blurred and he loses contact with reality by completely absorbing himself in the identity of the character whose role he has assumed.

This happened, for example, in the case of Mitchel Rupe who murdered two bank tellers in Bremerton, Washington, in 1982. His psychologist testified that Mitchel had gotten so involved with his character in D&D that he lost all contact with reality, leading him to murder two other men.[26]

James Dallas Egbert, aged seventeen, committed suicide by shooting himself in the head. Some of his fellow-students at Michigan State University suggested that his involvement with D&D was the factor that led him to end his life. Just prior to his suicide, Egbert wrote, "I'll give Satan my mind and power."[27]

In another tragic case, Jeffrey Jacklovich of Topeka, Kansas, committed suicide with a revolver. His suicide note read, "I want to go to the world of elves and fantasy and leave the world of conflict." This young man had been a football player and member of the Future Farmers of America prior to his untimely death. He had also been deeply involved with D&D.[28]

We will deal with more of the crimes and violence that have been associated with Dungeons & Dragons, and other fantasy role-playing games in our later chapter on satanic crime.

Tools of Destruction

In this chapter we have looked into Satan's toolbox and examined many of the instruments, schemes and devices he uses to ensnare and destroy people. We have dealt with many of the leading tools he employs, but we have not discussed every single item to be found in his workshop. There are so many that it is impossible to cover them in a single chapter.

The important thing to remember about each of these "tools" is that even though they may appear to be innocent and harmless, each one is used for destructive purposes in Satan's kingdom-building plans.

It is as C.S. Lewis wrote in *The Screwtape Letters:*

> **Bad angels, like bad men, are entirely practical. They have two motives. The first is fear of punishment: for as totalitarian countries have their camps for torture, so my Hell contains deeper Hells, its "houses of correction." Their second motive is a kind of hunger. I feign that devils can, in a spiritual sense, eat one another; and us. Even in human life we have seen the passion to dominate, almost to digest, one's fellow; to make his whole intellectual and emotional life merely an extension of one's own — to hate one's hatreds and resent one's grievances and indulge one's egoism through him as well as through one's self. His own little store of passion must of course be suppressed to make room for ours. If he resists this suppression he is being very selfish....It is (I feign) for this that devils desire human souls and the souls of one another.**

It is for this that Satan desires all his own followers and all the sons of Eve and all the host of Heaven. His dream is of the day when all shall be inside him and all that says "I" can say it only through him....[29]

C.S. Lewis goes on to employ the image of a bloated spider to describe Satan in his efforts to devour human beings. He cannot get enough; he is never satisfied because his hunger for control and worship and power is never-ending. For all these reasons we need to recognize that the enemy of our souls will employ any nefarious scheme he can devise to bring us down. He is practical, and the tools we've examined in this chapter are instruments he uses to fulfill his evil purposes.

> **The devil is no idle spirit, but a vagrant, runagate walker, that never rests in one place. — The motive, cause, and main intention of his walking is to ruin man.**
>
> **(Thomas Adams)**

8

Satan's Symbols and Signs

We perform human sacrifices, by proxy you might say
— the destruction of human beings who would, let's say, create
an antagonistic situation towards us — in the form of curses
and hexes, not in actual blood rituals because certainly the
destruction of a human being physically is illegal.

(Anton Szandor LaVey)

Symbology

In order to really understand occult symbols and their functions, it is necessary to first consider symbology in general. All of us think and communicate by means of symbols. The words we use in speaking and writing, for example, are symbols, and most of our physical gestures are symbolic as well. We often speak of the symbolism conveyed by art and literature when meanings deeper than the obvious, surface portrayals exist.

A symbol, therefore, is a representation of an idea, a person or a thing. The U.S. flag symbolizes freedom, democracy and other values associated with the United States of America. Since we cannot *see* freedom or democracy in the literal sense, we use the flag to represent those concepts.

In order for a symbol to be meaningful to us, however, we must understand the context in which it is used. The word "car" is a meaningful symbol for a particular kind of vehicle only because people in the English-speaking world know what that word represents. They are familiar with what a car is and they use the word as a symbol to convey something that is known and understood by most English-speaking people. Taken out of its context, however, the word "car" would have little meaning. An Australian aborigine who has never seen a car, for instance, may not have any idea of what the word means.

Likewise, if we took the U.S. flag to a place where the inhabitants had never seen one before, the flag would not be a meaningful symbol for them. The individual might be able to appreciate the design and colors of the flag, but he would not know what the stars, stripes and colors represent.

Most symbols are tangible representations of intangible things. Something that can be perceived by the physical senses stands in place of an idea, a concept or an abstract belief or value. Symbols are frequently used by religions to convey theological and ethical concepts.

The dove represents peace. The heart stands for love. An anchor is a symbol of faith. The cross stands for the death of Jesus Christ. It is also a symbol of hope.

In the world of the occult, symbols are used to represent spiritual concepts also. The meaning of the symbol, however, depends on the context in which it is used.

Many occultists take symbology one step farther than Christians and others do. Sometimes they believe that the symbol does more than simply represent something else; within the symbol itself there are often magical properties, according to their view. These meanings and interpretations differ among occultists, however, so it is impossible to understand them unless we look at the context in which they are used.

With this in mind, we must always consider three aspects of symbology in order to understand the meanings of specific occult symbols:

    1. In what manner is the symbol used?

    2. What type of occultism is practiced by the person or group using the symbol?

    3. What is the level of involvement of the person or group who is using the symbol?

Each of the above considerations is important in trying to determine the significance of occult symbolism. White witches and satanists, for example, may employ similar symbols, but they do so for different purposes and with different understandings. An individual at a superficial level of involvement may use these symbols without understanding their true meaning, and may even draw them incorrectly.

Types of Occult Symbols

There are three general types of occult symbols:

1. Symbols that are believed to have specific magical properties.

2. Symbols that identify a particular group or a particular expression of occultic interest.

3. Symbols that are part of a magical alphabet.

It is possible for an occult symbol to fall into more than one of the types listed above. In fact, many common symbols can be accurately described according to the first two types. These categories, though not absolute, help us to describe and discover the use of basic occult symbols.

Throughout this chapter, we will describe some of the various symbols as they are understood and used by most serious occultists. At the same time, however, it is important to realize that particular individuals and groups may alter the significance of a given symbol for their own purposes. Those who are at the superficial level of occult involvement may use symbols inappropriately out of ignorance or misunderstanding and/or carelessness.

Symbols With Magical Properties

A number of basic geometric figures are often associated with magical or spiritual ideas. The most common are shown as follows:

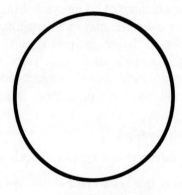

The Circle

The Circle — The circle is one of the most universal of magic symbols; it represents endlessness or infinity. A circle is often drawn on the floor (or ground) at a ritual site, and the ritual activity takes place in or around the circle. Also, circles are believed to contain magical power, which is why circles are often drawn around other symbols.

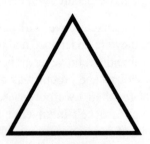

The Triangle

The Triangle — A triangle with one point facing upwards represents good, spirit, or the element of fire. (Prior to the modern discovery and classification of elements by the natural sciences, it was commonly believed that the physical world and everything in it were composed of four elements. These were earth, air, fire and water. In some cases, spirit or ether were considered to be the fifth "element.") A triangle with its point facing downward can represent evil, the physical or the element of water. Equilateral triangles, the sides of which are of the same length, symbolize wisdom. Triangles may also represent the Trinity, and may be placed within circles for protection.

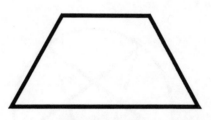

The Trapezoid

The Trapezoid — According to the Church of Satan, the trapezoid is a powerful, potentially destructive magical symbol. However, those who understand its power are supposedly able to use it effectively against others. *The Satanic Bible* recommends the use of a nude woman upon a trapezoidal table as an altar for group rituals.

The Pentagram ("Upright")

The Pentagram ("Upright") — A pentagram, or pentacle, is a five-pointed star. It is often used in ceremonial magic as a representation of man. The five points can represent the five senses, or they can represent spirit (the top point) and the four elements. In the upright position (one point facing up, two points facing down), it is most often employed by magicians who practice "white magic."

The Inverted Pentagram

The Inverted Pentagram — The pentagram in this position is almost universally a satanic symbol. Whereas the upright pentagram represents the supremacy of the spiritual over the physical, the inverted pentagram symbolizes the triumph of the flesh over the spirit. Also, the Temple of Set apparently uses the inverted pentagram within a circle to represent a doorway through which members can communicate with Set.

The Hexagram

The Hexagram — The hexagram, also referred to as the Seal of Solomon, is a six-pointed star formed from two triangles, one facing up and the other facing down. It is often used in ceremonial magic to represent the occultic maxim "As above, so below." The hexagram is used by a wide variety of occultic expressions, including witchcraft, Hermetic orders such as the Golden Dawn, and by some satanists. It is occasionally used as a talisman to protect the wearer against evil. The use of the six-pointed star (the Star of David) to represent the nation of Israel is separate and distinct from this specific occult use. This is one example of a situation in which the context of a symbol's use is of paramount importance.

The Lightning Bolt

The Lightning Bolt — The lightning bolt is often used as a "power symbol" by occultists. In other words, they believe that the proper use of this symbol gives the user control over others. Anton LaVey, high priest of the Church of Satan, occasionally wears a medallion with a lightning bolt superimposed over an inverted pentagram.

The Nine Satanic Statements Symbol

The Nine Satanic Statements Symbol — This symbol appears in *The Satanic Bible* together with "The Nine Satanic Statements" (See also page 46 of this book where we list these "statements.") A variation of this symbol also appears in a catalog for "The Magickal Childe," an occult mail order outlet. According to the catalog, the talisman with this symbol is to be used for the destruction of one's enemies.

The Eye of Lucifer

The Eye of Lucifer — In non-occult use, the eye within a triangle symbolizes "enlightenment." Within the occult, the emphasis is on Lucifer as the one who brings enlightenment. The "eye's" connection with the Illuminati, a group founded by Adam Weishaupt in 1776, is possible but not proven.

The Lemegeton

In a grimoire known as the *Lemegeton,* one may discover a group of names that are associated with demonic beings. (An occultist may not refer to these beings as demons, however.) The numerical symbol of 666 is often used in rituals designed to call forth or banish the demons.

Astaroth — Also known as Astarte, Astaroth is the Phoenician goddess of fertility and of sexual love.

Asmodeus — The word "Asmodeus" is derived from a Hebrew term that means "destroyer." Asmodeus was an evil being who was known as "the king of the demons." He is also identified with Beelzebul (see Mark 3:22).

Baal — Also known as Hadad, Baal was the supreme fertility god of Canaan. He was also the god of fire.

Belial — Belial is uniformly regarded as the proper name of the prince of evil — Satan.

Many of the symbols used in ceremonial magic are derived from these basic forms, and they incorporate names of angels, demons and sometimes even the names of God. They may be used to call forth or banish spirits, for protection or for a variety of other purposes.

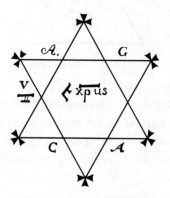

The Pentagram of Solomon

The Pentagram of Solomon — The Double Seal of Solomon

The Tree of Life

The Tree of Life — Although not technically a symbol that embodies magical power, the Tree of Life is a representation of the ten steps and twenty-two paths of the Cabala, a system of Jewish mysticism. (While mainstream Judaism does not accept the Cabala, most scholars do agree that it originated as a mystical form of Judaism.) A number of occultic expressions incorporate the Cabala in their teachings and practices. These include many witches, the Golden Dawn and the followers of Aleister Crowley.

Identity Symbols

Certain symbols are employed by occultists to identify particular groups and/or expressions of occultism. Most of the symbols that non-occultists frequently associate with satanism, witchcraft, and other forms of the occult are not primarily magical symbols. Rather, they serve to identify the type of occult expression followed by an individual or group, or they identify a particular group, such as the Church of Satan.

Many of these symbols serve a dual function by being both symbols of identification and magical symbols. Again, it is crucial to one's understanding of these symbols to look for the context in which they are used. Not everyone who uses these symbols is necessarily a committed follower of a particular occult expression, however.

Witchcraft Symbols

The Upright Pentagram

The Upright Pentagram — Although primarily a magical symbol, practitioners of "white witchcraft" often use this symbol to identify their affiliation. For example, it appears on the letterhead of the Witches' League for Public Awareness.

The Crescent Moon

The Crescent Moon — The crescent moon is occasionally employed to represent Diana, the moon goddess. Witchcraft is usually either matriarchal (an approach which places a goddess in preeminence over a god) or it recognizes an equality between a goddess (or goddesses) and a god (or gods). This symbol may also appear with a small star representing Lucifer, the morning star. (The Muslim usage of the crescent is not related to the occult.)

The Ankh

The Ankh — The ankh is an Egyptian symbol of life and fertility, and it is used by many witches. An ankh serimposed over an upright pentagram often denotes an interest in Gardnerian witchcraft.

Satanism's Symbols

The Inverted Pentagram

The Inverted Pentagram — The inverted pentagram is almost universally a satanic symbol, although its use among teenagers can often be attributed to its appearance on the album covers of certain rock/heavy metal bands. An unadorned pentagram within a circle is also the symbol for the Temple of Set, founded by Michael Aquino.

Church of Satan Symbol

Church of Satan Symbol — The inverted pentagram and goat's head within two circles is the symbol of Anton LaVey's Church of Satan, although non-members also have been known to use this symbol in a variety of ways. The figures between the two circles are Hebrew letters.

The Upside-Down Cross

The Upside-Down Cross — In Christianity, the cross is a symbol of Christ's atonement for our sins and His victory over death. Satanists often use an inverted cross to represent the defeat of Christ (and/or the defeat of Christianity).

666

666 — This well-known set of numerals is "the number of the beast," a biblical reference to the Anti-Christ that appears in the last book of the Bible, the Revelation. The number three represents God in the Bible, and the number six represents man. Therefore, three sixes can symbolize man claiming to be God, a claim that is often made by satanists. Many have become familiar with the significance of the 666 symbol through movies and rock music album covers.

The Satanic Goat

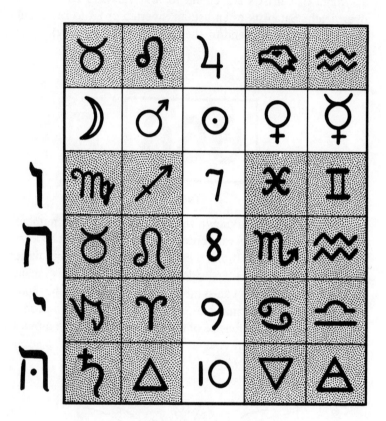

The Sign of Union

Other Occultic Groups

The Hermetic Order of the Golden Dawn — The Golden Dawn utilizes a great number of symbols on banners and on ritual dress. A few examples are shown below:

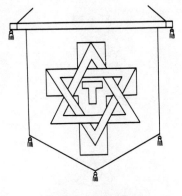

Banner of the East

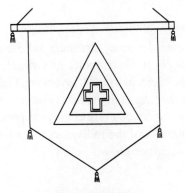

Banner of the West

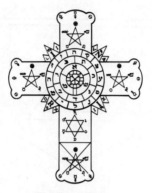

The Rose Cross

The Rose Cross — (This symbol is used by the Rosicrucians.)

Magical Alphabet Symbols

Occultists consider many alphabets to be magical, and they use these alphabets in their spells and rituals. The Hebrew alphabet is often used in rituals involving Cabalistic magic, especially in the writing of the various Hebrew names for God. However, a wide variety of alphabet usage is possible, depending on the occult interests of the individual or group. Some of the most common ones are shown below:

A =	H =	O =	**The Witch's Alphabet**
B =	I =	P =	
C =	J =	Q =	U =
D =	K =	R =	W =
E =	L =	S =	X =
F =	M =	T =	Y =
G =	N =	U =	Z =

The Witches' Alphabet

The Witches' Alphabet — This is taken from *Mastering Witchcraft* by Paul Huson.

Enochian	Title	English
Ѵ	Pe	B.
Ᏼ	Veh	C or K.
ᒐ	Ged	G.
✗	Gal	D.
⅄	Orth	F.
✗	Un	A.
⅂	Graph	E.
Ƹ	Tal	M.
ᒐ	Gon	I, Y, or J.
⊙	Na-hath	H.
⊂	Ur	L.
∩	Mals	P.
∪	Ger	Q.
⋝	Drun	N.
Γ	Pal	X.
⅃	Med	O.
Ƹ	Don	R.
Ᵽ	Ceph	Z.
ᑎ	Vau	U, V, W.
7	Fam	S.
/	Gisa	T.

The Enochian Alphabet

The Enochian Alphabet — This is taken from *An Advanced Guide to Enochian Magick.*

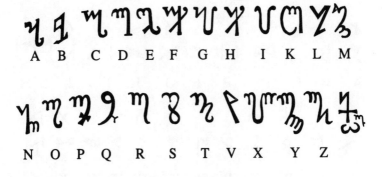

A B C D E F G H I K L M

N O P Q R S T V X Y Z

The Theban Alphabet

The Theban Alphabet — This is taken from *Man, Myth and Magic.*

Celestial Writing

Malachim

Malachim — This is taken from *Man, Myth and Magic.*

A   B   C   D   E   F   G   H   I   J   K   L   M

N   O   P   Q   R   S   T   U   V   W   X   Y

Z   □   □   □   □   □   □   □   □   □   □   □   □

The Runic Alphabet

The Runic Alphabet — In addition to their use in an alphabet, runes can also be symbols that represent words or ideas.

Although not actually part of an alphabet, Egyptian hieroglyphics (especially the ones used in the playing of "Dungeons and Dragons") can be considered in this category. Astrological symbols and symbols originating with alchemy (the power or process of transforming something common — such as a base metal — into something precious — such as gold) would also fit here.

Symbols Announcing a Ritual

Peace Symbol   **Anti-Justice Symbol**

Other Symbols

A number of occult symbols are often seen in conjunction with other kinds of symbols, especially when they are seen in the form of graffiti. Some of these non-occultic symbols are related to white-supremacist movements or "deviant youth" organizations. Around Halloween, one may see occult symbols in graffiti, but these may have been drawn by youths who are only superficially involved in satanism.

The "Peace Symbol" or "Cross of Nero"

The "Peace Symbol" or "Cross of Nero" — The evidence for a true occult use of this symbol is inconsistent, although many believe it to represent an upside-down cross with broken cross-pieces. This symbol does not appear in any of the serious occult literature.

The "Anti-Justice" Symbol

The "Anti-Justice" Symbol —

This symbol was actually meant by those who used it in the "Ban-the Bomb" movement (an early anti-nuclear weapons movement) to symbolize a circle of containment around an atomic missile.

The Cross of Confusion

The Cross of Confusion — The origins of this symbol are not completely known, but in modern usage it denotes an upside-down cross which questions the deity of Christ.

The Anarchy Symbol

Confusion Over Symbols

It is inaccurate to assume that someone is a satanist or even an occultist simply because one of the symbols we've cited in this chapter may be used by him or her as jewelry or in some other manner. Again, we must look for the context in which the symbol is used.

If someone has a statue of Buddha in his home, for example, it does not mean that this individual is necessarily a Buddhist. By the same token, if someone has a crucifix in his home, it does not prove that the individual is a Christian.

Several years ago a letter circulated among churches that accused the Proctor and Gamble Company of supporting the Church of Satan because of the "moon and stars" logo that was found on the packages of their products.

We immediately began to research this accusation when we heard about it. We called Proctor and Gamble as well as the producers of the "Donahue" program on which this idea was first aired. We were satisfied that there was no occult connection whatever in their use of the logo. Furthermore, the "moon and stars" logo, although somewhat similar to certain occult symbols, has no connection to any known occult group or practice.

From time to time, we hear this kind of rumor surfacing with regard to other occult symbols. For example, on the back of the one-dollar-bill of the United States, there is a pyramid within a circle that has an eye in a triangle above it. Some have claimed that this symbol is occultic in nature and they have tried to suggest that this is proof that our country is controlled by satanists!

Such fanatacism serves no useful purpose except to instill fear into the hearts of people. As Christians, we are not called to be reactionaries or alarmists. Rather, Jesus said we are to be "the salt of the earth" and "the light of the world" (Matt. 5:13-14). He went on to say, "Let your light shine before men, that they may see your good deeds and praise your Father in heaven" (Matt. 5:16).

Let us heed the words of our Master. Ours does not need to be a fortress mentality that seeks to hide from the world. Jesus said, "You are the light of the world. A city on a hill cannot be hidden. Neither do people light a lamp and put it under a bowl. Instead they put it on its stand, and it gives light to everyone in the house" (Matt. 5:14-15 NIV).

Instead of being knee-jerk reactionaries who look upon the darkness of our present age with fear, let us be the people of the light who lead occultists, satanists and others out of the darkness in which Satan has enshrouded them.

The true mark or "sign" of a Christian is love. Jesus said, "A new command I give you: Love one another. As I have loved you, so you must love one another. All men will know that you are my disciples if you love one another" (John 13:34-35 NIV).

When hate roars in, quench it with love.

When in darkness, turn on the light.

When faced with lies, tell the truth.

When surrounded by questions, give the answer.

It's not up to us to tell people what's wrong without telling them how to start doing it right!

9
Satanic Crime

When an offender is successful in abusing his victim he must try to conceal his deviate behavior from others. More likely than not, he will try to pledge the victim to secrecy in several ways. Secrecy strengthens the adult's power and control over the child, isolates the child from others, and helps perpetuate the sexual activity. It is important to understand that this technique is usually successful: Some children never tell anyone about sexual abuse. There are many reasons why the abuse is kept secret. The child is afraid of encountering disbelief, facing blame for the activity, or suffering punishment for disclosure. The child may fear that the adult offender will carry out his threats, or the child may even wish to protect the abuser. (From *Children Traumatized in Sex Rings* by Ann Wolbert Burgess, RN, DNSc, and Christine A. Grant, RN, PhD.)[1]

Crime, in Satan's Name

Essentially, all crime is governed by Satan. Therefore, in one sense, it would be accurate to state that all crime is satanic.

The Apostle Paul wrote to the church at Thessalonica:

For the secret power of lawlessness is already at work....The coming of the lawless one will be in accordance with the work of Satan displayed...in every sort of evil that deceives those who are perishing.

(2 Thess. 2:7-10 NIV)

The spirit of lawlessness is none other than Satan himself, and his handiwork is displayed in every daily newspaper. In our day, reports of murder, corruption, sexual immorality, and other criminal acts abound.

187

In newspapers around the world we can also read reports about another form of startling crime as well. This kind of crime is committed overtly in the name of Satan. In many localities and cities throughout the eighties and nineties we have read about murders, suicides and other violent acts committed by people who call themselves satanists.

Organized satanic groups will often dispute these reports by saying that there is no organized, behind-the-scenes network of satanists involved in criminal activity. Nonetheless, it cannot be disputed that satanic and occultic publications, teachings and practices have had an influence in the reported cases of satanic crimes.

One such case was reported by the Associated Press in November, 1990:

> Panhandle, Texas — It was Friday the 13th, a steamy night in July, when 17-year-old Frankie Garcia was taken to a barn outside an abandoned shack known locally as the "Haunted House" to meet his death.
>
> Witnesses who found the body say Garcia apparently was forced to kneel in the dirt and taste the barrel of a high-powered .223-caliber rifle as his killer pulled the trigger.
>
> Residents were shocked when word got out that a self-professed satanist had confessed to the murder.
>
> Kenneth Glenn Milner, a 19-year-old admirer of Charles Manson and Jack the Ripper, has been charged with murdering Garcia, a former friend. He is also charged with the attempted murders of Kenneth Williams, his former high school principal, and Jimmy Britten, a former girlfriend's stepfather, that same night.
>
> The 2,300 people who live in this farming town worry that there will be other attacks. Parents closely watch their children, keeping them off the dirt roads that crisscross the rolling wheat fields of the region.
>
> ::There is fear that there are more satanists out there," says Linda Salas, who has four children. "There are rumors that they are looking for a blond-haired, blue-eyed boy to sacrifice...."[2]

It is important to note that many of these events are taking place in small towns — in middle America. They don't occur only in New York or California where some people might expect them to be. There is no place to hide any more. Thanks to the media, there is no safe haven for raising kids left in rural America.

The experience of the people in Panhandle, Texas, has been shared by thousands of people in other communities that have been terrorized by satanic crime. This is one of Satan's schemes — to have people react out of fear rather than reason tempered by compassion.

Many cases of ritual abuse and satanic murder involve self-styled (solitary) satanists as opposed to members of specific occult organizations. This is not always the case, however. As we have already pointed out, satanists and occultists cannot excuse these crimes by "washing their hands of them" entirely because many times, the satanic criminal has been influenced by them and their teachings.

This was the case with Kenneth Milner who frequently read from the *Necronomicon* (a handbook of spells that reportedly involve the summoning of demons), and he was also greatly influenced by teachings about astral projection. One teen-ager who used to live next door to Milner reported, "He knew every horror movie by heart. He would make masks of characters in the horror movies — grotesque masks — like with blood and an eyeball hanging out." Obviously, neither can producers of media that glamorize and sensationalize sadistic themes of occultism excuse themselves from their responsibility by saying that their products play no role in influencing satanic crime.

At the outset of our look at occult crime in this chapter it essential for us to understand, however, that not all occult and satanic groups are overtly involved in criminal activities. Many witches, for example, while advocating a philosophy that is in direct contrast with Christianity and many of society's prevailing standards, may not ever engage in illegal activities. Even within satanism (which receives most of the blame for occult criminal activity), it is possible to identify a "satanic establishment" that seeks to maintain a level of public respectability.

The focus of this chapter will be on satanic activities that most strongly go against the grain of society. These behaviors include: anti-social activities, rape, child abuse, kidnapping, murder and suicide.

Anti-Social Activities

Technically, anti-social activities involve any behavior that is considered hostile or harmful by organized society. It is marked by participation in actions that deviate sharply from the norm.

While many of these activities may not be considered to be technically illegal, all anti-social behaviors are considered to be unusual, strange and undesirable by the majority of people.

The milder form of activities within this category might include such things as the wearing of bizarre clothing and jewelry; strange and frightening mannerisms; unfriendly behavior; the use of satanic symbols; and even nudity during rituals.

Sometimes anti-social behaviors go further than this. Obscene gestures and language may be one form. Satanic graffiti is another. In the extreme, some anti-social behaviors may involve self-mutilation. When I was involved in satanism, many of my friends cut off the little fingers of their left hands to show their allegiance to Satan.

In some cases, certain occult groups engage in "cult of confession" behaviors. This refers to activities that are deliberately designed to isolate an individual from society as a whole while, at the same time, binding him or her to the group more fully. To be effective, cult of confession activities must be extreme. In some cases they may lead participants to cross over the line into illegal activities; usually, however, the activities are simply strange and unusual without being actually illegal.

Such acts might involve orgies, homosexuality, bestiality (sex with animals), the drinking of blood and/or urine, the eating of feces, or other "kinky" behaviors.

Those occultists who engage in anti-social activities are frequently (and usually unknowingly) preparing themselves for participation in illegal activities in the future.

One of the letters we received at Warnke Ministries shows how initial involvement with anti-social activities through occult influences can lead one (a teen-ager in this case) in the direction of criminal activity.

> I know a 15-year-old boy who is involved in satanic practices. I do not know if he is in a cult. He listens to heavy metal (Sex Pistols, Grateful Dead, Motley Crue, Ozzy Osbourne, Metallica). I do not know all of the groups except that they are the ones who sing about death, mutilation, etc., and have pictures of things like skulls with worms hanging out of them. He is wearing all black clothing, skull earrings, and the chain-type stuff. He wanted his bedroom done all in black and was hanging up the pictures of the groups he likes. He is also drawing pictures of skulls with knives through them, a person holding a cross in fire and those types of things. . . . He said he isn't involved in a cult, that he was just interested and intrigued by the "Dark Side." He has skipped school for as much as three weeks in a row and is now staying out all night without leaving a note or calling which until recently, he has never done. He is also involved in drugs and alcohol. . . .

The young man who is described by this letter is rebelling by engaging in anti-social behavior. He tries to pass off this anti-social approach by saying that it is harmless. Already, however, it has led him into self-defeating, self-destructive patterns and the illegal behaviors of alcohol and drug abuse as well as truancy.

Lesser Criminal Offenses

By the term "lesser criminal offenses" we refer to illegal activities that do not result in direct physical damage to persons. In making this distinction, however, we realize that it is a somewhat arbitrary term; nonetheless, it is useful in a limited sense in helping us to see the different levels of criminal involvement in which an occultist may become engaged.

Common examples of these lesser criminal offenses include graffiti (that utilizes occult and satanic symbols), vandalism (frequently of cemeteries and church properties), trespassing, theft and cruelty to animals.

In some cases, the crime may be more or less incidental to an occult ritual. For example, a ritual site may be chosen for convenience rather than for a specific magical purpose. In such a situation, trespassing is frequently involved.

Vandalism and the drawing of graffiti are not usually part of a magical ritual, although certain symbols utilized in the graffiti may be employed to help identify a location or to give directions to a ritual site.

Theft may or may not be related to a ritual, but if the stolen items have religious significance, it is highly likely that the intent of the thieves is to use them in rituals. Many times, crosses or parts of a church's altar as well as consecrated hosts (communion bread) from Catholic churches, will be stolen for purposes of desecration in a Black Mass. Theft may also play a role in one's initiation into a group of self-styled satanists (as a requirement for entry into the group).

The mutilation of animals is seen by some satanists as a way to serve specific purposes. In some cases, the torture of animals is primarily a way to express violence or the desire to inflict pain without facing the penalties for doing such violence to a human being. There may also be a magical purpose for killing an animal:

> Most of the processes in the [magical] textbooks involve
> the killing of an animal, usually a young goat, at some stage
> in the operations.[3]

The sacrifice is sometimes done in advance of the actual
ritual to obtain "parchment" from the animal's skin or some
other needed item. This may not always be the case, however:

> In the later grimoires [books of spells] the sacrifice tends
> to be more closely associated with the ceremony itself and in
> modern rituals the victim is sometimes slaughtered at the
> height of the ceremony. This is done to increase the supply
> of [spiritual, "psychic," or magical] force in the circle.[4]

Reports of the ritual abuse of animals and their utilization
as satanic sacrifices are increasing in number. Oftentimes, these
activities take place in conjunction with occultic holidays — in
the days and weeks prior to and following them.

One lady wrote to us about such sacrifices that have recently
taken place in her home area in the Midwest:

> As my friend and her mother were mushroom-hunting,
> they ran into some strange scenes. There were two deer that
> were dead. One ear from each of the animals had been
> removed; the eyes were missing, as were all their insides. On
> the chests of the deer pentagrams had been carved.
>
> There was also a dead dog hanging in the tree and some
> kind of dead animal was wrapped up in a black tarp. (Its head
> and legs had been removed.)
>
> Needless to say, this really shook them up and they called
> the police. What really concerns them is to think that this is
> happening in our small town....

Police files in many cities and rural areas are getting thicker
with reports of such animal mutilations and sacrifices. During
the seventies and eighties, there were several reports of
midwestern livestock being mutilated for satanic ritual purposes.
In one issue of *Newsweek* during this period, for example, there
was a report of accounts of mutilated livestock in twenty-seven
states. Frequently these animals (usually sheep, cattle and horses)
were found with their reproductive organs removed and their
blood drained.[5]

In *Satanism — the Seduction of America's Youth,* Bob
Larson makes this observation:

> **The use of cattle is particularly noteworthy. In the more
> advanced stages of Luciferian worship, cows play an
> important ritualistic role. Many groups trace their origins to
> ancient agrarian cults. Egyptians, Canaanites, and
> Babylonians had pagan religions that revered the cow as a
> mother goddess and combined bestiality with bovine genital
> veneration. Even today, tourists to the Egyptian pyramids can
> walk through subterranean passages and witness row upon
> row of elaborate stone sarcophagi used to entomb sacred
> cattle. The Valley of the Kings in Luxor contains five-
> thousand-year-old wall paintings that picture humans
> cohabiting with cattle and consorting sexually with other
> livestock.**[6]

Many former satanists have reported to me that they
regularly participated in animal sacrifices and other forms of
ritual abuse of animals. In many of our counseling sessions we
have learned of increasingly extreme behavior that is taking place
in covens and groups throughout the United States, including
bestiality. Some individuals are capable of violence against
animals and other human beings prior to getting involved with
a satanic group. In most cases, however, a new recruit would
not consider himself or herself as being capable of committing
murder, and he or she would not be willing to participate in
a ritual involving animal sacrifices, kidnapping, rape or any
other form of violence — at first.

Something happens within the value system and
psychological outlook of the new recruit with the passing of
time. This is the desensitization process that we referred to
earlier. It also involves progressive entrapment and
indoctrination ("brainwashing"). Gradually, the individual loses
his perspective regarding the difference between right and
wrong. As this distinction grows blurrier and the values of a
particular occult group get clearer, the individual opens himself
or herself up to an entire array of behaviors he or she would
never have considered engaging in previously.

Such people may even become capable of participation in lust rituals including rape, homosexuality, bestiality, ritual sacrifices, and murder. For some, the ritual killing of an animal may serve as a step on the way to becoming capable of murdering a human being.

Often, it is blind allegiance to Satan that leads an individual into more severe kinds of crime. In much the same way that adherents of certain religions believe that they are honoring their deity by engaging in warfare or even suicide, the satanist may believe that he is honoring his "god" by committing murder!

The Altar of Sacrifice

In *The Satan Seller,* I describe the kidnapping of a young woman who was subsequently raped during a satanic ritual:

> "What do you mean, take my clothes off? In the first place, it's cold. Secondly, it's indecent. And thirdly, you can't make me!"
>
> "But that, my dear Mary, is the name of the game," Bert said. "I think I've seen you around school. If I remember right, you bulge out in just the right places. Let's find out...
>
> "Now, it's time for the fertility rites," I intoned. "Any of you guys who want to volunteer, stand up." Half the crowd stood up....
>
> Then Mary got the message. She started to roll off the altar. "Hold her!" I commanded sharply.
>
> Bert and James pinned her down fast. A guy slipped out of his robe and came up to the altar....[7]

As I mentioned in *The Satan Seller,* Mary later became a Christian thanks to the love shown to her by a group of believers. She was one of the first people in my life who told me about the love of Jesus.

After her conversion to Christ, Mary sought me out to let me know that she forgave me and to tell me that Jesus loves me. Because of His love, she was able to love me in Him.

The love of Jesus that I saw demonstrated by Mary was one of the things that God used to turn my life around.

Ritual abuse of a sexual nature has two purposes for those who engage in it. First, it gives the participants an opportunity to exercise control over another individual and to perceive themselves as being in a position of dominance. Secondly, the emotional response of the victim is considered to be a source of power for the magician. Participants in black magic regard the emotions of fear and pain as being equally potent. Thus, the emotional anguish of the victim and the emotions of the person performing the ritual provide a form of fuel for the spell:

> **The most important reason for the sacrifice....is the psychological charge which the magician obtains from it. The frenzy which he induces in himself by ceremonious preparations, by concentration, by incantations, by burning fumes, is heightened by the savage act of slaughter and the pumping gush of red blood.**[8]

Matamoras, Mexico

A drug cult in Brownsville, Texas, abducted Mark Kilroy, a twenty-one-year-old student at the Austin campus of the University of Texas in April, 1989. It was the apparent belief of cult members that the ritual sacrifice of a human victim would provide them with supernatural protection in their illegal activities. They had been running a metric ton of illicit drugs across the Rio Grande River each week.

It is now believed that this particular cult may have killed at least fifteen victims as ritual sacrifices. It is reported that some members of the cult would have sexual relations with their victims prior to their murder, and certain cult leaders had even learned how to rip the victim's heart from the chest cavity while he was still alive. In the case of Mark Kilroy, his brain was removed and cooked in a pot.[9]

This drug cult was not directly involved with voodoo, Santeria, Hoodoo, Yowba or satanism. It was most closely related to a sorcery cult somewhat akin to African black magic. The cult had a particularly violent approach to ritual abuse as reflected by the comments of Carlos Tapia, the Chief Deputy of Cameron County, Texas, the county in which Brownsville (a city near the Mexican border) is located:

> **I thought in my twenty-two years of law enforcement, I had seen everything. I hadn't. As we drew near, you could smell the stench...blood and decomposing organs. In a big, cast iron pot there were pieces of human bodies and a goat's head with horns....**
>
> **I was angry when I heard what they did to a private investigator working for the father of the American boy they murdered. They cut the skin off the bottoms of both his feet and made him walk on salt. Then they put him in a tub of water and boiled him alive. While he was screaming, they pulled pieces of raw flesh off his body....[10]**

Though this cult shares some similarities with Santeria (an occult movement that originated in Cuba) and Brujaria (a Mexican occult group), it is primarily a variant of a West African sorcery cult. Sorcerers gain power over spirits by elaborate rituals and sacrifices.

It is certainly appropriate to say that the Matamoras cult is satanic in that it is a black magic cult, a malevolent organization akin to our concept of "the left-hand path." It appeals to evil spirits instead of God for protection. The use of the goat's head in their ritual and inverted crosses tattooed on the chest of one of the cult's members also reveal its satanic leanings.

This cult, like hundreds that exist in the world today, was eclectic in the sense that it derived its practices from various occult and satanic orientations. The members borrowed ideas and approaches from many different philosophies, including:

> 1. *Voodoo* (also known as *voodun*) — originated with the Ibo tribe in Nigeria. It was then overlaid with older French Roman Catholicism by African slaves in Haiti. Voodoo in our present day is associated with sophisticated drug and herb use, and a particular group known as "The Zombie Cult." Many adherents

of voodoo may be found in Miami, New York City and other U.S. cities.

2. *Santeria* ("the saints") — also comes from Nigeria originally (the Yoruba tribe). In Cuba, it mingled with old Spanish Roman Catholicism. In South Florida primarily, and in several other U.S. areas there are more than 80,000 followers of Santeria.

3. *Hoodoo* — This approach involves U.S. southern black folk magic, involving the "root doctor" or "conjure man." Though it is a form of witchcraft, its background is English as opposed to African.

4. *Brujaria* — the sorcery cult of northern Mexico and the American southwest. It mixes Santeria-type elements with old European magic and the sorcery (or witch cults) of native American tribes. It has some similarity to the black (evil) witch cults of the Pueblo and Navajo tribes. These cults do not reflect traditional native American beliefs, however. The Navajos, for example, have always had a great fear of these witch cults. Many large Indian reservations of the Southwest are disturbed by the current resurgence of satanic activity in America, and are holding seminars in an effort to learn how to combat it.

5. *Macumba* — This is a Brazilian movement in which African tribal religion and the old Portuguese Roman Catholicism combine to form an occult expression. The word "macumba" literally means "to sacrifice to the gods."

6. *Quimbanda* — Brazilian black magic. This is actually the sorcery cult of Macumba.

7. *Pajelanca* — An Afro-Brazilian cult that was first known in the Amazon regions.

8. *Palomayumba* — Also an African sorcery cult, stemming from tribes in West Africa. Also known as *Pajelanca.*

All of the above groups practice ritual sacrifices. These are known as *Matanza,* and the animals utilized for sacrifices may include chickens, goats and turtles. All of these animals' carcasses were found at the Matamoras site. Blood offerings are important to each of the groups as well.

A cauldron (known as a *Nganga* or *Preuda*) was also found at the site of the Matamoras murders. The cauldron is considered to be the cultists' source of power in rituals. other items of occult significance were found there as well. These included:

1. *Cigars* — The smoke from which is used to attract their deities.

2. *Copper* — a symbol for *Oshunm,* an African deity. (Copper pennies were found in the cauldron at Matamoras.)

3. *Fire* — the symbol of Chango (the chief Yoruba deity). Chango is invoked in sorcery and he is associated with thunder, fire and cigars!

4. *Horseshoes* — symbols of the warrior god, Ogyum. There was a horseshoe at the Matamoras site.

5. *Pennies* — already mentioned as being associated with copper, the symbol of the African deity, Oshunm. Seven pennies symbolize the seven African power deities.

6. *A shed* — This is the sanctuary for the practice of these forms of occultism. It is also known as the *"Idbodu."*

7. *The skull* — The skull encases the brain. Generally, after a human sacrifice, the brain is left in the skull so it can "think."

8. *Sticks* — Sticks are stuck in the ground or placed in the cauldron to symbolize "communioning" (partaking of the power inherent in the sacrifice).

9. *Sword or machete* — Also known as the athamè, a sword or machete is frequently used in black magic, satanism and witchcraft. In the case of Mark Kilroy, a machete was used to kill him.

The Texas State Attorney General who was in charge of the investigation of the Matamoras horrors, Jim Mattox, has made this poignant observation:

> **What I saw in Mexico was unbelievable. My concern is for the growing influence of satanism. In a civilized nation, this should not be tolerated.**[11]

While many wish to deny the reality of satanism and its associated terrors in our land today, I am grateful that so many of our law-enforcement officials do recognize the serious reality of Satan's schemes. Deputy Sheriff Carlos Tapia gives good advice for all of us to consider:

Don't get caught unawares like we did. If you see any
signs of something that's out of the ordinary, notify your law
enforcement officers. Do yourself a favor: Save your kids![12]

Satan's Lust for Children

The ritual abuse of children and infants is one of the most
problematic of all occult crimes for several reasons. Most
reported cases of such abuse come from the testimonies of
children and/or adult "survivors" of ritual abuse. Some critics
would say that these bizarre tales cannot be believed.

My work with children and adult "survivors" leads me
to an entirely different conclusion. My own experience as a
satanist tells me that such stories are not only believable; they
are a terrible reality of the satanic scene.

Satan's lust for children is real. There is evidence to suggest
that he is behind the rash of child abductions, the increase in
child pornography, the sexual abuse of children and the
thousands of cases of ritual child abuse we read about.

Research indicates that one of every four girls and one of
every ten boys are sexually molested before the age of eighteen.
More than thirty-four million women in the U.S. are victims
of childhood sexual abuse.[13]

It has been established that there are actual sex rings that
seek children for their victims. Some of these are heterosexual
in nature; others are homosexual; some are bisexual.

Sex ring crime is a term describing sexual victimization
in which there are one or more adult offenders and several
children who are aware of each other's participation. There
are three different types of child sex rings. The solo sex ring
involves one adult perpetrator and multiple children. There
is no exchange of photographs, nor are there sexual activities
with other adults. By contrast, a syndicated ring involves
multiple adults, multiple child victims, and a wide range of
exchange items including child pornography and sexual
activities. At a level between these two types of rings is the
transition ring, in which the children and pornography are
exchanged between adults, and often money changes hands.[14]

One recent study reveals that child sex rings are increasing both in the United States and the United Kingdom. Some of these have satanic connections and other involve pedophiles (individuals who prefer to have sex with children). One well-known organization in the latter category is the Man-Boy Love Association.

Three reasons for ritual child abuse are generally proposed. First, children are more easily dominated than adults and can be manipulated (usually through fear) into concealing the abuse. Often, such manipulation involves threats of harm to the child and his or her family. Second, children represent innocence and the goal of many satanists is to destroy innocence as a way of showing their contempt for God. Third, involvement at a very young age in group activities can be seen as a way of influencing future recruitment into a satanic group. Even though a child's experiences with a group may be traumatic, they may become convinced that they have no other choice, especially if one of their own parents has been involved.

One father wrote to us to ask for help concerning his two children who were victimized through ritual abuse:

> Our two beautiful kids were sexually and physically molested. They also had to participate in satanic rituals. According to our kids and other kids (this happened at a day-care center), the following things happened:
>
> 1. They killed and sacrificed babies and animals.
>
> 2. They ate flesh and drank blood from babies and animals.
>
> 3. They chanted....

This distraught father, who is a very credible, committed Christian, went on to describe other traumatic events the children were forced to watch or engage in. They were used for the sexual gratification of the satanists, and they had to watch homosexual activities taking place. They were required to eat human excrement. Finally, they were threatened with knives, and they were told that their parents would be killed if they mentioned these events to anyone! We have investigated cases of ritual abuse of children all over the world, and for the most part, they all tell the same sort of stories. The chance that this is purely random or that somehow these kids have decided to tell the same lie is highly unlikely.

Child sexual abuse is a frequent problem at day care centers. The McMartin Preschool case in southern California has brought this matter to public awareness. Some cases involve individual pedophiles who have no occult connections. Other cases have ritual-abuse overtones, and children who have been victimized in these settings have reported similar experiences in different places around the country.

As Boise, Idaho's police occult investigator, Larry Jones, has pointed out:

> **The statements by victims from different parts of the country tally with each other...and it's being corroborated by therapists.**[15]

All too frequently, close relatives or friends initiate a child into the horrors of ritual abuse. Commonalities that are involved in most of these cases include practices that are too gruesome to describe — mutilations of animals and babies, cannibalism, pornography, etc.

In Los Angeles in 1985, the body of a young girl who had been the victim of ritual abuse was found with a pentagram carved in her chest. A pediatrician familiar with the case, Dr. Gregory Simpson, said, "The conclusion I reached is that satanic abuse of small children does exist, and it's something that needs to be dealt with by the medical community."[16]

Ritual abuse, like so many other forms of satanic and occult crime, has caused many people to retreat into a denial reaction in much the same way that an alcoholic or other addict will deny his problem. In a recent interview, Dr. Carl Raschke addressed this response by comparing our society to the society of Nazi Germany during the rise of Hitler. He said that we are like the Germans were in many cases when they heard about Nazi atrocities; they did not want to hear about them, chose to disbelieve them, and tried to ignore them.[17] Hoping that ritual abuse is not true will not make it go away!

Child Abuse

There are three forms of child abuse that have become a national issue and societal concern: physical abuse, emotional abuse and sexual abuse. All three of these forms may be a part of ritual abuse in a satanic setting.

Emotional abuse usually takes the form of verbal abuse. It often involves parents screaming at their children with harsh criticism, foul language and constant put-downs. When a child is treated in this manner, he is robbed of all self-esteem. The child becomes an emotional cripple. Always looking for love and acceptance, he or she may forever chase illusions.

Physical abuse involves harsh corporal punishment that is administered in anger and hate. Like emotional abuse, physical abuse hinders proper emotional development and it usually stays with a person well into adulthood. The physically abused child often becomes a child abuser himself.

In a satanic setting, it is sexual abuse that seems to be perpetrated on child victims most of all. Deep scars and hidden hurts remain with such a victim throughout their lives as a result of sexual abuse.

The November 14, 1990, issue of *USA Today* discloses the case of a trusted teacher who will be sentenced for sexually abusing several boys:

> Donald Marks, a teacher for more than 30 years, will be sentenced in Boulder, Montana, today for sexually molesting four elementary school boys....

> Court records show 22 accusations against Marks for molesting male students — some dating to 1956. County prosecutors have said there may have been up to 45 victims....[18]

The article goes on to show how Marks may have molested boys for more than two generations. In one case, a father of a boy who was molested by Marks reported that he had been molested by the same teacher when he was a boy!

Leslie Mitchel, a spokesperson for the National Committee for the Prevention of Child Abuse, explains how such a scenario could develop:

> **Victims may feel "dirty" or blame themselves. Often when children are abused, 90%, 80% of the time it's from people they trust, people they love.[19]**

Kenneth V. Lanning, a supervisory special agent at the FBI Academy in Quantico, Virginia, has written a very helpful behavioral analysis of child molesters. He addresses the problem of denial that we have already alluded to:

> **You'll find that the community does not universally condemn this problem. One of the real issues has to do with a certain societal attitude. In all the many years that I've talked to different groups about this problem, if someone were to say to me, what is the most common response you get from an audience, I would have to say in all honesty the most common response is denial: the refusal to accept it, the refusal to perceive it, the refusal to process it. This is true of police offices; this is true of mental health professionals; this is true of citizens, parent groups, and everybody else. People refuse to accept this.**
>
> **As a result of this denial, two myths continue to be perpetuated. The first myth is that child molesters are dirty, old, evil men, and that only dirty, rotten, evil, vicious, horrible people commit this crime. And because this man who is accused of committing the crime is not old and evil and rotten and mean, he can't possibly have committed the crime. And this is what we hear over and over again: "It can't be true! I know that guy. He's a nice guy."**
>
> **To that I say, "What does that have to do with whether or not he molested the child?" But that is the perception. If he's a nice guy, he didn't molest the child....**
>
> **And the second myth that's equally horrible and equally false is that children want or initiate this sexual activity. This**

myth is much more subtle in nature. You can get very few people who will openly admit that they believe this. But yet, when you see their reaction and their response to this person, you'll have to come to the realization that that's exactly what they believe, that children want and initiate this activity....

A psychopath may be involved in all forms of antisocial behavior, including chid molestation. These people operate under a philosophy I refer to as "If it feels good, do it."[20]

Mr. Lanning's observation reminds me of Aleister Crowley's maxim — "Do whatever thou wilt shall be the whole of the law."

Mr. Lanning concludes with the philosophical statement that governs the lives of many occultists and satanists. It is important for us to understand this and to be aware that Satan has no regard for the age or background of his victims.

I am convinced that the ritualized sexual abuse of children occurs much more frequently than any of us would want to believe. I base my belief on the hundreds of letters we've received, the countless victims I've talked with and the cases I've studied.

Many experts in the field agree with me. Dr. Lawrence Pazder, PhD, has worked with victims who have experienced, "Repeated physical, emotional, mental, and spiritual assaults combined with a systemized use of symbols, ceremonies, and machinations designed and orchestrated to attain malevolent effects."

Ken Wooden has studied this problem and presents seminars of his findings to those who work with children. He describes ritualized sexual abuse as follows: "A bizarre, systematic and continuing mental, physical, and sexual abuse of children for the purpose of implanting evil and giving a form of sacrifice to a force or deity."

Let me share with you one of the letters we received from a mother whose daughter was ritualistically abused in a day-care setting:

This ritualistic abuse of our kids is bigger than even we know. I worry about the other young folks that have been dragged into this stuff, trying to get recognition, be different and have power to fit in with some group.

A friend of mine knows a young guy that got tangled up with satanism. As a part of his initiation, they stuck a live rat in his anus and left it there until it died. That is the kind of stuff....Lots of parents have kids that are being abused and don't know like I did. It is not easy to accept. Then when you do accept it, you suspect everything and everyone. A couple of weeks after we found out for sure that our little girl was not coming back, we found a dead dog in our yard....

Satanists pick what pleases them at the moment. With some, the more sickening the better....

My little girl cried again today about being placed in a ring of candles and being made to sit there all day. She didn't dream that up, nor did she dream up the nude pictures they took of her.

On top of all this, because our abuse case has been reported to the Department of Human Services, as is the law, they are investigating *us* instead of the Day Care Center....Separation is something the satanists threatened her with if she talked....

Other cases have been reported to me of families who have been falsely accused of child abuse themselves after they have reported ritual abuse to authorities. Thankfully, however, this is not usually the case. Upon learning of the abuse of a child, it is of paramount importance to report the situation to the police and the agency that deals with children's services.

It is also a sad note that in some divorce cases accusations of abuse are leveled at one spouse by the other in order to influence the judge's custody decisions. In cases of this nature, it is a form of abuse in itself when one uses children as a means to "get even" with his or her spouse.

Certainly, if such accusations are true, they should be taken very seriously. When they are false accusations, however, the situation always becomes very damaging to the children. It also damages the fabric of justice in our society and further criminal investigations of a serious nature.

Ritual Murder

Dr. Al Carlisle of the Utah State Penal System suggests that as many as 50,000 to 60,000 occult murders occur each year in the United States alone. While this is only an estimate, it does provide a strong basis for believing in the seriousness of the problem. To some satanists, the murder of a human being represents the highest form of sacrifice and service to Satan.

A large number of cases exist in which individuals have been convicted of ritual murder, their only motive being advancement in satanism or the acquisition of supernatural powers.

Not far from my home, in Bardstown, Kentucky, a recent murder was proven to be essentially ritualistic. In this case, a young man named Anthony Gowan was convicted of the murder of Carol Mudd, an employee of The Stone Castle, a novelty and curio shop. His goal in committing the murder was to serve the prince of darkness.

Another letter we received describes a satanic ritual murder that was witnessed by a young woman:

> During the night I was awakened by a noise. I got up and went to the bathroom and while I was on the toilet, the shower curtain was suddenly whipped open, to reveal a big man standing there with a butcher knife. While he raped me, Joe [her former boyfriend who had taken her there] was watching. He shot a drug into my arm. I tried to resist him. It made me feel dizzy, but I was aware of what was going on around me. I was taken to a vacant apartment upstairs. When we walked in they were saying, "We have been waiting for you." Plus a whole lot of raunchy talk. What I saw was awful. Candles burning, people in black robes with hoods on them. There were about a dozen men and women.
>
> They were all praying to Satan. Then they sacrificed a baby boy. They then laid me on a table, naked, and started

putting their hands on me and praying to Satan. This went
on for a while. I remember looking up and seeing Joe drinking
from an ornate cup and red liquid dripping on his beard. I
remember the evil feeling and looking up and seeing a white
glow on the ceiling. Next they made me take a vow with Satan,
while an ornate white knife was held to my throat.

They told me to look on the other side of the room, and
there was a young man hanging there. I know I saw him when
I went in, but I didn't want to deal with it. They spread plastic
on the floor and put him on the plastic and took turns
chopping at his body. Then they tried to hand me his penis,
I wouldn't take it, so they [description of sexual abuse deleted].
I vomited. I was still on the table, then the leader, who had
red around the collar of his robe, came into the room with
a girl. She was crying and screaming, "You have killed my
baby!". . . .

This young woman goes on to describe how she was forced
into lesbian activities with the mother of the sacrificed baby,
directed to kill the woman (which she refused to do), and
witnessed the satanists burning this woman at the stake. She
concluded her letter with these remarks: "I share this with you
because your book helped me and my family. . . . Others may
need help to. I was afraid because Satan said that he would kill
my family if I told anyone. I know the Lord wants me to tell
people about this. . . . Jesus said He would protect me and my
family."

This is just one of many letters of this kind we receive
every month. The nay-sayers would like us to believe it's not
happening — but according to those who are in contact with
us — it is!

In an earlier chapter we alluded to the effects of fantasy-
role playing games, such as Dungeons & Dragons, and how
many who started out with these games have gone on to commit
murder and suicide. Pat Pulling, President of B.A.D.D.
(Bothered About Dungeons and Dragons), has compiled a
booklet that describes some of these cases. One story comes
from *The Tampa Tribune,* dated February 3, 1983:

> Ed Forter knew he'd be on someone's hit list as he began stalking a fellow University of Tampa student one morning last week in a game that challenges student "assassins" to kill before being killed.
>
> Forter, 22, spent that night and the next six in Tampa General Hospital suffering from a lacerated kidney, facial cuts that required six stitches, a black eye, and bruises where he was kicked and beaten by students in a fight that campus police said was "peripherally" related to the assassin game.[21]

Fortunately, this situation was stopped just in the nick of time before someone was killed. The university officials prohibited the "Killing as an Organized Sport" game the day after 140 students armed themselves with toy dart guns.

Similar situations, however, have resulted in death and destruction. Satan is behind each of these tragedies. As a matter of fact, his symbol — the pentagram — is to be utilized in conjunction with the casting of spells and summoning demons outlined in the *Dungeon Master's Guide,* that is used by players of Dungeons and Dragons.

Pat Pulling, President of B.A.D.D., lost a son as a result of his involvement with Dungeons and Dragons. She writes, "The large majority of the information in D&D manuals is violence-oriented. It consists of detailed descriptions of killing, including satanic human sacrifice, assassination, sadism, premeditated murder, and curses of insanity. Much of the material comes from demonology including witchcraft, the occult, and evil monsters. The game details curses of insanity including suicidal and homicidal mania.[22]

Is it any wonder, then, that numerous murders and suicides have resulted among those caught up in the fantasy world created by this role-playing game? The Associated Press reported one of these murders as follows:

> Juan DeCarlos Kimbrough, 14, died January 1, 1985, shot by his 15-year-old brother, Anthony Kimbrough. Oakland police homicide detective Jerry Harris said that the 14-year-old's death was ruled accidental. Detective Harris

stated, "It was really a tragic thing; they were playing a game that deals heavily with fantasy death and used the gun as a kind of prop."

The brothers were playing "Dungeons and Dragons," a fantasy game set in medieval times that involves role-playing and magic. Juan had assumed the role of "dungeonmaster," a powerful individual who directs the play of the game.

Detective Harris said, "I'm told that to die in combat while playing the game is nothing because there are spells which can be cast to bring you back....Unfortunately, that's not the way it works in real life."[23]

To date, most of the convictions for criminal activity in the realm of the occult have been of solitary satanists or satanists working in small groups. Organized satanic groups frequently deny that any sort of criminal activity takes place under their influence. When it does, they endeavor to assure everyone that they are not at fault.

Laurie Cabot, chairperson for the Witches' League for Public Awareness, has often maintained that witches are bound by their principles to refrain from harming any living thing. She claims that anyone who does so is no longer considered to be a witch.

Despite protestations to the contrary from Laurie Cabot, Anton LaVey, Michael Aquino and other occult leaders, there is considerable evidence that links some criminal activities to some satanic organizations.

Maury Terry points out one obvious example in *The Ultimate Evil*. The book uncovers the role of a satanic organization with branches in New York, California, North Dakota and Texas that was apparently responsible for the Son of Sam murders as well as a number of other killings.[24]

Satanic secrecy enshrouds many suspicious murders and cases of ritualistic abuse. It makes it difficult for law-enforcement officials to obtain sufficient evidence to convict the satanic criminal.

The members of our staff and myself have talked to hundreds of police officers around the United States who are concerned about satanic crime. They have seen it. They are aware of its horrifying reality. Many are currently investigating cases of ritual criminal activity. The problem all too frequently is the lack of evidence because of satanic secrecy.

Many indictments of ritual crime have been made in recent years, however, and as our knowledge of this field continues to expand, it will become increasingly difficult for satanists and others to maintain the aura of secrecy that hides them from the rest of society.

Suicide

In the *TSR Dungeon Master's Guide* (used in conjunction with the playing of Dungeons and Dragons) one finds this description of "Suicidal Mania":

> **This form of insanity causes the afflicted character to have overwhelming urges to destroy himself or herself whenever means are presented; a perilous situation, a weapon, or anything else. The more dangerous the situation or item, the more likely the individual is to react self-destructively.[25]**

Satan has seduced thousands of young people to commit suicide through several schemes, including Dungeons and Dragons. Note the following newspaper reports:

> **Straight-A student Irving Lee Pulling II put a loaded gun to his heart and pulled the trigger — because he'd been cursed by a wizard in the eerie game of Dungeons and Dragons.[26]**

> **Steven Loyacano, 16, October 14, 1982, Castle Rock, CO. Suicide by carbon monoxide in an automobile. Police reported satanic writing and a suicide note link the death to D&D.[27]**

> **Jeffrey Jacklovich, 14, died, 2/8/85, self-inflicted gun shot wound. He left behind a box containing a note and 3 dice from the game, Dungeons and Dragons.[28]**

> **Timothy Grice, 21, died January 17, 1983, Lafayette, Colorado. Suicide by shotgun. A detective report noted,**

> "D&D became a reality....He thought he was not constrained to this life, but could leave and return because of the game."[29]

These obituaries form a roll call that represents only a few of the victims of Satan's schemes. These boys died as a direct result of Satan's seductive lures. They are the casualties of the satanic revolution, victims of the spiritual warfare in which we are engaged.

As many as fifteen young people and children kill themselves every day! While 5,000 teen-agers succeed in committing suicide each year, another 500,000 are unsuccessful in their attempt to do so.

As in most societal problems, there is a multiple causation at work behind the scenes that leads a young person to take his or her life. Whatever the specific reason, however, it is important to realize that it is Satan who plants the seeds of self-destruction in multitudinous ways.

One well-known psychiatrist, Dr. Mary Griffin, has made the following observation regarding teen-agers who kill themselves. She states that they are, "...killing the hopelessness. They really don't mean to be killing themselves. The act of suicide says, 'The only way I can see to be helped is to kill myself. Please find another answer for me.' "[30]

A teen-ager who became involved with satanism, Tommy Sullivan, made this pact with Satan prior to killing his mother and himself:

> To the greatest of demons. I would like to make a solemn exchange with you. If you will give me the most extreme of all magical powers, I will kill many Christian followers. Exactly twenty years from this day, I will promise to commit suicide. I will tempt teenagers on earth to have sex, have incest, do drugs, and worship you. I believe that evil will once again rise and conquer the love of God.[31]

Tommy was only fourteen years old when he sold his soul to Satan. The king of evil accepted his offer, and two lives were destroyed.

Clues to Occult-Related Deaths

Police investigators look for several clues to help them determine if a homicide or suicide has occult-ritual connections. Some of those clues include the following:

1. Location of the Body. Most cult rituals take place in deserted areas — woods, deserts, cemeteries, abandoned buildings, churches, etc.

2. Position of the Body. The direction of the body and the way it is laid out may provide important information. If it has been positioned in the shape of a circle or a cross, if it has been nailed to a cross, or if the body hangs from a tree (by its feet, hands or neck), there is a likely possibility that ritual abuse was involved.

3. Missing Body Parts and Organs. In occultic blood rituals (such as the one that took place in Matamoras, Mexico), parts of the human body may be removed. Sometimes they are eaten (cannibalism) or simply kept on hand for use in some other way. The body parts that are most often used in these ways are the head, heart, hands, genitalia, eyes, ears, nose, tongue and lips.

4. Clothing an/or Nudity. Since many occult rituals are performed "skyclad" (in the nude), a nude body may be a clue to ritual abuse. Likewise, if the body was dressed in some sort of ritual garb, such as a ceremonial robe or mask, it is likely that the victim was subjected to ritual abuse.

5. Stab Wounds or Cuts. The location, number and pattern of all contusions on the body may provide a clue for investigators. Certain patterns and symbols of stab wounds may reveal that the blood was drained for ritualistic purposes. numbered patterns of cuts and bruises (i.e., threes, sixes, sevens or thirteens) may be significant as well. Incisions on the sex organs and/or teeth marks on he body also suggest ritual abuse.

6. Ink Marks or Tattoos. Sometimes ink marks (symbols) and tattoos show ownership or membership with regard to a particular occult group. These may be in the form of patterns, symbols, or a message written in an unknown alphabet or code.

7. The Use of Paint or Special Colors on the Body. If the body has been painted entirely in one color or several colors, occult activity was probably involved. Another clue may be found when the body is smeared with a particular substance.

8. *The Use of a Branding Iron or Burns.* Sometimes a branding iron is used as a form of sadistic torture. Any unusual burns on the body may be a clue of occult involvement.

9. *Jewelry on or Near the Cadaver.* The use of special occult-related rings, charms, amulets, stones, talismans, etc. may provide the investigator with important clues.

10. *Jewelry That Is Missing.* When it is suspected that jewelry has been removed from the body, the investigator looks for cuts, scratches and abrasions that may indicate that the jewelry was forcefully removed.

11. *Colored Ropes on or Near the Body.* These items are probably instruments of bondage, a particular aspect of some satanic rituals. The different colors of the ropes represent various magical powers.

12. *Ritual Items Near the Body.* These may include any of the items we have already discussed in association with occult rituals: candles (note colors); cords or ropes; containers of salts and herbs; an altar or central object with occult symbols carved in it; an Athamé; a circle or triangle drawn nearby (possibly on the ground); a chalice; the four elements (earth, water, air and fire); animal parts and organs; a book of shadows (book of spells or grimoire); a censer; a sword (or ritual knives); parchments; a cauldron (usually an iron pot); coins; statues; stones; jewels; and effigies or voodoo dolls.

13. *Oils or Incense on the Body.*

14. *Wax From Candles on or About the Body.*

15. *Human or Animal Feces on the Body or Consumed by the Victim.* Many satanists use human or animal excrement in their rituals.

16. *Rope Burns, Other Signs That Victims Hands or Feet May Have Been Tied.* One occult group, for example, was known to have used a strong, thin piano-type wire that was tied and pulled tight to the altar, then attached to the victim's toes, fingers and genitalia. Through other forms of torture, they made the victim move and shift positions, causing the parts of the body that were tied to be severed from him.

17. *Stomach Contents of Urine, Feces, Semen, Blood, Drugs, Wine or Potions.*

18. *Lungs With Ingested Matter.* Some cults will use fire as one of their elements (sometimes known as "balefire") while conducting their rituals. They may burn herbs, incense, or belladonna in the process. If the victim was forcefully required to drink blood or some other liquid, some may have collected in his or her lungs, and the breathing of smoke filled with other substances would cause certain particles to remain in the lungs as well.

19. *The Absence of Blood in the Cadaver or on the Ground (or Floor).* Blood is extremely important (even precious) to many occult groups because they believe that the life force is found in the blood. The lack of blood in a body, therefore, is very important in determining if occult involvement was present because many cultists will drain the blood from the body in order to drink it or bathe in it. They try to avoid wasting any of it.

20. *Semen on, Near or Inside the Cadaver.* Acts of perverted sexual abuse are also common among various occult groups. Sex with a dead body (necrophilia) is sometimes an initiation rite for new members of certain groups.

21. *Occult Ritual Paraphernalia and/or Christian Artifacts.* Another indicator of occult involvement is found in desecrated religious items, such as symbols and utensils used by Christians and Jews. The use of occult symbols is significant as well.

22. *Biblical Verses and Graffiti Written in Blood.*

23. *Unusual Alphabets or Cabalistic Writing.* These may be in the form of Runic, Witchcraft or Theban alphabets or they may be Hebrew and Greek. Secret codes may be employed as well.

24. *Animal Body Parts.*

25. *Drawings or Photographs of Victims.*

26. *Dates of Rituals, Calendars, Etc.*

27. *Computer Ties in the Home.* If you suspect occult involvement, and the victim utilized a computer in his home, it is advisable to check the data stored in the computer. Many cults and groups are highly organized and they use computers to store information and send messages.

28. *Photography of Mock Weddings, Child Pornography or Sexual Activities (Especially Involving Anal Practices).*

29. *The Mark of the Beast.* The number of the Anti-Christ (666), and other symbols that show allegiance to Satan.

NOTE: Some of the above clues, when looked at singly, are not clear indicators of occult involvement (i.e., location of the body). Others are. When several of these clues are observed together, however, ritual abuse is unmistakable.

To attribute such activities to "nut cases" is wrong. These people are serious, and they know what they are doing.

The Shroud of Darkness

How I wish this chapter — indeed, this entire book — were not necessary, but we must not, we cannot ignore what is taking place in our society today.

When Hitler's S.S. was committing its hideous crimes against humanity, few people took a stand against the evil that was deliberately being perpetrated against innocent victims. Those who did so were silenced. Many who heard the alarm they sounded tried to ignore it. It would appear that they did not want to believe that such things could happen. The result? More than six million innocent victims were killed!

The same was true just a few years back when some people took a stand against the secretive activities of the People's Temple. Those who were not directly involved with the cult did not want to hear about its enslavement of people and its leader's paranoia. Many simply chose to ignore the alarm that was sounded by some. As a result, nearly 1,000 people lost their lives through murder and suicide under the misguided leadership of Jim Jones.

In Matamoras, Mexico, many people lost their lives as a result of the deranged beliefs of individuals involved in a nightmarish drug cult inspired by Satan. And in many places around the world, the victims of satanic crime are being found almost daily — their bodies mutilated beyond recognition or their souls forever scarred by Satan's schemes.

In this chapter I have tried to portray the harsh reality of satanic crime in an effort to help all understand that it *is* taking place. The shroud of secrecy prevents us from knowing all that goes on behind the scenes. It is my hope that this book will help to lift the shroud, to let in the light, to expose the works of darkness.

The Bible says:

> For you were once darkness, but now you are light in the Lord. Live as children of light (for the fruit of the light consists in all goodness, righteousness and truth). Have nothing to do with the fruitless deeds of darkness, but rather expose them. For it is shameful even in mention what the disobedient do in secret. But everything exposed by the light becomes visible, for it is light that makes everything visible. This is why it is said:
> "Wake up, O sleeper,
> rise from the dead,
> and Christ will shine on you."
>
> Be very careful then, how you live — not as unwise but as wise, making the most of ever opportunity, because the days are evil....
>
> **(Eph. 5:8-16 NIV)**

I once lived in the darkness of satanism, but now I am light in the Lord. God has called me to expose the works of darkness through the light of His love and His will. It is time for us to wake up, to let our light shine in the darkness, because the days are evil.

10

On Stage With Satan

A rock concert is really nothing else but a ritual....At a Led Zeppelin concert the aim is to release energy for the performers and the audience. To achieve this you have to tap the sources of magical power, however dangerous that may be.[1]

(Jimmy Page, lead guitarist for
Led Zeppelin, now disbanded)

Marketing Gimmick, Satanic Scheme or Both?

Actually, the connection between rock music and occultism is both a marketing gimmick and a satanic scheme. As we have already pointed out, Satan can use anything for his glory, and it is abundantly clear that he sometimes uses rock music and other entertainment to fulfill this purpose.

On the other hand, it is important for us to maintain a realistic, well-balanced appraisal of Satan's influences in the entertainment field, especially when we consider rock music. Too many have become "knee-jerk reactionaries" when it comes to rock music. The issue is often clouded by misinformation, misunderstandings and half-truths.

It is my earnest desire to be fair, and as objective as possible, in my treatment of all the sensitive issues discussed in this book. I avoid making any generalizations because I know that each occultist is an individual who utilizes his or her free will in every given situation. Similarly, it would be wrong to make sweeping generalizations concerning Christians because each individual approaches his or her faith in a unique way.

219

Almost any presentation of satanism as a social issue in the past decade has included a discussion of the alleged connection between rock music and the occult. Media accounts of teen-age occultism, for example, portray the music of groups and artists such as Black Sabbath, Motley Crue, Ozzy Osborne and others as tools of recruitment used by satanists. many conservative Christians hold to this view even though there is very little evidence to suggest that it is true, at least on a general scale.

It is important for us to realize that the case against most rock and heavy-metal artists is often overstated. Even among groups that actively employ occult and satanic imagery, very few members are actually satanists. One notable exception to this, however, is King Diamond, who is a member of Anton LaVey's Church of Satan.[2]

For the most part, the satanic symbolism and extremist behaviors (such as biting the head off a bat), are marketing gimmicks that increase sales of recordings and concert tickets. This is not to say, however, that Satan cannot use these "gimmicks" to his advantage in the lives of rock musicians and fans.

Backward Masking

This subject has been the focus of many diatribes against rock music in recent years. Much that has been reported about alleged backward masking is questionable and difficult to prove.

By backward masking we refer to the placement of reversed words or messages into audio recordings. There are two types of these backward messages — those that are consciously perceived by the listener and "subliminal messages" of which the listener is not aware. In both cases, it is necessary to ask two questions:

    1. What is the intent of the message?
    2. What effect, if any, does the backward message have on the listener?

Sometimes it is difficult to find the answers to these questions, especially regarding the presumed effects such messages may have on listeners. Many have tried to prove a connection between subliminal messages in rock music to the rising tide of teen-age suicide in America. Thus far, the proof of this supposed cause-and-effect relationship has not been so firmly established that courts have been able to concur with its allegation.

The use of consciously perceivable reverse recording is relatively common in the music field. It is, in fact, a simple procedure that enables one to create a backward message in a standard music studio. In multi-track recording, simply turning the tape over on the machine causes any tracks that have already been recorded to be played in reverse. Any instrumental or vocal tracks recorded with the tape turned over, therefore, will sound reversed when the tape is played in the usual manner.

The use of this technique was introduced into the field of popular music by groups like the Beatles who did use backward masking in a number of their album projects. Many artists (including Christian artists like Paul Clark and Petra) have since utilized this technique. In most cases, the effect is used purely for aesthetic purposes; instrumental sounds or meaningless words or phrases are recorded backward in order to achieve a particular artistic effect. Very few people object to this. Controversy surrounding backward masking usually centers on the use of meaningful words or phrases that may or may not be intended to send a persuasive message to the listener.

It has been reported that a wide range of blasphemous statements have been backward masked on rock recordings. Some of these accusations include the following:

> "Turn me on, dead man" — the Beatles.
> "Evil, the master of God, rules over you" — Alphaville.
> "Heaven is hell!" — Motley Crue.
> "To hell with the Bible. All I want is magic." — Queen.
> "Satan, Satan, Satan. He is god. He is god." — Black Oak Arkansas.

"The devil himself is your god." — K.I.S.S.[3]

It is not possible to prove that these statements were intentionally recorded in backward form by the artists involved. Some backward messages of even more blasphemous and profane content have been alleged to have been recorded by other groups as well.

Psychological Research

In a book entitled *Satanism,* Ted Schwartz and Duane Empey recount the views of John Kappas, PhD. According to Dr. Kappas's research, the use of both types of backward masking has been widespread in the music industry, but the ability to influence behavior in this way is very questionable.[4] Kappas conducted studies in which subjects listened to backward phrases containing both positive and negative messages. The subjects responded similarly in both situations; although they became irritated or depressed because of the discordant sounds, their reaction was the same regardless of the content of the messages.[5]

There is little doubt that consciously perceivable backward masking has been successful for most of the artists who have used it. However, the success is in the form of album sales, not in the gaining of "converts" to satanism and occultism. Backward passages on albums resulted in widespread speculation about the intent of performers by both fans and critics, and this increased the publicity and visibility of the artists. No evidence exists, however, to suggest that the messages themselves covertly influence behavior.

In saying this, however, it is important for us to remember that certain impressionable people can be influenced to engage in all sorts of behaviors as a result of what they see, hear and read. In most of these cases, however, the stimulus that leads one into questionable behaviors is usually overt and obvious as opposed to being hidden and covert.

The other type of backward masking, the kind in which the listener is not aware of the message, is somewhat more problematic, however. The influence of subliminal messages recorded in the normal way (consciously perceivable) is well-documented. However, as Dr. Kappas's studies suggest, the assertion that the mind is capable of understanding a backward message, either consciously or subconsciously, is highly questionable.[6]

Critics of rock music who discuss backward masking will occasionally claim that studies have demonstrated that the ability to influence behavior through backward masking of subliminal messages is real. They are never able to produce empirical data to confirm these claims, however.

Additional research on the role of suggestion in backward masking was undertaken by two psychologists, Stephen Thorne and Philip Himelsten. In their study, three different groups listened to portions of songs often associated with backward masking:

1. **"Revolution No. 1" by the Beatles.**
2. **"Stairway to Heaven" by Led Zeppelin.**
3. **"Black Sabbath" by Black Sabbath.**

The control group was told to listen to the tape and keep track of its members' reactions. The second group was requested to record any words or phrases they heard, and the third group was told that satanic messages had been recorded on he tapes, and they were to find them.

According to this research, only one member of the control group claimed to be able to find words, phrases or satanic messages, and this person was familiar with popular opinion about backward masking. In the second group, 95% of the subjects found the words or phrases, but only 18% found satanic messages. In the third group, 59% found words or phrases not related to satanism, while 41% found satanic messages.

Clearly, the subjects who expected to find words or messages were likely to find them, and those who weren't specifically listening for them did not. Interestingly, I have witnessed an informal demonstration of a similar nature. A passage from "Stairway to Heaven" was played for the audience in reverse. The listeners were asked what they heard. Then the audience was told to listen for the phrase "my sweet Satan," and the passage was played again. Most people hear this backward message only after they have been told about it. This indicates that most people do not even detect the "backward message" when it is reversed for them, let alone when it is played in its normal context!

Rock Musicians and the Devil

The life styles of certain rock musicians who have become role models for many young people do influence the behavior of others. This is an area of important concern because people often try to become like their heroes.

It disturbs me when I hear someone like Mick Jagger, a well-known rock star with the Rolling Stones, make this statement: "I am deliberately presenting myself as a personification of the devil."[7] At concerts, while singing "Sympathy for the Devil," Jagger sometimes rips off his shirt to display a tattoo of the devil on his chest.[8]

Although this may simply be a marketing device he uses to impress impressionable fans, the issue it presents can be easily misunderstood by young people. It is the matter of perception that is of paramount importance as we look at the satanic connection to rock music.

Themes of sexual suggestiveness and satanic seduction are woven into the styles and lyrics of some rock musicians. Alice Cooper, for example, has stated, "My audience wants me to treat them like a sex maniac taking his victim....The relationship between me and my listeners is extremely sexual. To dominate an audience in this way is a tremendous and satisfying experience."[9]

The manager of the Rolling Stones stated, "Rock music is sex and you have to hit teenagers in the face with it."[10]

The lead singer with the group called Queen made the comment: "On stage I'm a devil," and the lyrics sung by Queen deal with sexual assaults, blasphemy and homosexuality.[11]

The ambiance created by rock musicians at concerts is oftentimes filled with satanic images. Black Sabbath, for example, has been known to present black masses and invocations to the devil. Some groups have attempted to glorify suicide and cannibalism. King Diamond, who is a member of the Church of Satan, has expressed surprise over society's inability to understand why babies are sacrificed.[12] Many times it seems that audiences attending rock concerts are fueled with a demonic frenzy. Sometimes this violence results in physical harm and death.

The Drug Connection

The widespread use of illicit drugs by both rock musicians and their fans is well-known and documented. The smell of marijuana smoke is a familiar part of the ambiance at many rock concerts.

Satan uses drugs to devour the lives of young people and adults. Drug abuse is a self-defeating, self-destructive activity, and as Derek Prince has pointed out, "If there is self-destructive activity going on in an individual's life, you can be sure the devil is behind it."

Many rock musicians have succumbed to self-annihilation through alcohol and drug abuse. The roll of Satan's victims in this field is long and depressing. Jimi Hendrix, John Bonham (of Led Zeppelin) and Bon Scott (of AC/DC) all choked to death on their own vomit as a result of alcohol and/or drug abuse. Overdoses of heroin claimed the lives of Janis Joplin (once known as the "queen of rock"), Sid Vicious of the Sex Pistols (who overdosed on heroin after stabbing his girl friend to death),

Pete Farndon of the Pretenders, and possibly Brian Jones of the Rolling Stones. Alcoholism conquered Ron McKernan of the Grateful Dead, and Roy Buchanan who hanged himself in a jail cell while sobering up.[13]

At least twenty additional rock stars have died from drug abuse. Still others have committed suicide or died in mysterious ways. Marc Bolan, for example, who was lead guitarist for T-Rex, died in a mysterious car accident. (He had attributed his success in the field of music to black magic.)[14]

Entertainers and the Church of Satan

Critics of rock music, particularly those who speak to conservative Christian audiences, occasionally associate rock music with Anton LaVey's Church of Satan. Sometimes they go so far as to state that the Church of Satan is responsible for the use of satanic imagery in rock music, or that the organization uses rock music as a tool for recruiting young people.

Rock music is not necessarily a feature of rituals in the Church of Satan, but Anton LaVey does take credit for inspiring the growth of satanic themes in music as well as the movies. Nikolas Shreck, leader of the Werewolf Order of Satanism, has created an album of satanic music that is more akin to classical styles than rock.[15]

Quite often, rock music is the only musical style mentioned with regard to occult themes. Such themes appear in other types of music as well. For example, in the classical music of Wagner one finds occult imagery, and Berlioz's "Symphonie Fantastique" makes reference to a black mass.

In a recent interview, Bob Larson spoke with Zeena LaVey (the daughter of Anton LaVey) and Nikolas Shreck (leader of the Werewolf Order of Satanism). They reported that several well-known entertainers are affiliated with the Church of Satan, but refused to disclose their names.[16]

Zeena stated that her father had once had an affair with Marilyn Monroe, and that Jane Mansfield was a member of the Church of Satan at the time of her death.[17] According to Zeena LaVey, Jane Mansfield died as the result of a curse that had been placed on her boy friend by Anton LaVey. LaVey reportedly had warned Ms. Mansfield to stay away from the man he had cursed. While driving with her boy friend, Ms. Mansfield and the gentleman were killed in a mysterious auto accident. Ms. LaVey states that the wreck was a result of the curse that was placed on the man by her father. If Jane Mansfield had heeded his warning, LaVey believes that she would have remained alive.[18]

Zeena LaVey also stated that Sammy Davis, Jr. was at one time involved with the Church of Satan.[19]

Both LaVey and Shreck are prophesying the emergence of a satanically ruled society. They believe that many well-known individuals who are "closet satanists" will be emerging from their "closets" in the nineties to take part in what they believe will be the final victories of the satanic revolution. It is their belief that the Church of Jesus Christ is experiencing its dying throes at the present time.[20]

Is the Music Evil?

Critics of rock and heavy metal music often make claims concerning the alleged harmful or evil nature of certain types of music. According to one story (attributed to an anonymous missionary) a tribesman who had recently been delivered from demonic influences claimed to be able to see demons rising out of a tape recorder that played contemporary Christian music. Such stories are often used to suggest a similarity between certain ethnic or tribal rhythms and occultic religious rituals and rock music. However, as one leading music researcher has observed, no one to date has been able to document this allegation, nor has anyone been able to find the missionary who first shared this tale!

To ask a teen-ager not to listen to rock music is very much the same as asking him or her not to listen to music at all. The rock music idiom is part and parcel of the teen-age sub-culture. In this understanding we see how attitudes toward musical styles are formed. They are culturally induced.

There is nothing inherently evil about rock music any more than there is something inherently good in all four-part male harmony. It is not the rhythm, the beat or the style of music that counts; it is how that music is used.

God is the author of music. In light of this fact, Martin Luther was able to use a popular bar-room ditty to form the score for the triumphant hymn, "A Mighty Fortress Is Our God." He was criticized for doing so in the sixteenth century just as Christian rock artists are criticized today. And yet, I've been present at several concerts where Christian rock groups led scores of young people to the Lord Jesus Christ. I am convinced that many of those kids would not have found Jesus in the traditional way, so God used Christian rock music to reach them.

Sometimes we get very parochial in our approach to ideas and styles that differ from our own. The old adage, "Beauty is in the eye of the beholder" may be rewritten with regard to music as follows, "Beauty is in the ear of the listener." It is the individual's perception of a musical style or beat that is a paramount importance.

Again, it is more important to be aware of how a certain style of music is used rather than to react to the style itself. What do the lyrics have to say? What is the life style of the musician(s)? How has the music affected others?

In dealing with our young people, it is important to help them find the answers to these questions instead of issuing a blanket prohibition of a given style of music.

I've found that this approach to my own children has worked best of all. In the process, I've learned a lot about them, myself and other people. No form of music in inherently evil, but many forms of music can be used for evil purposes.

The Occult Connection

During presentations to junior high and high school students I am frequently asked, "How does listening to rock music make a person become a satanist?" (Presumably, the teen-agers have been told that this happens.)

I always answer, "Listening to rock music does not *make* anyone do or become anything at all. However, music can exert a strong influence in a number of areas as can the media, other forms of art and peer pressure."

For example, rock music does not *make* someone commit suicide. In fact, one cannot even blame the devil by saying that he *made* me do wrong. Flip Wilson was fond of that excuse, "The devil made me do it!" No one, and certainly no form of music, can make a person do anything. James wrote, "When tempted, no one should say, 'God is tempting me.' For God cannot be tempted by evil, nor does he tempt anyone; *but each one is tempted when, by his own evil desire, he is dragged away and enticed.* Then, after desire has conceived, it gives birth to sin; and sin, when it is full-grown, gives birth to death." (James 1:13-15, NIV, italics mine).

The theme of personal responsibility for one's own actions is too often downplayed. When one voluntarily chooses to respond to the temptation to do wrong, sin always follows and the end result is death, as Paul indicated in the book of Romans:

> **For the wages of sin is death, but the gift of God is eternal life in Christ Jesus our Lord.**
>
> **(Rom. 6:23 NIV)**

In stressing the importance of personal responsibility and individual accountability, I do not want to minimize the reality that listening to rock music (and other styles of music) can exert a strong influence in a number of areas. The same is true of any art form, the media and peer-group pressure.

The fact that celebrities in the music field (such as Michael Jackson, Madonna, Phil Collins and Ray Charles) are paid enormous sums of money to endorse products suggests that advertising agencies believe strongly in their ability to influence people. Anyone who has attended a concert of a major musical celebrity can attest to the manner in which an artist's dress, speech, mannerisms and life style are imitated by the fans. Certainly the biggest stars in the music industry have been the cultural heroes of the latter part of the twentieth century.

As we have already pointed out, most of the groups and artists who employ occult or satanic imagery in their song lyrics and/or in their cover art, do so mainly to sell albums. However, some of their fans may take this symbology quite seriously. When a group such as Motley Crue is idolized by its fans, the use of occult symbolism may be taken at face value by certain admirers. Regardless of the performers' intent, therefore, some fans' initial exposure to occult/satanic themes often does come from rock groups.

At the same time, it is possible to point out specific groups and artists who are either practicing occultists or who have an interest in the area of occultism. One well-known example is Jimmy Page of Led Zeppelin who became so fascinated with occultist Aleister Crowley that he purchased Crowley's castle in England.

The lyrics of much rock music often advocate a life style that is based upon self-indulgence (one of the satanic statements), sexual promiscuity, rebellion against authority, and substance abuse. (It is important to remember that rock and heavy metal are not the only forms of music that advocate these activities, however.) Nonetheless, the anti-establishment message of much of today's rock music is very much consistent with the satanic ideals of self-interest and self-indulgence.

It is also true that the music of some rock and heavy metal artists has been incorporated into satanic rituals, particularly by self-styled satanists and satanists who were already a part of the drug sub-culture prior to becoming satanists.

Professor Carl Raschke of the University of Denver notes the connection between cult recruiting and drug use.[21] Other studies substantiate the evidence that those who use drugs prior to interest in the occult or satanism usually incorporate drug use into their religion.

My personal experience and numerous counseling situations indicate that the same is true for both rock music and the life style associated with it. In many cases, criminal or drug-oriented gangs may become exposed to satanism via their interest in rock or heavy-metal music and begin to incorporate a superficial form of satanism into their activities. Although the commitment of some remains superficial, others go beyond the beginning stages to a more serious level of involvement.

In concluding this chapter, I would encourage each one of us to take a serious look at what the tolerance given to the anti-establishment message of the rock sub-culture says about our society. By making this observation, I do not mean to imply that our wonderful freedom of speech should be curtailed, however, our ability to tolerate such strong messages that promote immorality, satanism, evil, drug abuse and other anti-establishment values tells us a great deal about the present state of our society.

The Coming of the Lawless One

The condition of our society in the present day should be a matter of grave concern to every citizen. The Apostle Paul referred to the age in which we live in his second letter to the Thessalonians:

> Don't let anyone deceive you in any way, for that day will not come until the rebellion occurs and the man of lawlessness is revealed, the man doomed to destruction. He opposes and exalts himself over everything that is called God or is worshiped, and even sets himself up in God's temple,

proclaiming himself to be God....For the secret power of lawlessness is already at work; but the one who now holds it back will continue to do so till he is taken out of the way....The coming of the lawless one will be in accordance with the work of Satan displayed in all kinds of counterfeit miracles, signs and wonders, and in every sort of evil that deceives those who are perishing. They perish because they refused to love the truth and so be saved.

(2 Thess. 2:3,7,9-11 NIV).

The secret power of lawlessness is already at work. The work of Satan is being displayed in all kinds of counterfeit miracles, signs and wonders, and in every sort of evil.

It is time for us to expose lawlessness for what it really is: rebellion against God, our Creator. In the forthcoming chapters we will endeavor to show how we can help to rescue those who are perishing by leading them to truth instead of deception. The god of this evil age (Satan) has blinded the hearts of many — it is our responsibility to show them the truth.

I like the approach taken by John Newton, the writer of "Amazing Grace":

Many have puzzled themselves about the origin of evil. I am content to observe that there is evil, and that there is a way to escape from it, and with this I begin and end.

11

Dispelling the Darkness

There are two equal and opposite errors into which our race can fall about the devils. One is to disbelieve in their existence. The other is to believe, and to feel an excessive and unhealthy interest in them. They themselves are equally pleased by both errors, and hail a materialist or a magician with the same delight.... [but] God turns servants into sons, so that they may be at last reunited to Him in the perfect freedom of a love offered....[1]

(From *The Screwtape Letters*
by C.S. Lewis)

Freedom From Fear

Most people I meet are very fearful about satanism and occultism. This is understandable in light of the hyped-up and sensationalistic media coverage recently given to this topic. This fear of the unknown causes some to engage in denial, leading them to disbelieve in the existence of the devil and his minions. This reaction is a defense mechanism that stems from the realization that whatever one accepts, one becomes responsible for.

On the other hand, there are those who become driven by fear into an almost-obsessional preoccupation with the devil and his minions. I've encountered some folks who seem to feel that every problem in life is somehow related to demon possession. For them, the resolution of many of life's problems, therefore, can be found in the "quick fix" of exorcism.

A very distraught couple — middle-aged parents of a teen-aged boy — came up to me after a concert one evening.

"Mike, can you help us with our son?" the father asked, with tears welling in his eyes. "He is demon possessed. The psychiatrist says he has multiple-personality disorder."

I listened carefully as the boy's frantic mother interjected, "He calls himself a skin head and his life is totally out of control. He's so violent and very hateful to his father and me. We don't know what to do. Satan has him under his direct control."

Realizing I had to be in a city 500 miles away the next morning, I told these caring, fearful parents that I would not be able to work with their son directly, but I would refer their situation to a clergyman in their community who is highly respected in the field of counseling. Then I prayed with the couple specifically asking God to give them wisdom in dealing with their son.

Two months later I heard from the pastor who agreed to help this boy. This is what he reported to me, "Mike, I began to work with the family. The parents were so convinced that their son was demon-possessed, but I felt all along that he had a different problem."

"We're so attuned to an instant-answer approach to our problems, aren't we, Jim? In my experience, very few problems are actual demon possession. Most problems have several influences behind them," I observed.

"Yes, and in Billy's case I learned that his biggest problem was not spiritual at all. It wasn't even primarily a mental problem."

"What did you find out, then?" I asked.

"Well, one night while I was counseling with Billy at the kitchen table, I noticed a peculiar behavior. Every few minutes he would take a teaspoon, dig it into the sugar bowl and eat raw sugar! Spoonful after spoonful!

I interjected, "Then the kid was wired! His problem was sugar, not Satan!"

"That's right, and I asked his parents how long he had been consuming sugar like this, and they said matter-of-factly, 'Oh, since he was about ten years old.' For six years Billy has been eating raw sugar by the bowlful every day! It's no wonder he behaves the way he does; I would too!"

"Did the doctor concur with your findings, Jim?"

"Yes, he sure did. He feels that a change in Billy's nutrition, along with intense personal counseling will enable him to overcome his problems."

"That's great, Jim. Thanks for your help in this. I know Billy's parents must be very pleased. Satan may have been behind Billy's poor choices, but the boy certainly wasn't demon-possessed."

That kind of story has been repeated countless times in our work with young people. The fear that Billy's parents experienced caused them to react to his problems in an unreasonable, confusing way. Satan had blinded them through fear.

God does not want us to be fearful. As C.S. Lewis pointed out, there is an antidote for fear: "the perfect freedom of a love offered." That love is a free gift of God. He sent His only begotten Son to be a sacrifice for our sins:

> **For God so loved the world that he gave his one and only Son, that whoever believes in him shall not perish but have eternal life.**
>
> **(John 3:16 NIV)**

It is in the certainty of God's love for us that we are able to find freedom from fear. The phrase "Fear not . . ." appears 450 times in the Bible. One of my favorite passages concerning God's power over fear appears in the book of First John:

> **God is love. Whoever lives in love lives in God, and God in him. . . . There is no fear in love. But perfect love drives out fear, because fear has to do with punishment. The man who fears is not made perfect in love.**
>
> **(1 John 4:16b-18 NIV)**

There is no reason for a Christian to be fearful when dealing with someone who is involved in satanism or occultism. We should always be wise and careful, but there is never a need for fear.

Once when I was ministering at a large midwestern church, a group of fourteen young satanists decided to attend the concert. The church was almost packed full when these young people who were dressed in hooded black robes appeared at the entrance.

The ushers were somewhat taken aback by these unusual visitors. The men began to fear what might happen if they were to allow the occultists to come in. I was praying in the pastor's study when someone knocked on the door to apprise me of what was taking place. I asked to see the head usher.

When the usher came into the office, I could see fear written on his face. "I won't let them come in," he explained.

"Look, I can understand your concern, but if you don't let the satanists in, I won't do the concert. Those kids need to hear about the love of Jesus too."

"But they're wearing black hoods and everything!" he interjected with a sense of panic.

"One of our staff members will talk to them," I directed.

My assistant went out a side door, walked around the large church and went up to the group of satanists who were huddled on the front steps. Their leader emerged from the circle and confronted him, "Why won't they let us in? Isn't your concert open to the public?"

The leader of the coven was a priestess who appeared to be about nineteen years old. She seemed to be very much into herself and her attitude was as belligerent as a scalded cat's. "Why won't you let us in?" she screamed. "You have to let us attend!"

It was clear that she was a dominant leader who controlled her group through power forms that probably included sexual power over the guys.

"I came out here to invite you to the meeting," my staff member explained. "We welcome you."

One of the young men who accompanied her spoke up, "We've heard of Mike Warnke, and we've come to find out if he's for real."

"It's Mike's personal pleasure to have you here," my helper assured them. "But I do have one favor to ask of you."

"What's that?" the priestess shot back, almost defiantly.

"Would you mind taking off your robes? I think your apparel would upset others and that could have a negative effect on the concert. I would really appreciate it if you would comply with my request."

She agreed to do so somewhat reluctantly, and the ushers escorted her and her entourage to seats right in the front of the auditorium. I paid close attention to them throughout the concert, and I noticed how attentive they were. They seemed to soak in every word.

I was especially impressed with the way the priestess's facial expressions changed as she listened to the gospel. Her harsh demeanor had been replaced with a look of peace and her eyes sparkled with interest.

None of the fourteen responded to the altar call, but I heard from the church's pastor two weeks later. "Mike," he reported, "eight of the satanists who came to your concert have received Jesus as their Savior and five of them have started to prepare for church membership! They asked me to thank you, and one of the five wanted me to let you know that he was glad to discover that you are real and so is Jesus!"

It thrilled me to hear this pastor's report, especially the part about being real. To me, this is the greatest compliment of all because I know that spiritual reality is what each person seeks. Occultists have experienced some spiritual realities through their rituals and studies. This shows that many of them are looking for truth. It is our privilege to be able to show them the greatest reality of all — the love of Jesus Christ. When this becomes our focus, we will not be afraid of them. Our fear will be replaced with the love of God.

"If You're Not Radical, You're Not Spit!"

We have a responsibility to those who live in darkness. Essentially, there are two kingdoms: the kingdom of light and the kingdom of darkness. I've lived in both. The kingdom of darkness is governed by Satan; the kingdom of light is ruled by Jesus Christ.

The light of Jesus shines in the darkness, but many people fail to perceive it. People today are like those of New Testament times who were described by John:

> **In the beginning was the Word, and the Word was with God, and the Word was God. He was with God. He was with God in the beginning. Through him all things were made; without him nothing was made that has been made. In him was life, and that life was the light of men. The light shines in the darkness, but the darkness has not understood it"**
>
> **(John 1:1-5 NIV).**

Those who live in darkness still do not comprehend the light. In most cases that divine light is revealed to people by individuals who know Jesus, people who are "the children of light."

Jesus said, "You are the light of the world. A city on a hill cannot be hidden. Neither do people light a lamp and put it under a bowl. Instead they put it on its stand, and it gives light unto everyone in the house. In the same way, let your light shine before men, that they may see your good deeds and praise your Father in heaven" (Matt. 5:14-16 NIV).

We are the "lamps" or "flashlights," if you will, that have the capacity to provide the light that will lead satanists and occultists out of their darkness. This becomes possible when we learn to walk in the light and to live in accord with the supremacy of love. Being lights that dispell the darkness requires a radical commitment to Jesus Christ.

Let's replace fear with faith, panic with passion and criticism with caring in our dealings with occultists. It is the truth that sets men free. Someone has correctly observed, "We are only as sick as our secrets." As God's people learn to walk in the light through openness and honesty and truth, those in the darkness will find the pathway that leads to God's glorious light.

Too many have been hindered from finding this path by the phoniness and judgment they have perceived in Christians and received from those who call themselves followers of Jesus. By the way we live, let us declare the truth of the Bible:

> **This is the message we have heard from him and declare to you: God is light; in him there is no darkness at all. If we claim to have fellowship with him yet walk in darkness, we lie and do not live by the truth. But if we walk in the light, as he is in the light, we have fellowship with one another, and the blood of Jesus, his Son, purifies us from all sin"**
>
> **(1 John 1:5-7 NIV)**

Walking in the light, then, is walking in the truth and love of God. It is our responsibility to "let our light shine" before others so that they will learn the importance of Jesus' statement: "Then you will know the truth, and the truth will set you free' (John 8:32 NIV).

This is what I mean by being radical, and remember, if you're not radical, you're not spit! It is a radical commitment to Jesus Christ exhibited by the church that dispells the darkness in our world.

How to Know if Someone Is Involved

I've written this book for three primary purposes:

1. To expose the works of darkness by bringing them into the light.

2. To help people who have been blinded by the darkness to find their way to the light.

3. To help everyone who is concerned about the problems we've discussed understand those problems better so that they can help others.

The focus of this chapter is on the third purpose. There are countless parents who are concerned about their children. Counselors and pastors are working with people who have been influenced by the occult. Young people care about their friends who are being seduced by the schemes of Satan. Law enforcement officials need to understand occultism and satanism in order to know how to deal with specific crimes and individuals affected by occultism. Dispelling the darkness is important to every concerned citizen.

In the previous chapters we have endeavored to show how people get involved in occultism and what happens when they do. In order to find out if someone you are concerned about has gotten involved, it is important to be familiar with the levels of involvement, philosophies, practices, symbols and tools of satanists and occultists. It is also important to learn how one may get involved.

When you suspect that someone is getting involved with satanism, it is essential to look for specific clues that will help to confirm or discount your suspicions. In so doing, however, be sure to remember that these are only clues and they do not necessarily mean that the person is a satanist.

For example, as we have already pointed out, someone may use certain satanic signs and symbols without being an actual satanist. We must not jump to conclusions. How we handle the delicate issues surrounding occult involvement is of paramount importance. There is no place for making accusations, for example, nor should one ever put someone down who may be interested in satanism or occultism.

Clues of Satanic Involvement

The following list serves to remind us of some of the issues we've already discussed, and it can be used as a helpful guide in spotting some of the clues of occult involvement. It is not a complete list of all possible signs, but it does highlight some of the main indicators.

1, *Obsession with fantasy role-playing games.* (Such an obsession may be the starting point of occult involvement in the life of a teenager. These "games" are of particular interest to boys.)

2. *Obsession with heavy-metal rock music.* (Please note that the emphasis here, and in the preceding clue, is upon the word "obsession." This word literally means "a persistent, disturbing preoccupation....")

3. *Books on magic, witchcraft, paganism, satanism, grimoires, a personal "book of shadows" or spells.*

4. *Objects used for spells or rituals.* These have already been listed in a previous chapter, but they may include candles (especially ones that have been tapered or carved in the form of a human figure), candle holders, incense, knives, an inverted pentagram, an inverted cross and the number 666.

5. *Symbolic jewelry.* (See the chapter on symbols.)

6. *Drug use.* While many satanists are drug abusers, not all drug abusers are satanists. Incense is used often as a common cover-up for the odors of some drugs.

7. *Unexplained paranoia or fear of the world.*

8. *Extreme secretivity.* The individual may begin stashing things away and will refuse to talk about anything that relates to his or her involvement. When the subject of satanism is brought up by a parent who suspects his or her teen-ager of being involved, the young person is likely to be unresponsive.

9. *Fear of discussing involvement.* A young satanist may be sworn to secrecy and threatened with harm (to self or others) if he or she ever discloses anything about the group.

Let me reiterate two things about the above list. First, it is by no means complete. Second, the existence of any one of these clues (or even more) does not necessarily mean that the individual is involved in satanism. Whether the individual is involved or not, however, many of these clues are indicators of possible problems in the person's life.

A Typical Profile of a Young Satanist

Most young people who become involved in satanism are intelligent and creative. These innate qualities drive them to become curious about the mysteries of the universe. Quite possibly, the individual satanist may be considered an underachiever in school despite his or her intelligence.

Boys more often than girls become interested in satanism. On the other hand, girls more often than boys become interested in witchcraft. Most come from middle or upper-middle class families.

The typical satanic recruit enters the group with a low sense of self-esteem or a shattered self-image. He or she may have a difficult time relating to his or her peers. Frequently, the individual has become alienated from his or her family's values and religion.

In the early phases of involvement, the young satanist suffers from stress and its accompanying anxiety and fear. He or she experiences frequent feelings of inadequacy and a sense of having lost control over his or her life.

To summarize, then, the typical young satanist is a boy who, although intelligent, does not do particularly well in school. He experiences anxiety from fear of failure in school and relationships. He is in a state of rebellion against traditional family and religious values, and he does not think well of himself. He turns to satanism in an effort to find answers to (or ways to deal with) his problems.

Warning Signs of Ritual Abuse

The preceding list and profile deals with teen-agers who may be recruited into satanism. Another area of acute concern relates to children who have been victimized through ritual abuse. The following list identifies some characteristics that are frequently exhibited by preschool children who have been abused.

1. *Accident Proneness.* The accident-prone child hurts himself seemingly unintentionally. His or her frequent "accidents" may be a subconscious means of punishment inflicted on the child by himself.

2. *Acting Out.* By "acting out" we mean attention-seeking, hyperactive behavior that may be even violent or destructive in nature. Such behavior may be directed against the child's teacher, parents, other children, animals or even toys. The child may pull down his or her pants, pull up her dress or take his or her clothes off at inappropriate times. Sometimes the child may even touch others sexually or ask for "sex."

3. *Talking About Animals.* If the child is preoccupied with animals being hurt or if he or she refers to "scary animals," he or she may have witnessed ritual abuse of animals.

4. *Bodily Signs (Including Pain).* These physical symptoms of ritual abuse may include balding, rectal or anal pain, strange facial grimacing, unusual bruises, vaginal pain, bleeding, lacerations, scarring, etc. A physician's examination may reveal a relaxed sphincter muscle and other symptoms of sexual abuse. Other signs of sexual abuse may include childish sexual provocativeness, his or her referring to blood or "white stuff" in the genital area (of self or others), and coming home from school "dirty" or "wet."

5. *References to Bondage.* These references might involve the child or someone else being tied up or caged. Sometimes this is expressed as, "I (or another child) was put in jail."

6. *Cognitive Problems.* A victim of ritual abuse is likely to experience learning problems. His or her play may become unfocused, disorganized or even non-existent.

7. *Wearing Costumes.* The child may refer to the wearing of costumes, especially black, brown, white or purple robes,

police costumes, "religious-type"' costumes, scary or monster costumes, and TV-character costumes.

8. *Drugs and Alcohol.* The ritually abused child may be forced to take drugs or drink alcohol. He or she may refer to such substances as "bad candy" or "medicine." Other references may include the eating of mushrooms, receiving shots, smoking tobacco, or consuming alcohol.

9. *Toilet Habits.* If a child begins to use new language for urine and feces (especially "poo-poo" and "wee-wee"), he or she may have experienced ritual abuse that focuses on bodily processes of elimination. Sometimes this preoccupation with such subjects involves making noises (as if passing gas) with the mouth, a strange preoccupation with urine, feces, expelling gas or diarrhea. Other unusual habits such as smearing feces on walls or leaving toilet paper with feces on it strewn on the bathroom floor may be indicators of ritual abuse as well. Tasting, touching or swallowing urine and feces also occurs.

10. *Emotional Symptoms.* Emotional extremes that may include anger, anxiety, phobias, guilt, apparent feelings of low self-esteem, rapid mood swings and separation anxiety are often exhibited by ritually abused children.

11. *Unusual Fears.* If the child expresses fears of being harmed or killed by "bad people" or taken away by "bad people," he may have been threatened by someone. Other seemingly irrational fears may include fear of the dark, fear of dying, fear of the genital area being washed, the house burning down, monsters, ghosts, mutilation, other children being harmed or hurt at school, parents being killed or hurt, something foreign in his or her body (i.e., ants, bombs), and even references to his or her heart turning to ice.

12. *References to Killing.* It is unusual for a pre-school child to be preoccupied with death or thoughts of harming, being harmed or mutilation. When playing, the ritually abused child may emphasize death and/or mutilation themes. He or she may refer to physical abuse of children or babies at school, sexual abuse of others, burials of dead children, dismembered body parts, disposing of bodies or body parts, killing or mutilating children (sometimes this may even include references to crucifixions.)

13. *References to Photographs.* The ritually abused child may refer to movies being made (sets, costumes, cameras, etc.).

He or she may talk about photographs of nude children and/or adults or of pictures being taken of naked children.

14. *References to Drawings.* The child may talk about drawings he has seen that depict ritual abuse, satanic symbols, etc. When drawing, the ritually abused child may exhibit an obsession with monsters, ghosts, devils, penises, men with penises, etc.

15. *References to Other Places.* Sometimes ritually abused children are taken to hidden places such as cemeteries, forests, caves, etc. If the child talks about visiting such sites or mentions having gone to a different school, circus or hospital, there is a possibility that he or she did go to an unusual place for purposes of ritual abuse.

16. *References to Sexual Abuse.* If the child talks about an adult abusing him or her sexually or in any other way, it is essential to take that expression seriously. The child may talk about someone touching him or her inappropriately, witnessing sexual activity, penile penetration, etc. If a physician's examination confirms such sexual abuse, law enforcement officials should be informed immediately. The sexually abused child may refer to the abuse as, "Mr. or Mrs. So-and-So touched my bottom (or my pee-pee)," etc.

17. *Sleep Patterns.* Extraordinary nightmares and/or night terrors may be symptomatic of ritual abuse.

18. *Changes in Speech Habits.* The sudden development of speech impediments and/or disorders may signal ritual abuse. Talking in strange, deep voices may also be a symptom.

19. *Strange References.* When a child begins to use unusual references such as "other daddy" or "other mommy" or "other family" at school or give TV character names for people at school (i.e., Fred Flintstone, G.I. Joe), he or she may have been subjected to ritual abuse.

Please remember that the existence of these warning signs in a young child's life may not have anything to do with child abuse. Several of these signs appearing all together and suddenly, however, is a definite reason for concern. When you suspect ritual abuse, you should do the following:

1. Get medical attention for the child.

2. Inform law-enforcement officials of the possible abuse and your suspicions regarding the perpetrators.

3. Remove the child from the school or group where it is believed the abuse takes place.

4. If you suspect that a family member is involved, be certain that the child is never left alone with that individual.

5. Get psychological help for the child.

6. Confront the perpetrator(s).

Of primary importance in helping someone get out of occultism or satanism and/or helping the victim of ritual abuse is the building of a strong and caring relationship with the person you are concerned about. The existence of such a relationship between a parent and child goes a long way in preventing many of these problems. The next section deals with the skills involved in developing such a caring and trusting relationship.

"I Care — I Really Do"

It has often been said that parenthood is one role in life that most of us assume in adulthood but very few of us ever have any training at all in parenting skills. The foundation block of good parenting, in my opinion, is a strong relationship. Such a relationship is built with trust, love, and good communication skills (including listening).

Possibly nothing sounds so empty to a child or young person than "I care — I really do" when it is not backed up with caring actions and the commitments involved with loving, spending time with the child and listening to him or her.

The core dimensions of any effective relationship involve the following:

1. *Unconditional love.* This is the kind of love that God, the Father, has for us. It involves loving someone for who they are rather than for what they do. There are no strings attached in this kind of love.

2. *Active listening*. This kind of listening goes beneath the surface. It involves listening for the feelings, the hurts, the stirrings of the heart instead of just hearing the words someone says. It is listening with the heart.

3. *Being real*. There can be no relationship with a phony. Children and young people are especially adept at being able to spot a phony. We need to let people we truly care about know who we are, what we think and feel as openly and honestly as possible.

4. *Empathy*. This is a quality that enables one to truly understand what the other person feels and experiences. It permits one to identify with the struggles and feelings of others. Through empathy, one is able to see the world through the other's eyes and to walk in his or her footsteps.

All of the above guidelines form the framework for ongoing communication. Through communication, many problems can be understood and resolved.

We cannot change another person, but we can accept him or her as we find him or her. Sometimes, the act of accepting another person (without conditions) is the trigger that enables the other to take steps to change his or her own life. In the atmosphere of acceptance and love, like a tender plant in the sunshine, one is able to grow and to change.

It is our relationship with Jesus that helps us to build relationships with others. When someone has been involved in satanism or occultism or has been the victim of ritual abuse, there are no quick fixes or instant cures. The process of growth toward wholeness is slow and it requires great patience from the one who is trying to help.

Patience is one of the fruits of the Spirit of God that is produced in the Christian life. (See Gal. 5:22). As someone has said, ''Patience is a virtue; possess it if you can. Seldom found in woman, never found in man . . . .'' One cannot exhibit this kind of patience on his own; it comes from learning to lean on Jesus for all that we need. Without Him we can do nothing. (See John 15:5). Patience, then, as is true with all aspects of our relationship with Jesus (and with others), is cultivated through prayer.

Young people who have been affected by satanism or occultism have to learn to crawl before they can walk. As Christians, we need to take careful time to help them to get grounded in the truth. The lack of grounding and discipling results in one becoming like a big balloon on a little thread. When the first crisis comes, such a person is likely to return to the occult.

The Love of Jesus

For most of us, it was the love of Jesus that drew us to Him. People who are coming out of the world of the occult need to develop a renewed sense of self-worth. They need to learn that God truly loves them. Many times they may feel that God can't forgive them for what they've done. It is our responsibility to show them that He does forgive them, accept them, love them.

As early as possible, it is important to separate the individual from his old friends and surroundings. It will be quite some time before he or she is able to follow through on his or her desire to share Jesus with old friends. I've heard many former satanists tell me with great exuberance, "Mike, now that I'm saved, I will go back to my old friends and tell them about Jesus." I always dissuade them from doing so until much, much later in their spiritual growth.

Through the love of Jesus and the patience He provides for us, we help the former satanist to rethink and reprogram his mind and body. He or she needs to relearn how to eat, sleep, feel and think. He or she must associate with Christian people because fellowship will most likely be the sustaining factor in his or her Christian life.

Be Reasonable

I've watched some parents literally push their children away from them without realizing it. These parents expected perfection of their children, and were harshly critical of their kids whenever they failed to measure up.

As parents, we need to learn to respect our children and to lead them to make good choices in their lives. At all costs, we need to avoid discounting the choices, feelings and tastes of our teen-agers. Instead of showing contempt for their choices by making statements such as: "How can you listen to this garbage?" or "How can you read such trash?", we should respect our child's hunger for spiritual truth, his need to individualize and develop an identity all his own and listen for his feelings.

So many of the young people I've worked with have ended up in satanism out of rebellion against the values and rules that their parents have harshly and arbitrarily required of them.

Let's show interest in the things that are of interest to our children. Let's ask why they are interested in those things out of a sincere desire to learn about them and their interests. Let's listen to their thoughts and feelings and always endeavor to keep the lines of communication open.

Communication is always blocked when one person judges another. Our responsibility is not to judge others (especially members of our own family); rather, it is to love them.

Above all else, we must strive to be real. Our concern for another must be genuine. On one radio show I was being interviewed along with a male witch. The host seemed to want to encourage controversy between us. I've lived long enough to know that few people are ever persuaded by argumentation, so I simply asked my fellow-guest, "What do you want to do about Jesus?" That's the fundamental issue in the spiritual life. Eventually, I was able to pray with the male witch, "Lord, let this man know that you love him. Reveal yourself to him as he continues his search." At the conclusion of my prayer, the man looked at me with tears in his eyes and said, "Thank you for loving me."

Slavery Versus Freedom

The young satanist who seeks a way out of his despair has been involved in a very negative life style. He and his fellow satanists have been engaged in selfish pursuits that involve using others and taking in as much as possible for themselves, but relatively little giving out.

In the occult, all service is either from fear or it is designed for personal gain. It is slavery of the most severe form. Satanists don't realize it, but Satan (the master of hate) wants to see people go to hell! He lies, he kills and he destroys whatever he can to accomplish this goal. The satanist has believed the devil's lie. Everything else that happens is symptomatic of that lie.

Christianity, on the other hand, is freedom and truth. There are three kinds of love in the world:

> 1. *The love a slave has for his master.* This is impure love because it is based on fear.
>
> 2. *The love an employee has for his employer.* Also impure, this kind of love may be based on greed and the need for security.
>
> 3. *The love a child has for his father.* This is pure and genuine love. It is based on trust. When you ask a child to identify his grandfather, you might say, "Who's that man?" In all likelihood, the child will respond, "He's my grandpa." When you ask, "Why do you love him?" you are likely to get the same response, "He's my grandpa." What better reason could there be to love him?

The third category of love typifies our relationship with God. We love Him for who He is — and that's enough. We are not His slaves; we are His children, and what freedom there is to know that He has chosen us! Jesus said:

> **My command is this: Love each other as I have loved you. Greater love has no one than this, that one lay down his life for his friends. You are my friends if you do what I**

command. I no longer call you servants, because a servant
does not know his master's business. Instead, I have called
you friends, for everything that I learned from my Father
I have made known to you. You did not choose me, but I chose
you to and bear fruit — fruit that will last. Then the Father
will give you whatever you ask in my name. This is my
command: Love each other.

(John 15:12-17 NIV)

Through His love, we will be able to lead satanists and
occultists into the glorious liberty of the sons and friends of
God. (See Gal. 5:1).

The One, True Sacrifice

The above quote from the Gospel According to St. John
reveals the central sacrifice of life: "Greater love has no one
than this, that one lay down his life for his friends" (John 15:13
NIV).

The gods of the occult kingdom continue to require
sacrifices. In Christianity, the one, true sacrifice has already
been provided by God who offered His Son — the Lamb of
God who takes away the sins of the world.

He is the Light of the world. Because of His sacrifice on
the cross, the darkness of sin and evil can be dispelled.

Accentuate the Positive

In helping a former occultist or satanist find the way to
God, it is advisable to be as positive as possible. Whenever
appropriate, incorporate humor into your discussions with him
or her.

Remember that he or she has come out of an exceptionally
dark and foeboding milieu in which everything is taken very,
very seriously. Lead him or her into the light of God's love
by being very positive and happy. Reflect the joy of the Lord
and the freedom from guilt and fear that God provides.

Don't Expect Too Much

Sometimes we aren't successful in helping a satanist or occultist find new life and freedom in Jesus. As a case in point, I remember a young lady who came to our offices in Kentucky. She had been a member of the First Church of Satan in San Francisco.

One of our counselors at that time was a warm and wonderful Christian lady named Dot Green. She befriended the young woman and began to counsel with her. The former satanist was about twenty-three years old and her name was Carol.

Before long, Dot began to realize how manipulative Carol could be. She had learned techniques of manipulation through her involvement with satanism. She tried to use the sympathetic reactions of Dot and the other Christians she encountered to her advantage. She thrived on any ego-stroking and other forms of attention she received.

One day, everyone was thrilled to hear Carol announce, "I used to be a satanist, but now I'm a Christian!" Dot and several others prayed with Carol, shared the Scriptures with her, and made certain that her physical needs were provided for.

Eventually, it was decided that Carol could greatly benefit from the training provided by a center we knew about. Carol agreed that it would be a good idea for her to go there. We prayed for her, provided her with some new clothing, and gave her transportation to the center.

A few weeks later we learned that Carol had left the center. We grew concerned about her. Was foul play involved?

We received our answer within a couple of months. A call came from Berkeley, California. The caller reported that Carol had gotten satanists to issue a contract on my life and the lives of my wife and children.

Carol was a con-artist. She had used Christians to her advantage. It is important for us to be careful when we're dealing with a former satanist. If we see that the individual's spiritual progress is unusually slow, it is possible that we are experiencing satanic infiltration. The infiltrator's job is to disrupt the lives of members of the Church. If we learn that this is the case, we need to take a hard-line approach toward the infiltrator through confrontation.

What Should the Church Do?

In face of the growing occult movements in our society, there are three primary things for the Church to do:

1. *To get out of denial.* We must stop pretending that the problem does not exist.

2. *To get educated.* We need to know all we can learn about our enemy, Satan, and what schemes he employs to accomplish his purposes.

3. *To rededicate ourselves to Jesus and His gospel.* We must not forget that Christianity is for the people who need it (i.e., satanists, occultists and others), not just for a select few who meet our personal criteria.

The noted theologian, Carl F.H. Henry, has pointed out that there are three primary forces that are in conflict over the minds and souls of people today:

1. *Secular Humanism.* This is basically naturalism, the belief that man has within himself the potential to improve himself. To them, there is no supernatural realm and no after-life; no God and no Satan.

2. *Occultism* — Belief in hidden knowledge and supernatural forces that include eastern mysticism, spiritualism, satanism, etc. It is marked by superstition and fear.

3 *Christianity* — A belief in Jesus Christ as our risen Lord and Savior, the one who has defeated the realms and powers of death and darkness. In Christianity there is supernatural power that goes above and beyond anything the world has to offer.

Sometimes Christians fall victim to Satan's lies too. We fail to see the power we have available to us through the Holy Spirit. We can easily fall back into humanism, naturalism and materialism at times when we are confronted by the forces of evil in the world.

How can we ever forget that we do have the answer the world is looking for? We have a story to tell to the nations. We have the greatest power on earth.

Whether we are aware of it or not, we *are* engaged in a spiritual warfare. Read the words of St. Paul:

> **Finally, be strong in the Lord and in his mighty power. Put on the full armor of God so that you can take your stand against the devil's schemes. For our struggle is not against flesh and blood, but against the rulers, against the authorities, against the powers of this dark world and against the spiritual forces of evil in the heavenly realms. Therefore put on the full armor of God, so that when the day of evil comes, you may be able to stand your ground, and after you have done everything, to stand. Stand firm then, with the belt of truth buckled around your waist, with the breastplate of righteousness in place, and with your feet fitted with the readiness that comes from the gospel of peace. In addition to all this, take up the shield of faith, with which you can extinguish all the flaming arrows of the evil one. Take the helmet of salvation and the sword of the Spirit, which is the word of God. And pray in the Spirit on all occasions with all kinds of prayers and requests. With this in mind, be alert and always keep on praying for all the saints.**
>
> **(Eph. 6:10-18 NIV)**

The Power of Prayer

Much of this warfare is accomplished through prayer. We do need to take a stand against criminal activities by contacting the police whenever we are aware of such crimes. We need to do all we can to help young people and adults find their way out of the darkness. Whenever possible, we should be available for spiritual dialogue with those who are in occult movements. But above all we should pray.

In recent years I have been moved by my personal encounters with people who have been victimized by the schemes of Satan in particularly painful ways. For example, I was personally asked to investigate the case of an eight-year-old girl in Oklahoma who had been kidnapped, raped, crucified and stabbed to death. I went to the small rural community where her parents lived and, as I listened to them tell their painful story, I felt the love Jesus has for them more powerfully than I'd ever felt His love before.

I wept as I prayed with these grief-stricken parents, and I felt Jesus was saying to me, *"Mike, I need you and everyone who will work with you to get involved in helping children and young people whose lives the enemy seeks to devour."*

I could share thousands of stories with you in graphic detail about how Satan is destroying the lives of children, young people and adults in our society today. The problem is real.

At Warnke Ministries, we sense that God is leading us to get involved in helping children who have been victims of child abuse and their families. We are getting involved in education regarding this problem. The numbers of cases of child abuse are growing each year, and we can make no mistake about it, Satan is behind every one of these cases whether ritual abuse is involved or not.

I visited in a hospital in California and stood and prayed at the bedside of a five-year-old boy who has been in a coma for several weeks because of child abuse, and I felt compelled to do everything I could to stand against this terrible tragedy that Satan is visiting upon our children. I sensed Jesus' great love for children everywhere.

Even when I visited a prisoner in a penitentiary in Wyoming I felt the love of Jesus. This man had been incarcerated for molesting children. In a very real sense, he and thousands of other child molesters are victims of Satan's schemes as well.

As a Church, we need to remain alert to all the enemy's devices. We do have a responsibility to our society to be the light of the world. There is much we can do to stem the rising tide of satanism in the world today. It is our job to dispell the darkness.

The words of Cotton Mather, who wrote during the seventeenth century, form a fitting conclusion for this chapter because the are as valid today as they were when he wrote:

> **That there is a Devil is a thing that is doubted by none but such as are under the influences of the Devil. For any to deny the being of a Devil must be from an ignorance or profaneness worse than diabolical.**

(From *A Discourse on the Wonders of the Invisible World* by Cotton Mather.)

12

The Future Generation

Many critics are concerned about the effect on children growing up with such sexually explicit and violent material casually available. Any child with access to a phone can call "dial-a-porn." There are sexually explicit comic books. And, in youth-oriented films like "Halloween," "Friday the 13th," and "Nightmare on Elm Street," it's usually young women who are victims.[1]

(Catherine Foster, staff writer,
The Christian Science Monitor.)

Satan's Twins — Sex and Violence

Our culture is saturated with graphic portrayals of sex and violence. An FBI study of thirty-six mass murderers who were involved in sex-serial crimes reveals that 81% of them ranked pornography as the highest of their sexual interests.[2] When Dr. James Dobson interviewed mass-murderer Ted Bundy prior to the criminal's execution, he learned that Bundy attributed his violent sexual proclivities to an addiction to pornography. And yet the pornography industry is growing richer every day; it is now a ten-billion-dollar-a-year business that grows at the rate of one billion dollars a year.[3]

The Attorney General's 1986 Commission on Pornography disclosed this important finding: "In both clinical and experimental settings, exposure to sexually violent materials has indicated an increase in the likelihood of aggression."[4]

At one time such materials could be found only in the dark and dirty "adult" bookstores, but now it is appearing in motion pictures, music videos, novels, advertising and other forms of "entertainment." As we have already pointed out, our society is undergoing Satan's desensitization process regarding the issues of sex and violence. What used to be obscene is now considered harmless. "Anything goes" — the satanic motto — has become an accepted tenet of our times.

Norma Ramos, a representative of Women Against Pornography, has pointed to the effects of this desensitization in our society: "The technological expansion of pornography has made it omnipresent.... Women in rape crisis centers and battered women's shelters are telling us there's a relationship between pornography and violent behavior. They've seen it."[5]

It is encouraging to know that many diverse groups within our culture are beginning to recognize the harmful effects of these satanic schemes. Throughout the centuries, the Church of Jesus Christ has taken the vanguard in addressing many of the harmful issues of society. At first, society will often react against the Church's stand, but usually, after many years pass, society will recognize that the Church was right all along. This was true with regard to slavery, health-related issues such as smoking and drinking, women's rights, civil rights, etc. The time will come when the same thing will happen to society with regard to the issues surrounding satanism, occultism, violence and the misuses of the gift of sex.

Perhaps the primary motivator in all of this will be the monetary costs to society. For example, it is estimated that there will be thirty million cases of AIDS worldwide by the year 2,000! How tragic that statistic is — and how costly! Yet it is one of the disastrous effects of free sex.

The Innocent Victims
Our children are being victimized by people who want to realize financial profits. There is violence in the cartoons they watch on TV. "Teen-age Mutant Ninja Turtles" and "G.I. Joe" — two of the hottest cartoon characters and toys available on

today's market — openly advocate violence. Many times, cartoons deal with occult magic and mystery as well.

The rising interest in comic books is also an area of concern. Comic books are considered valuable collectibles today. Comic-book stores are opening in many cities and shopping centers. A casual glance through the shelves and racks of these shops reveals Satan's schemes to open kids' minds to the themes of illicit sex and violence. Many comics contain satanic imagery and portray occult rituals and magic. Some have enticing drawings of nude men and women. Some of these shops also carry Dungeons & Dragons and related paraphernalia.

Added to all this, there is the graphic violence and sexual seductiveness exhibited in music videos shown continually on cable networks like MTV. Other cable channels offer outright pornography and many show films with R ratings at any time during the day and night. Advertising is laced with nudity, sexual provocativeness and substance abuse. Television programs — even many that specifically appeal to young audiences — are filled with sexual innuendoes, profanity and violence.

All of this is part of the daily fare for children in our society. How confusing it must be for children even when they have parental guidance. Even adults are confused and manipulated by these schemes of Satan.

All too often, producers and performers of the various media will deal with the effects of their products upon children in Pontius Pilate fashion by saying, "If you don't want to look and listen, you don't have to," or "If you don't want your child to see and hear these things, you must make sure that he doesn't." This is the cop-out they give in the name of freedom of speech.

In pointing to this problem, it is not my desire to discount or minimize the importance of parental responsibility. There can be no substitute for caring parents who patiently and lovingly help their children make wise decisions. But at the same time, there is a need for society in general to recognize that we *all* have a responsibility to *all* of our children. Producers and entertainers have to realize that they *do* have a responsibility to the children.

Very few parents are able to supervise all the activities of their children within every twenty-four-hour period. Whenever the child steps foot outside the home (and sometimes within the home as well) he is literally bombarded with profanity, obscenity, sexual provocativeness and violence via graffiti, billboards, periodicals and other media. These influences have infiltrated the schools, the marketplace, the libraries, etc. Truly, our culture has become so saturated with sex and violence that it is unavoidable!

Regrettably, there is a vast market for hard-care pornography. There is an even vaster market for vulgarity, profanity and open licentiousness. Comedians create jokes for this market that are so base and vulgar they wouldn't even be accepted in typical locker room banter!

Even in situation comedies on television, one can see how society's values are being eroded, piece by piece, year after year. Adults are victimized by this undermining of traditional values and children are being destroyed.

Encouraging Signs

It is encouraging to note that some secular journalists and writers are beginning to sound an alarm about the effect all of this will have (and is having) on our children. MTV executives, for example, have rejected Madonna's video — "Justify My Love" — that graphically portrays erotic fantasies that include group sex, voyeurism, sado-masochism and bisexuality. The MTV producers defend their decision as follows: "We respect her work as an artist and think she makes great videos. This one is just not for us."[6]

In a similar vein, Simon & Schuster has dropped the planned publication of *American Psycho* by Bret Easton Ellis. This novel contains some forty references to violence against women; the female editorial staff at Simon & Schuster protested against its publication and the publisher listened. Another publisher, however, has picked it up.

A recording company — Geffen Records — has refused to distribute a new release by Geto Boys (a rap group) because of its violent and sexual lyrics.

Those who know me well realize that Mike Warnke is anything but a prude. I do believe in freedom of speech and freedom of artistic expression. But I also know that true art involves creativity that produces aesthetic grandeur. True art is never destructive because it stems from the creativity God gives to His people. When art becomes destructive, it is clear to me that the power behind it is not the Creator, but the destroyer.

I do not believe in censorship either. That is not the answer to this problem. The answer is found in taking a stand against those things in our society that are harmful to our children and young people. If enough of us take a stand together and raise our voices loudly enough, we will be heard. Let us never be afraid to take a stand against evil. Let us confront it whenever it appears.

At the present time, evil is spreading like a metastasizing cancer throughout society. It can be stopped. The unsolved cases of so-called serial murders in Massachusetts, Washington and Florida along with the gang rape that occurred in New York's Central Park in 1989 are symptoms of this fast-spreading cancer. In Boston on Halloween night of 1990, eight youths participated in the gang rape, robbery and murder of a young woman in Franklin Park. And in cities too numerous to mention, violence and sexual assaults keep police departments busy twenty-four-hours-a-day.

We can stem this advancing tide through prayer and action. The time is now to stop this undermining of the traditional values that have made our society strong. All of us have a tremendous responsibility in this area. For too long we have allowed satanists, occultists, pornographers and others to get off the hook by their hypocritical stand on "freedom." We all know that when one person's freedom begins to harm others, it is no longer freedom but licentiousness.

Let us be courageous enough to lift God's standard for the world to see:

> **Finally, brothers, whatever is true, whatever is noble, whatever is right, whatever is lovely, whatever is admirable, if anything is excellent or praiseworthy, think about such things.**
>
> **(Phil. 4:8 NIV)**

Penetrating the Culture

One of the problems we face as Christians near the end of the twentieth century is that we have failed to significantly impact our culture with the values that are important to us. We have become "knee-jerk reactionaries" to the developments within society instead of being the "salt of the earth" that we have been called to be. The salt of the earth gives society a pleasant-tasting seasoning that preserves, purifies and heals.

One of the chief properties of salt is to produce thirst. Have we made people thirsty for the truth of Jesus Christ? In too many cases, our "fortress mentality" prevents us from doing so. Instead of penetrating the culture with the Good News, we have withdrawn from it. This is a false view of the Scriptures and it too frequently makes the Church impotent when it comes to meeting the real needs of society.

Jesus said, "You are the salt of the earth. But if the salt loses its saltiness, how can it be made salty again? It is no longer good for anything except to be thrown out and trampled by men" (Matt. 5:13).

C.S. Lewis issued a call for Christians to become excellent in everything they do. He pointed out how Christians took the lead in all areas of the arts and culture prior to the twentieth century. The best music, literature, art and other forms of creativity were produced by Christians. Christians were the leaders. Unfortunately, that is no longer true. Much work produced by Christians today stems from a "copy-cat mentality" that leads the producer to imitate and reflect what he sees in society at large rather than to create original material. Have we become followers instead of leaders?

Paul McGuire, a Hollywood film-maker and writer, pointed to this problem in a recent interview: "The root problem is that Christians don't take Christianity's role seriously. We don't penetrate the major power centers of society — film, education, television, politics. It's one thing to stand on the outside and complain; it's another to be integrally involved with society coming up with alternatives. Francis Schaeffer taught me that the flaw in contemporary evangelical culture is pietism, the false view of spirituality which says being in church is spiritual, while working for the New York Times, for example, is not spiritual. This false view permeates the Christian culture...."

He goes on to point out, "I've been all over the United States and found New Age everywhere. When I was in a small town in California not long ago to speak about the New Age Movement I was shocked to find out there was a witches' coven at the high school. The students were actively involved in witchcraft. Subliminal tapes, self-hypnosis, meditation centers and occult activities are in many communities in the United States."[7]

The Future Generation

As the return of Jesus Christ approaches, we need to be very alert to all that is taking place around us. What is the societal inheritance we are leaving to our children? Many are concerned about America's national deficit and Social Security, but how many are concerned about our spiritual bankruptcy? We are concerned about environmental issues such as pollution, but how concerned are we about moral pollution?

The angel of the Lord appeared to Zechariah to announce the coming of John the Baptist. The angelic messenger said, "Many of the people of Israel will he bring back to the Lord their God. And he will go on before the Lord, in the spirit and power of Elijah, to turn the hearts of the fathers to their children and the disobedient to the wisdom of the righteous — to make ready a people prepared for the Lord" (Luke 1:17).

A recent survey of teenagers' attitudes reveals that young people value one quality above all others in their parents: treating children like real people and showing them that you understand them. It is this that bridges the generation gap. This study goes on to reveal that teenagers value their parents most when their parents:

1. Listen as well as talk.

2. Appear to value the son/daughter without conditions or qualifications.

3. Don't impose too many restrictions, but discuss and establish ground rules and guidelines.

4. Allow a "reasonable" degree of independence and demonstrate they trust their children.

5. Offer emotional support when it's required, and stand back when it isn't.

6. Talk to them like an adult and respect their point of view.

7. Accept the fact that times have changed, and not always talk about their own upbringing.

8. Act "sensibly" by being neither too indulgent nor too moral.

9. Refrain from being too pushy about schoolwork.[8]

The same study reports that teenagers become critical of their parents when parents:

1. Are overprotective.

  2. Are over-interested in their child's schoolwork or social life.

  3. Treat brothers and sisters unequally.

  4. Provide no discipline and no restrictions.

  5. Don't respect the young person's privacy.

  6. Always react to the bad instead of the good.

  7. Betray confidences (even to the other parent).

  8. Use cliches to justify their attitudes or values (i.e., "It's only for your own good.")

  9. Ask the same questions over and over (i.e., "How was school today?;;)

  10. Don't explain their reasons for saying no.

  11. Compare their children with those of other parents.

  12. Interfere in the child's choice of clothes.

  13. Live in the past.[9]

As we have already pointed out, developing a good relationship with our children will go a long way in helping them to avoid many of the problems we've covered in this book. This will turn the hearts of the parents to their children and the hearts of the children of their parents.

Greater Power, Wisdom and Love

We have focused this book on the schemes Satan has devised to destroy individuals, society and the Church in an effort to better understand how he works and how we might confront him. Our particular emphasis has been on occultism and satanism, but it is clear that Satan is at work behind the scenes in many other arenas as well.

Of particular concern to me, for example, is the issue of abortion. Again, this is one of Satan's schemes to destroy individuals and to undermine the traditional values of our society. This tragic situation needs to be addressed along with many other issues that exist in our world today.

The prophet Daniel in the Old Testament had to face a society that believed in and practiced magic and occultism and evil. Moses had to deal with the same problem. They didn't just complain and rage against those who were involved. They didn't fight them. They didn't put them down.

All both men had to do was to demonstrate God's superior wisdom and power. This is what we need to do today as well. First, we commit our lives unreservedly to the Lord Jesus Christ. In Him we find ultimate wisdom, love and power. Then, we let Him do His work in and through us.

This was the approach Daniel took, and he bathed it all in prayer:

> So I turned to the Lord God and pleaded with him in prayer and petition, in fasting, and in sackcloth and ashes. I prayed to the Lord my God and confessed, 'O Lord, the great and awesome God, who keeps his covenant of love with all who love him and obey his commands, we have sinned and done wrong. We have been wicked and have rebelled; we have turned away from your commands and laws....The Lord our God is merciful and forgiving, even though we have rebelled against him; we have not obeyed the Lord our God or kept the laws he gave us through his servants the prophets....O Lord, listen! O Lord, forgive! O Lord, hear and act!
>
> **(Den. 9:3-5, 9-10,19 NIV)**

Daniel began with a confession that was both personal and corporate, and God heard him. God responded with a promise, "Daniel, ...As soon as you began to pray, an answer was given...for you are highly esteemed" (Dan. 9:23).

As a direct result of his knowing and loving God, Daniel received superior insights and understanding that far exceeded the occult wisdom of the king's seers and prophets. Daniel praised God for these spiritual gifts:

> Praise be to the name of God for ever and ever; wisdom and power are his. He changes time and seasons; he sets up kings and deposes them. He gives wisdom to the wise and knowledge to the discerning. He reveals deep and hidden things; he knows what lies in darkness, and light dwells with him. I thank and praise you, O God of my fathers: You have

given me wisdom and power, you have made known to me
what we asked of you....

(Dan. 2:20-23 NIV)

Like Daniel, you and I can receive special wisdom and power from on high. Ultimately, that is the answer to all the problems we've discussed.

Never forget the words of John who wrote, "You, dear children, are from God and have overcome them, because the one who is in you is greater than the one who is in the world" (1 John 4:4 NIV).

The schemes of Satan are nothing in comparison to the plans and purposes and power of our God! He is great and awesome!

NOTES

Chapter One — "Origins of Occultism"

1. *Mystic Places.* 1990. Alexandria, Virginia: Time-Life Books.

2. *Ibid.*

3. *Ibid.*

4. Cavendish, Richard. 1967. *The Black Arts.* New York: G.P. Putnam's Sons.

Chapter Two — "Satanism in Today's Society"

1. LaVey, Anton Szandor. 1969. *The Satanic Bible.* New York: Avon Books.

2. *Ibid.*

3. *Ibid.*

4. Farrar, Stewart. 1971. *What Witches Do.* New York: Coward, McCann & Geoghegan.

5. Lyons, Arthur. 1988. *Satan Wants You.* New York: The Mysterious Press.

6. LaVey, Anton Szandor. 1969. *The Satanic Bible.* New York: Avon Books.

7. Larson, Bob. 1989. *Satanism — The Seduction of America's Youth.* Nashville, Tennessee: Thomas Nelson, Inc.

8. *Ibid.*

9. Terry, Maury. 1987. *The Ultimate Evil.* New York: Bantam Books.

10. Sellers, Sean. 1990. *Web of Darkness.* Tulsa, Oklahoma: Victory House, Inc.

Chapter Three — "The Satanic Revolution"

1. Moody, Edward A. 1974. "Magical Therapy: An Anthropological Investigation of Contemporary Satanism." (Pages 355-382 in *Religious Movements in Contemporary America,* edited by Irving I. Zaretsky and Mark P. Leone. Princeton, New Jersey: Princeton Press.)

2. Wilson, Clifford & Weldon, John. 1980. *Occult Shock and Psychic Forces.* San Diego, California: Master Books.

3. Terry Maury. 1987. *The Ultimate Evil.* New York: Bantam Books.

4. Nelson, Lawrence D. and Diane E. Taub. 1990. "Contemporary Satanism: Establishment or Underground?" Prepared for presentation to the Society for the Study of Social Problems Convention.

5. Cavendish, Richard. 1967. *The Black Arts.* New York: G.P. Putnam's Sons.

6. LaVey, Anton Szandor. 1969. *The Satanic Bible.* New York: Avon Books.

7. *Ibid.*

8. *The Scranton Times.* October 27, 1990. Scranton, Pennsylvania.

9. United Press International. January 15, 1985. Reported in *Daily News,* Van Nuys, California.

10. Frederickson, Bruce G. 1988. *How to Respond to Satanism.* St. Louis, Missouri: Concordia Publishing House.

11. Alfred, Randall H. 1976. "The Church of Satan." (Pages 180-202 in *The New Religious Consciousness,* edited by Charles Y. Glock and Robert N. Bellah.) Berkeley, California: University of California.

12. Modica, Terry Ann. 1990. *The Power of the Occult.* Avon-by-the-Sea, New Jersey: Magnificat Press.

13. Lyons, Arthur. 1970. *The Second Coming: Satanism in America.* New York: Dodd, Mead and Company.

14. Chesterton, G.K. 1985. "The Unnaturalness of Natural Religion." *Spiritual Counterfeits Project Newsletter* 11(3):18-21.

15. *Ibid.*

16. Cavendish, Richard. 1967. *The Black Arts*. New York: G.P. Putnam's Sons.

17. Durkheim, Emile. 1965. *The Elementary Forms of the Religious Life*. New York: Free Press.

18. Raschke, Carl A. 1985. "Satanism and the Devolution of the New Religions." *Spiritual Counterfeits Project Newsletter* 11(3):22-29.

19. Larson, Bob. Discussion on radio broadcast, "Talk Back." October, 1990.

20. Manning, Al G. 1972. *Helping Yourself With White Witchcraft*. West Nyack, New York: Parker Publishing Company, Inc.

21. Sellers, Sean. 1990. *Web of Darkness*. Tulsa, Oklahoma: Victory House, Inc.

22. Chesterton, G.K. 1985. "The Unnaturalness of Natural Religion." *Spiritual Counterfeits Project Newsletter* 11(3):18-21.

23. Scott, Gini Graham. 1983. *The Magicians*. New York: Irvington.

Chapter Four — "Surrendering the Soul"

1. LaVey, Anton Szandor. 1969. *The Satanic Bible*. New York: Avon Books.

2. Peck, M. Scott. 1983. *People of the Lie*. New York: Simon & Schuster, Inc.

3. *Ibid.*

4. "Satan Worship Called Dangerous, Growing." *Chicago Tribune*. April 27, 1986.

5. Lofland, John and Rodney Stark. 1965. "Becoming a World-Saver: A Theory of Conversion to a Deviant Perspective." *American Sociological Review* 30:862-75.

6. Fleming, Jon. *Rocky Mountain News*. November 18, 1984.

Chapter Five — "Satan's New Age"

1. Sire, James W. 1988. *Shirley MacLaine and the New Age Movement*. Downers Grove, Illinois: InterVarsity Press.

2. *Ibid*.

3. Keyes, Ken. 1975. *Handbook to Higher Consciousness*. Coos Bay, Oregon: Living Love Publications.

4. *Ibid*.

5. *Psychic Powers*. 1990. Alexandria, VA: Time-Life Books.

6. *Ibid*.

7. Alexander, Brooks. 1988. *Spirit Channeling*. Downers Grove, Illinois: InterVarsity Press.

8. LaVey, Anton Szandor. 1969. *The Satanic Bible*. New York: Avon Books.

9. Larson, Bob. 1989. *Satanism — The Seduction of America's Youth*. Nashville, Tennessee: Thomas Nelson, Inc.

10. Sire, James W. 1988. *Shirley MacLaine and the New Age Movement*. Downers Grove, Illinois: InterVarsity Press.

11. Truzzi, Marcello. 1972. "The Occult Revival as Popular Culture: Some Random Observations on the Old and the Nouveau Witch." *The Sociological Quarterly* 13:16-36.

12. Lyons, Arthur. 1970. *The Second Coming: Satanism in America*. New York: Dodd, Mead and Company.

13. Truzzi, Marcello. 1972. "The Occult Revival as Popular Culture: Some Random Observations on the Old and the Nouveau Witch." *The Sociological Quarterly* 13:16-36.

14. *The Tampa Tribune-Times.* Sunday, November 4, 1984.

15. *The Tampa Tribune-Times.* January 20, 1985.

16. Cabot, Laurie. 1988. Letter for the Witches' League for Public Awareness to Larry Jones, editor of the "File 18" Newsletter.

17. Cavendish, Richard. 1967. *The Black Arts.* New York: G.P. Putnam's Sons.

18. *Newsweek.* July 23, 1984.

19. Sellers, Sean. 1990. *Web of Darkness.* Tulsa, Oklahoma: Victory House, Inc.

20. *Ibid.*

21. Cooper, John C. 1985. *Throwing the Sticks.* Bristol, Indiana: Wyndlam Hall Press.

Chapter Six — "The Witch's Calendar"

1. *Mystic Places.* 1990. Alexandria, VA: Time-Life Books.

2. *Ibid.*

3. Phillips, Phil and Joan Hake Robie. 1987. *Halloween and Satanism.* Lancaster, Pennsylvania: Starburst Publications.

4. *The Scranton Times.* October 28, 1990. Scranton, Pennsylvania.

5. *The Scranton TImes.* October 27, 1990. Scranton, Pennsylvania.

6. Phillips, Phil and Joan Hake Robie. 1987. *Halloween and Satanism.* Lancaster, Pennsylvania: Starburst Publications.

7. *Mystic Places.* 1990. Alexandria, VA: Time-Life Books.

8. *Ibid.*

9. *Ibid.*

10. Phillips, Phil and Joan Hake Robie. 1987. *Halloween and Satanism.* Lancaster, Pennsylvania: Starburst Publications.

Chapter Seven — "Inside Satan's Toolbox"

1. MacNutt, Francis. 1990. Christian Healing Ministries Newsletter.

2. Huson, Paul. 1970. *Mastering Witchcraft.*

3. Phillips, Phil and Joan Hake Robie. 1987. *Halloween and Satanism.* Lancaster, Pennsylvania: Starburst Publications.

4. Manning, Al G. 1972. *Helping Yourself With White Witchcraft.* West Nyack, New York: Parker Publishing Company, Inc.

5. *Ibid.*

6. *Ibid.*

7. *Ibid.*

8. *Ibid.*

9. "The Quest." Autumn, 1990. Wheaton, Illinois: Theosophical Society in America.

10. *Ibid.*

11. *Ibid.*

12. "New Age Journal." July-August, 1990. Brighton, Massachusetts: Rising Star Associates.

13. *Ibid.*

14. *Ibid.*

15. *Ibid.*

16. *Ibid.*

17. *Ibid.*

18. *Ibid.*

19. Gaynor, Frank (editor). *Dictionary of Mysticism.* New York: Citadel Press.

20. *The New York Times,* December 27, 1933.

21. Barrett, William. 1918. *On the Threshold of the Unseen*. New York: Dutton.

22. *Psychic Powers*. 1990. Alexandria, Virginia: Time-Life Books

23. *Ibid.*

24. *Ibid.*

25. "NCTV News." January-February, 1985. National Coalition on Television Violence.

26. Bremerton, Washington Newspaper. April 23, 1982.

27. *New York Times*. August 18, 1980.

28. *Capitol Journal*. February 8, 1985. Topeka, Kansas.

29. Lewis, C.S. 1961. *The Screwtape Letters*. New York: Macmillan Publishing Company.

Chapter Nine — "Satanic Crime"

1. Burgess, Ann Wolbert. *Children Traumatized in Sex Rings*. March, 1988. Washington, DC: National Center for Missing and Exploited Children.

2. Brown, Chip. Associated Press. "Sadistic Murder of Teenager Is Stuff of Horror Movie." *The Sunday Times*. November 4, 1990. Scranton, Pennsylvania.

3. Cavendish, Richard. 1967. *The Black Arts*. New York: G.P. Putnam's Sons.

4. *Ibid.*

5. "Tracking the Cattle Mutilations." *Newsweek*. January 21, 1980.

6. Larson, Bob. 1989. *Satanism — The Seduction of America's Youth*. Nashville, Tennessee: Thomas Nelson, Inc.

7. Warnke, Mike. 1972. *The Satan Seller*. South Plainfield, New Jersey: Bridge Publishing, Inc.

8. Cavendish, Richard. 1967. *The Black Arts*. New York: G.P. Putnam's Sons.

9. "Geraldo!" television program. November, 1990.

10. Larson, Bob. 1989. *Satanism — The Seduction of America's Youth.* Nashville, Tennessee: Thomas Nelson, Inc.

11. *Ibid.*

12. *Ibid.*

13. Sandford, Paula. 1988. *Healing Victims of Sexual Abuse.* Tulsa, Oklahoma: Victory House, Inc.

14. Burgess, Ann Wolbert. March, 1988. *Children Traumatized in Sex Rings.* Washington, DC: National Center for Missing and Exploited Children.

15. Larson, Bob. 1989. *Satanism — The Seduction of America's Youth.* Nashville, Tennessee: Thomas Nelson, Inc.

16. *Ibid.*

17. "Larry King Live!" television program. Cable News Network. November, 1990.

18. Ciacchi, Betty. *USA Today.* November 14, 1990. "Teacher for 30 Years Faces Sex Abuse Sentence."

19. *Ibid.*

20. Burgess, Ann Wolbert. March, 1988. *Children Traumatized in Sex Rings.* Washington, DC: National Center for Missing and Exploited Children.

21. *The Tampa Tribune.* February 3, 1983.

22. Pulling, Pat. *Articles Relating to Dungeons & Dragons.* Richmond, Virginia: B.A.D.D., Inc.

23. The Associated Press. January 1, 1985.

24. Terry, Maury. *The Ultimate Evil.* New York: Bantam Books.

25. Pulling, Pat. *Articles Relating to Dungeons & Dragons.* Richmond, Virginia: B.A.D.D., Inc.

26. Stewart, Jane. September 20, 1983. *Weekly World News.*

27. "NCTV News." Volume 6, No. 1-2. January-February, 1985. National Coalition on Television Violence.

28. *Capitol Journal.* February 8, 1985. Topeka, Kansas.

29. "NCTV News." Volume 6, No. 1-2. January-February, 1985. National Coalition on Television Violence.

30. Sellers, Sean. 1990. *Web of Darkness.* Tulsa, Oklahoma: Victory House, Inc.

31. Larson, Bob. 1989. *Satanism — The Seduction of America's Youth.* Nashville, Tennessee: Thomas Nelson, Inc.

Chapter Ten — "On Stage With Satan"

1. Schlink, M. Basilea. 1990. *Rock Music — Where From? Where To?* Darmstadt-Eberstadt, West Germany: Evangelical Sisterhood of Mary.

2. LaVey, Zeena. 1990. "The First Family of Satanism." Video Production of Compassion Connection, Inc., Denver, Colorado.

3. Schlink, M. Basilea. 1990. *Rock Music — Where From? Where To?* Darmstadt-Eberstadt, West Germany: Evangelical Sisterhood of Mary.

4. Schwartz, Ted and Duane Empey. 1988. *Satanism.* Grand Rapids, Michigan: Zondervan.

5. *Ibid.*

6. *Ibid.*

7. Schlink, M. Basilea. 1990. *Rock Music — Where From? Where To?* Darmstadt-Eberstadt, West Germany: Evangelical Sisterhood of Mary.

8. *Ibid.*

9. *Ibid.*

10. *Ibid.*

11. *Ibid.*

12. *Ibid.*

13. *Ibid.*

14. *Ibid.*

15. LaVey, Zeena, and Nikolas Shreck (leader of the Werewolf Order of Satanism). "The First Family of Satanism." Video production of Compassion Connection, Inc., Denver, Colorado.

16. *Ibid.*

17. *Ibid.*

18. *Ibid.*

19. *Ibid.*

20. *Ibid.*

21. Raschke, Carl A. 1985. "Satanism and the Devolution of the New Religions." *Spiritual Counterfeits Project Newsletter* 11(3):22-29.

Chapter Eleven — "Dispelling the Darkness"

1. Lewis, C.S. 1961. *The Screwtape Letters.* New York: MacMillan Publishing Company.

Chapter Twelve — "The Future Generation"

1. Foster, Catherine. December 4, 1990. *The Christian Science Monitor.* Article entitled, "Porno, Violence in Media Targeted."

2. *Ibid.*

3. *Ibid.*

4. *Ibid.*

5. *Ibid.*

6. *Ibid.*

7. Chandler, Russell and Paul McGuire. May, 1989. An interview in *Charisma and Christian Life.*

8. Gibson, Noel and Phyl Gibson. *Deliver Our Children From the Evil One*. 1989. Freedom in Christ Ministries Trust: Australia.

9. *Ibid.*

GLOSSARY OF OCCULT
TERMS & CONCEPTS

Abraxas | A Gnostic term for their supreme deity. In a few Gnostic sects, also the name of a minor deity. Using the Greek number system, Abraxas has a numerical value of 365, representing a cycle of divine action (also the number of days in a solar year).

Abyss | To the Egyptians, it was the abode of the dead; to the Babylonians, the chaos from which the universe came into existence.

Adept | One who is skilled in the magical arts. In Theosophy, a spirit being who sends messages to this world.

Aeromancy | Observations of air (one of the original four "elements"), sky, clouds, shapes, or other atmospheric phenomena for purposes of divination; weather forecasting, of course, is not considered divination.

Agrippa | A grimoire written in black or purple pages, and shaped like a man.

Alchemy | The attempt to turn base metals into gold or silver.

Alexandrian Witchcraft | A system of witchcraft founded by Alex and Maxine Sanders.

Alraun | An image made of rowan wood.

Altar | A table (or naked female body) used for the practice of magic or for worship.

Alter	An occultist who has multiple personality disorder.
Alectryomancy	Divination by observation of a bird picking grains from a circle of letters.
Aleuromancy	Possible answers to questions are placed in balls of dough and baked. One is chosen at random, and will presumably be the correct answer. Modern "fortune cookies" come from this practice.
Alomancy	Divination by salt.
Alphitomancy	Divination by means of special cakes, which are presumably digestible by a person with a clear conscience but are distasteful to others.
Amulet	An ornament or charm used to ward off spells, disease, etc.
Anachitis	A stone used for conjuring water spirits.
Anacithidus	A stone used for calling up demons.
Ancient One	The officiating priestess as a Black Mass is sometimes known as "The Ancient One," regardless of her age.
Ancient Ones	Evil gods who wish ill for mankind, counterparts to the Elder gods.
Animism	Worship of the spirit that presumably animates all things.
Ankh	A symbol or amulet in the shape of a "T" or a cross with a loop on top — the Egyptian sign of life.
Anolist	In ancient times, someone who conjured up demons at an altar for divination.
Anthropomancy	An ancient form of human sacrifice.
Anthropophagy	The practice of eating human flesh, particularly by witches at a Sabbat.

Apantomancy	Divination based on seemingly chance meetings with animals or creatures; for instance, Mexico City was founded on the spot where Aztec priests saw an eagle on a cactus holding a live snake; black cat superstitions may also come from this practice.
Apotropaion	Charm that protects someone against evil spirits or "the evil eye."
Apotropaism	Defensive or protective magic.
Apport	The sudden appearance of an object in or from other objects, usually in seances or other spiritistic practices.
Arcana	A secret process or formula; in Tarot, twenty-two pictorial cards comprise the Major Arcana and fifty-six (or fifty-two) cards divided into four suits are the Minor Arcana.
Archetype	A symbolic idea that comes from the overall experience of mankind and is present in each person's subconscious; the concept has been developed by Jung and others.
Archons	According to Gnostic thought, deities less powerful than God but hostile to Him or unaware of Him, who rule the world.
Arithmancy	Divination by numbers; usually by attaching significance to number relationships such as birthdates; "lucky numbers," the number values given to letters.
Ascendant	The astrological sign rising on the horizon at the time a subject is born.
Astrogyromancy	Divination with dice bearing numbers of letters.

Astral Travel/ Astral Projection	A person's spirit temporarily departs from his body and travels to other places.
Astrology	The belief that people are controlled by the position of the planets and of certain stars, or that events can be foretold by the observation of celestial bodies.
Athamé	A ceremonial knife used by witches.
Augury	Observing the flight of birds as a means of divination, or any interpretation of the future based on signs and omens.
Aura	An energy field that presumably surrounds all living things.
Austromancy	Divination by studying the winds.
Automatic Writing	Written messages produced by the supposed spirit of a dead person through a medium while in a trance.
Averse	Black or evil.
Axiomancy	Divination by observation of the quivers of an ax or hatchet.
Baculum	A witch's wand, staff or broomstick.
Bahir	A sourcebook of the Cabala; presents some of the basic teachings of Judaic mysticism.
Balefire	Ritual coven fire.
Barrow	Celtic burial ground.
Basilisk	A legendary dragon, serpent, or lizard whose breath or look was considered fatal.
Belomancy	Divination by tossing or balancing arrows.
Beltane	A witch's holiday on May Eve.
Bibliomancy	Divination by books.
Bind	To cast a spell on someone or something.

Black Dragon	A popular grimoire attributed to Honorius, an occultist of the 15th century.
Black Magic	Negative, harmful or destructive magic, as opposed to white magic.
Black Mass	A ritual by which satanists or witches blaspheme God and ridicule Christianity, usually by observing a perverted Catholic Mass.
"Black Pope"	A reference to Anton LaVey, high priest of the Church of Satan.
Black Pullet	A grimoire that probably dates from the late 1700's.
Bolline	An athamé, often sickle-shaped.
Book of Enoch	An extra-biblical work, apparently written in the second century BC, which forms the basis for much of the mythology associated with witchcraft.
Book of Moses	The standard magician's code of the Middle Ages; it contains a complicated ritual for the induction of neophytes.
Book of the Dead	An Egyptian handbook for guiding the souls of the dead through the underworld.
Book of Toth (Thoth)	A book containing the wisdom of the Egyptian gods; possibly the origin for the Tarot.
Botanomancy	Divination by observing burning tree branches and leaves.
Breeder	A woman who bears a child to be used for ritual sacrifice.
Brigid	A witch festival held on February 2nd Eve.
Cabala (Kabbalah or Qabala)	Occultic material that apparently originated in Chaldea and Mesopotamia and was incorporated into ancient Jewish works and traditions; also refers to practices of magic that are derived from those works.

Cancer	An astrological sign.
Candelmas	See Brigid.
Cantrip	A spell cast by a witch.
Capnomancy	Divination by observing smoke as it rises from a fire, such as from a burnt sacrifice or from incense.
Cartomancy	Divination or fortune-telling by means of cards.
Catoptromancy	Divination by means of gazing at a mirror tilted towards the sun.
Causimomancy	Divination by observing how an object placed in fire burns (or fails to burn).
Cephalomancy	Divination by using the head or skull of a donkey or goat.
Ceraunoscopy	Observation of thunder and lightning for signs and omens.
Ceroscopy	Melted wax is poured into cold water, and the resulting shapes are interpreted as a means of divination.
Chalice	Magic cup used in the preparation of philters or libations.
Channeling	A New Age term for spiritualism. The channeler becomes the medium through which contact is believed to be established with the dead.
Charm	Chanted or spoken words used to invoke a spell, or a physical item said to possess supernatural power.
Chiromancy	Divination from studying the lines of the hand. Palmistry.
Chirognomy	The study of the general shapes or formation of the hand.

Christian Spiritualist Church An organization that promotes mediums and spiritists, and spiritualist teaching.

Church of Satan An organization founded in San Francisco by Anton Szandor LaVey, a satanist priest. (Founded in 1966.)

Church of the Satanic Brotherhood Founded in 1972 by ex-members of the Church of Satan.

Clairaudience The ability to hear sounds made in the spirit realm such as voices, etc.; or the ability to hear things distant in time or space.

Clairvoyance The ability to see people or events distant in space or time. (Extra-sensory perception)

Cleromancy Casting lots using pebbles or other objects, often of different colors.

Conjuration The act of summoning a demon.

Coven A group of satanists or witches, not exceeding thirteen, that come together for worship purposes.

Covencom The area within three miles of the coven's domain.

Covenstead The place where a coven meets.

Critomancy Observation of barley cakes for possible omens.

Crystallomancy Gazing into a crystal ball or other crystal object for purposes of divination.

Curse A spell or charm invoked against someone or something.

Cyclomancy Divination from a turning wheel.

Dactylomancy A dangling ring indicates words and numbers by its swings back and forth.

Daphnomancy	Listening to branches, particularly laurel branches, burning in a fire; the louder the crackle, the better the omen.
Demon	A non-human spirit; according to the Bible, they are angels who rebelled against God.
Dendromancy	Divination using oak or mistletoe.
Devil	Synonymous with demon; the devil refers to Satan.
Diakka	Spirits that communicate with or materialize for mediums and spiritists.
Divination	The attempt to gain information about people or events by supernatural means.
Eastern Religions	Religions of Asia, including Hinduism, Taoism, Shintuism, Buddhism, etc.
Ectoplasm	A substance that supposedly comes from a medium during a seance.
Elder Gods	Gods that occasionally come to rescue men from the ''Ancient Ones.''
Elemental	A familiar, or one of four classes of demons.
Elements	The early Greeks considered Earth, Air, Fire and Water to be the four elements.
Elf Fire	Fire produced without the aid of metals, used to light a balefire.
Enoch	According to Genesis, Enoch was a man who ''walked with God'' and was taken to heaven without suffering death; occultists attribute various powers and special abilities to him.
Erebus	According to Greek mythology, a dark region through which souls traveled on their way to Hades.
Esbat	A weekly or bi-weekly meeting of witches.

Esoteric Doctrines	Mystical occult teachings known to the most highly evolved adepts, parts of which can be found in various religions but these teachings are contained in no single one; these doctrines are presumably given by seers to the world in times of great need.
Evil Eye	A superstition which credits certain people with the ability to dispense bad luck with a gaze; people hope to counteract it by wearing charms or amulets.
Exorcism	The act of removing demonic control from someone who is demonized; in witchcraft, purifying something from alien influences.
Extra-sensory Perception	Known as ESP, gaining special knowledge through clairvoyance.
Familiar or Familiar Spirit	A demonic spirit that serves a witch or medium, or an animal that it may inhabit.
Fascination	The act of charming or casting a spell on someone nearby by a projection of power through the eye, etc.
Fetish	An inanimate object presumably inhabited by a spirit.
Gardnerian Witchcraft	Traditional witchcraft system founded by Gerald Gardner in England.
Gastromancy	An ancient form of ventriloquism; prophetic utterances were delivered in this way.
Geloscopy	Divination from the tone of someone's laughter.

Genethialogy	Observation of the position and influence of the stars at a person's birth to predict their future.
Geomancy	Interpretation of figures or dots drawn on the ground, or perhaps on paper, according to accepted designs.
Ghost	According to occultists, the spirit of a dead person; most Christians consider ghosts to be demons masquerading as the dead.
Glamour	A fascination.
Gnome	An elemental who lives in the earth.
Gnosticism	A religious and philosophical system which seeks after hidden mystical knowledge.
Goat of Mendes	A satanic symbol, the opposite of the Lamb of God (Jesus).
Graphology	A psychic analysis of someone's handwriting.
Grimoire	A book of spells that belongs to a witch or a coven.
Gyromancy	Someone walks in a circle marked with letters until they become dizzy; their stumbles "spell out" a prophecy.
Halloween	A November Eve witch's holiday; considered to be the day of the year most suitable for magic or demonic activity. (The Vigil of Samhain).
Hermetic traditons	Occult teachings that arose during the first three centuries AD.
Haruscopy, Heiromancy, Huroscopy	Various names for observation of cuts, cracks, or markings in very old objects and drawing prophetic conclusions from the same.

Hellfire Clubs	During the 18th and 19th centuries, these small groups in Europe reintroduced the Black Mass and other satanic practices, including sexual immorality.
Hexagram	A six-point talismatic star.
Hippomancy	Divination from the neighing and stamping of horses.
Horoscope	A chart showing a person's destiny as determined by astrological practice. (The signs of the Zodiac.)
Hydromancy	Observing any number of several aspects of water, including its color, ebb and flow, or ripples caused by pebbles dropped into a pool.
Idolatry	Worship of an idol.
Incantation	A charm or spell.
Incubi (plural), Incubus (singular)	A demon or wraith in male form sent for sexual purposes.
Invocation	Calling power in general or calling a demon.
Karma	The idea that our station in this life is a result of good or bad things done in previous lives.
Key of Solomon	Probably the most famous grimoire ever written; some legends hold that it was written by demons and hidden under Solomon's throne. Various versions in different languages survive today.
Lady	Female leader of a coven.
Lammas	August witch celebration.
Lampodemancy	Observing lights or torches for omens.
Lemegeton	A particular grimoire that contains symbols of demons.

Ligature	A spell which prevents a person from doing something.
Linking	A mental identification with a person or spirit; usually as part of a practice of magic.
Lithomancy	Divination using precious stones, possibly colored beads; usually stones are thrown on a flat surface, and whichever reflects the most light is considered the omen. Blue means good luck, green means realization of a hope, red means happiness in love or marriage, yellow means disaster or betrayal, purple means a period of sadness, and black or grey means misfortune.
Lucifer	Satan — the rebellious angel who was cast out of heaven.
Lycanthropy	The assumption of an animal form by an occultist.
Magic	The attempt to influence or control people or events by supernatural means.
Magick	Used by Aleister Crowley and others to distinguish between what was often practiced by "weaklings seeking an escape from reality" (magic) and Crowley's more systematic occult lifestyle and endeavors (magick).
Magistellus	An elemental servant or familiar.
Magister	Male leader of a coven.
Magus	A male witch.
Maiden	Title sometimes conferred upon a Lady's daughter.
Mare	A demon which sits on the chest and causes a feeling of suffocation.

Margaritomancy	Divination using pearls which were supposed to bounce upward beneath an inverted pot if a person was guilty.
Materialization	The physical manifestation of a spirit being.
Metagnomy	Divination by viewing events while in a hypnotic state.
Meteoromancy	Observing meteors or similar phenomena for omens.
Metoposcopy	The reading of character from the lines of a person's forehead.
Mighty Ones	Ancient gods revered by witches.
Molybdomancy	Divination by observing the hissing of molten lead.
Myomancy	Drawing prophetic conclusions from rats and mice, particularly their cries or the destruction they cause.
Necromancy	Communication with the supposed spirits of the dead, usually with the use of bones or some part of a corpse.
Necronomicon	A handbook of spells that involves the summoning of demons.
Numerology	Use of numbers associated with a person's name and birthdate as a means of divination.
Object Link	An object that is supposedly impregnated with the magnetism of a proposed victim or subject or a spell.
Occult	Phenomena or practices associated with the supernatural or the paranormal.
Oculomancy	Divination by observing a person's eyes.
Officer	Third leader in a coven, after Magister and Lady.
Olinomancy	Looking for omens from wines.

Omen	A prophetic sign.
Oneiromancy	Interpretation of dreams.
Onomancy	Finds meanings and omens in the names of persons and things; onomnacy is seldom used today, except for interpreting a person's proper name.
Onomantics	Onomancy applied to personal names.
Onyomancy	Interpretation of various characteristics from a person's fingernails as one aspect of Palmistry.
Oomantia, Ooscopy	Ancient practice of divination by eggs.
Ophiomancy	Divination from serpents.
Orniscopy, Ornithamancy	Observation of the flight of birds for omens.
Ouija Board	A board with letters and numbers with which supposed spirits can communicate.
Ovomancy	A type of divination from eggs.
Pact	The vow of secrecy given by a witch who joins a coven.
Pact with Satan	Selling one's soul to the devil; promising to serve him.
Palmistry	The interpretation of lines and formations of the hand.
Pantheon	A temple dedicated to all the gods.
Para-psychology	The study of paranormal, supernatural, or psychic powers in a scientific vein.
Pegamancy	Divination by observing spring water or bubbling fountains.
Pentacle, Pentagram	A five-pointed star, with one point up, it signifies deity, or rule of nature by mind. With two points up, it represents Satan. "Pentacle" may also refer to a talisman.

Pessomancy	Divination by pebbles.
Philosopher's Stone	A psychic substance used in Alchemy.
Phrenology	Divination from interpreting head formations or bumps on the head.
Phyllorhodomancy	A means of divination that comes from ancient Greece; a person slaps rose petals against his hand, and the success of a venture is judged by the loudness of the sound.
Physiognomy	Analysis of a person's character through observation of a person's features or physical characteristics.
Poltergeist	"Rattling ghost," a ghost that tends to throw or break objects or generally cause mischief, presence of a person who has strong mediumistic tendencies.
Power Object	An object with "witch power" placed in a subject or victim's vicinity to complete a spell.
Precognition	The psychic ability to see the future.
Premoniton	A foreboding of the future.
Psychic	Pertaining to phenomena which are supernatural, or perhaps actually demonic; or a person who has this power.
Psychic Surgery	Surgery by a medium having no ordinary medical knowledge, while in a trance.
Psychography	A form of mysterious writing, usually of a divinatory type.
Psychometry	The gaining of impressions from a physical object usually having to do with the owner or the object's history.
Pyromancy	Divination by fire, usually involving powdered substances thrown in.

Readings	Information or revelations gotten during a seance.
Reincarnation	A belief that holds to the idea that the soul reappears throughout various lifetimes in different bodies.
Repercussion	Injuries received from a projected form that appear on someone's body.
Rhabdomancy	Divination by means of a rod or stick; the probable forerunner of the divining rod.
Rhapsodomancy	Opening a book, usually poetry, and reading words or passages at random, looking for omens.
Ritual Abuse	Victimizing someone (usually sexually) in a satanic ritual.
Sabbat, Sabbath	A quarterly or semi-quarterly meeting of witches for celebration or for observance of the Black Mass.
Salamander	An elemental who lives in fire.
Samhain	A Celtic holiday corresponding to Halloween — "feast of the dead."
Satan	"The Adversary." Satan was the chief of the angels who rebelled against God and were cast out of heaven.
Satanism	The religion devoted to the worship of the devil.
Sciomancy	Various forms of divination involving direct communication with spirits.
Seal	A demon's summoning diagram or signature.
Seance	A ritual by which a medium calls upon the supposed spirits of the dead.
Servitor	A familiar.
Shade	The supposed spirit of a dead person.

Shaman	A witch doctor or "medicine man."
Sideromancy	Divining by observing the forms made by burning straws with a hot iron.
Sigil	A symbolic signature inscribed on a talisman.
Sigil of Baphoment	A symbol of the Church of Satan — two concentric circles with a pentagram within the smaller one. Within the five-pointed star there is a picture of the Goat of Mendes.
Soothsayer	A medium.
Sorcery	Magic, usually of the black variety.
Sorilege	Casting lots, hoping to find a good omen.
Spell	An incantation designed to bring about magic.
Spiritism	Worship of or communication with the supposed spirits of the dead; the Bible seems to indicate that these spirits are demons in disguise.
Spiritualism	The belief that spirit is a prime element of reality — communicating with the departed by way of a medium.
Spodomancy	Findng omens in soot or cinders.
St. John's Eve	The midsummer witch's celebration.
Stichomancy	A form of Rhapsodomancy.
Stolisomancy	Observing oddities in a person's dress for omens.
Succubus (singular), succubi (plural)	A demon or wraith in female form sent for sexual purposes.
Superstition	Trust in magic or chance; a belief resulting from fear of the unknown.
Sycomancy	Divination by writing possible responses to questions on tree leaves, and observing which one dries the fastest; a modern equivalent is

to cut responses on pieces of paper, roll them up, and place them in a strainer above a steaming pot to see which opens first.

Sylph　　　　　An elemental who lives in air.

Talisman　　　A power object, an amulet.

Tarot Cards　Cards used as a means of divination.

Tau Mega
  Therion　　　A reference to the anti-Christ, literally means "the Great Beast." Appellation used by Aleister Crowley.

Telekinesis　The psychic ability to move objects without touching them.

Telepathy　　Mind-to-mind communication.

Temple of Set　A satanic organization founded by Dr. Michael Aquino. ("Set" is the Egyptian god of death.)

Tephramancy　Divination by looking for messages in ashes, often burned tree bark.

Theosophy　　Literally "wisdom of God"; a religion incorporating some Christian concepts along with reincarnation, karma, and spiritistic practices.

Thurible　　　Also known as the witch's censer, the thurible holds incense that is used in ritual observances.

Tiromancy　　A form of divination using cheese.

Transvection　Levitation, or the projection of a wraith form.

Trumpet Speaking　Music notes supposedly made by spirits through a special trumpet during a seance.

Undine　　　　An elemental who lives in water.

Uroboros　　　A serpent depicted as eating his own tail; the symbol being used to show the unity of the sacrifice and the sacrificed.

Vampire	According to legend, one who rises from the grave by night to consume the blood of persons.
Vauderie, Vaulderie	The witches' Sabbat.
Venfica	A witch who uses poisons and philters.
Vibrations	A magical aura or atmosphere.
Voodoo	An occultic religion that utilizes magic, spiritism, fetishes.
Walpurgis Night	Beltane.
Warlock	Originally meaning 'one who breaks faith,' it is more often used by non-witches to refer to a male witch.
Werewolf	According to legend, a person who has been turned or turns himself into a wolf-like creature.
White Magic	Magic that is helpful or beneficial; the Bible makes no such distinction, and neither do most dedicated occultists.
Wicca	An Old English word from which we get the word "witch."
Witch	One who practices magic.
Witch's Cord or Girdle	Also known as the cingulum, the witch's cord is used for ritualistic purposes.
Witchcraft	The practice of sorcery or magic.
Wizard	"Wise One," a male witch.
Wraith	A projected astral body or mobile form of witch power.
Xylomancy	Divination using pieces of wood, either by interpreting their shape or noting the order in which they burn in a fire.

Yule	Midwinter witch festival.
Zodiac	The pattern of stars and planets used in astrology.
Zombie	A corpse that moves and acts as if it were alive; or a person completely controlled by a magician.

INDEX

Moses 29
Mother goddess (-es) 147
Motley Crue 220,221,230
MTV 259,260
Multiple Personality Disorder(s) 48,50
Murder(s) 14,48,63,67,68,155
Murder(s), ritual 45,60,113,207-211
Murphy, Bridey 98
Music 147
Mutilation(s) 202
Mutilation(s), animal 192,193
"Mysteries of the Unknown" 13
Mystery schools 26,27
Mystic 70
Mystical forces 37
Mysticism 32
Mythology (-ies) 20

National Coalition on Television
   Violence 154
National Committee for the Prevention
   of Child Abuse 204
National Spiritual Alliance of the USA
   151
National Spiritualist Association of
   Churches 151
Native American(s) 20,24,198
Navajo tribes 198
Nazi(s) 202
Nazi Germany 202
Necromancy 21,24,29,151
Necronomicon, The 189
Necrophilia 215
Nelson, Lawrence 60
Nergal 147
New Age 96-100
New Age bookstores 13,103
"New Age Journal" 149
New Age Movement 21-24,96,97
New Age, Satan's 47,93-119
New Age subculture 100
New Cumberland, Pennsylvania 125
Newton, John 232
New Year's Eve 122
New York City 47
Nganga 198

"Nightmare on Elm Street" 13,257
Nine Satanic Statements symbol 166
Nirvana 99
Norse 20
Nudity 30,55,72,146,213

Obsessive-compulsive disorder(s) 77
Obsidian 153
Occult 9,13,14,19,21-27,29,33,34,
   37,42,44,48,53,54,63,68,71
Occult arts 64,69
"Occult establishment" 11
Occult games 10,48
Occult Shock and Psychic Forces 57
Occultic 22-27,48,71
Occultism 9,11,14,17,19-23,34-37,
   69,253
Occultist(s) 19,20,21,26,27-29,33,
   34,37,56,61,68,71,73,115
Ogyum 199
Oil(s) 23
Oimelc 130
Old Testament, the 21
Omen(s) 17,21
"Omen" 104
Omnipotent 64
Omnipresent 64
Omniscient 64
On the Threshold of the Unseen 150
Ordo Templi Orientis 33
Orgy (-ies) 73,191
Osbourne, Ozzy 103,220
Oshunm 199
Osiris 33,147
Ouija Board(s) 10,149-152
Out-of-the-body experience(s) 98

Pagan(s) 44
Paganism 44
Page, Jimmy 219,230
Pajelanca 198
Palomayumba 198
Pan 135
Panhandle, Texas 188,189
Parchment 144
Past-life recall 98